and the intermittent efforts of chance relatives. In short, lacking a home and a homeland, spiritually as well as materially, he readily followed his natural bent and became more at home with himself than with his age or any one in it—to our instruction and delight. He can speak to the whole world because he was its child.

The calm, penetrating intellect which watched but never guarded him had under its disabused and passionate eye a creature about as capricious as Puck. He was emotionally a weather vane, alternately veering between gayety and spiritual loneliness. He was ambitious and lazy. He understood politics but had little knowledge of how to be a politician. He plunged into solitary researches for months on end over a period of years to produce a vast work on religion, which when it appeared was long outmoded; and many more months throughout his entire life into the futile service of women. He was physically and morally courageous; he fought twenty duels, the last when he was crippled and seated in an armchair. During the July revolution of 1830—the year of his death—Lafayette sent a message to his sickbed: "A terrific game is being played here. Our heads are at stake. Bring yours along." Which he did at once—though he had to come in an ambulance. He gambled assiduously at cards—he was badly in debt at fourteen; and throughout his life he gambled at love, at politics, and with his career. "Vogue la galère"—let's chance it —was his rule as well as motto. But he rarely found the courage to stick out an undertaking to the point of success, to rein in and slap down his caprices, or to break with the women who dominated him to his hurt.

This bare résumé of his character—like Mr. Nicolson's witty foreword—might imply that Constant was an unmitigated ninny, and more the butt than the subject

lations with women. These affairs occupy the greater part of Mr. Nicolson's book not merely for their unusual substance or their presumed appeal to the reader, but because they occupied—or, rather, consumed—so much of Constant's life.

During his unsuccessful efforts to escape from the toils of Madame de Staël he wrote to his aunt: "When the truth is certain to cause pain, then it is pride, not duty, which forces one to tell it. . . . True morality consists in avoiding, so far as one can, the infliction of suffering." This moral position may have served at the moment as an excuse; for, as his biographer observes, he was "an adept at deferred solutions,' and stouter hearts than his quailed at any solution which involved a showdown with Madame de Staël. But his apparent follies, indecisions and ineptitudes were in general due less to the feebleness of his will than the strength of his sensitivity. As he saw and felt the minutest tremors of his own being, he saw and felt those of others. He was often paralyzed because he was alive to too many things; he often left his actions to chance—"vogue la galère!"—because he was conscious of the multiple determinants at play in any dilemma. Perhaps this is why he considered himself among the realest of men: so inordinately much of himself and of others was real to him.

Though many love-lights came and went and he was married twice, two extraordinary women—neither of them his wife—dominated his existence. Madame de Charriere, a matronly blue-stocking who outdid him in tortuous self-analysis, took over his early manhood. Mr. Nicolson seems ill-disposed toward her; a kindlier and exquisite portrait of the lady will be found in Geoffrey Scott's memorable "Zélide"—a

…dant to any biography of …nstant. Next, Madame de …ël pre-empted his mature years, … comes altogether alive in Mr. …olson's hands. Indeed, it is … he or any writer could do to …p this flamboyant million-…ess, true Renaissance virago …d virtuoso, a woman who nearly …mpelled Europe to believe that … and Napoleon were the cru-…l figures of the age, from run-…ng away with the story in the …me manner as she made off with …nstant. Despite his eventual …arriage to some one else ("ob-…ously I must marry, if only in …der to get to bed at a reason-…ble hour"), it took him three …ars thereafter to be rid of her …, and he succeeded only then …cause her fancy had turned to …other. "Life," he once wrote, …consists of getting out of …ings." He was thinking of …adame de Staël.

These intricate experiences in …e ways of love, as well as the …ographer's discerning treatment …f them, should entice us back to …Adolphe." This singular mas-…erpiece holds the key to its au-…hor's character, explains why, to …im and to many others, the real …roblem of love is not conquest …ut extrication; and, more than …hat, transmits the essence of …onstant's famous *dédoublement*. …s a result, we shall be doubly …rateful to Mr. Nicolson for his …wn performance, which ranks …igh among his works—a hearty …nd enthusiastic recommendation …when we remember that his best …s the incomparable volume called …'Some People."

Marvin Lowenthal

UNIVERSITY OF PITTSBURGH AT BRADFORD

THE MARVIN LOWENTHAL MEMORIAL LIBRARY

BENJAMIN CONSTANT

BOOKS BY HAROLD NICOLSON

BENJAMIN CONSTANT

THE CONGRESS OF VIENNA
A Study in Allied Unity, 1812–1822

BYRON: The Last Journey

TENNYSON

DWIGHT MORROW

CURZON: The Last Phase

HELEN'S TOWER

THE DESIRE TO PLEASE

PEACEMAKING: 1919

MARGINAL COMMENT

SOME PEOPLE

SMALL TALK

COMMENTS: 1944–1948

LORD CARNOCK
A Study in Old Diplomacy

BENJAMIN CONSTANT, DEPUTY FOR THE SARTHE

INCONSTANTI PECTORE SENTENTIA CONSTANS

Benjamin Constant

HAROLD NICOLSON

Garden City, New York
DOUBLEDAY & COMPANY, INC.
1949

COPYRIGHT, 1949, BY HAROLD NICOLSON

ALL RIGHTS RESERVED

PRINTED IN THE UNITED STATES
AT
THE COUNTRY LIFE PRESS, GARDEN CITY, N. Y.

FIRST EDITION

AUTHOR'S NOTE

THIS biography is not a work of original research. It contains scarcely any material which has not either been published already, or rendered available to students in the libraries of Geneva and Lausanne. I must express my thanks to the directors and staff of those libraries for the courtesy extended to me. I am also indebted for advice and assistance to Mr. and Mrs. Ronald Armstrong, to M. Pierre de Lacretelle, to M. Ronald de Margerie, to Madame Dorette Berthoud, to Sir Edward Marsh, to Mr. Pocklington Senhouse and to Professor Marchand.

I am aware that it is pretentious for a foreign admirer of Constant to revisit ground which has already been so scrupulously mapped, annotated and surveyed by two such distinguished authorities as Gustave Rudler and Jean Mistler. Every student of Constant must proclaim his deep debt to these two masters of critical scholarship.

I have not sought to follow in the footsteps of the ever lamented Charles Du Bos or to give a psychological interpretation of Constant's personality. I have sought rather to provide, by objective narrative, a simple cautionary tale.

A cautionary tale addressed to parents who seek to gratify their vanity by imposing on their children an eccentric form of education: to parents who imagine that, by snubbing their children in private, they can mitigate the damage

AUTHOR'S NOTE

caused to them by being shown off in public: to fathers who are too impatient, shy or indolent to establish relations of confidence with their sons: to children who allow their own precocity, and the applause of their family, to generate conceit: to boys and girls who are tempted by the chance that they can speak foreign languages to suppose that they are more gifted than other boys and girls: to people who are unable to make men friends: to young men who, not being endowed with spontaneous physical appetites, seek to find gratification in cerebral attachments: to young men who commit the grave error of falling in love with love: to young men who are afflicted by satiety following upon sexual impatience: to authors who devote their lives to subjects which are too vast for their powers of application, and which become out of date by the time they are completed: to adults of weak will who allow their decisions to be determined by chance: to people who gamble: to men of sensitive natures who excuse their cowardice by attributing it to pity: to liberals who compromise with their own convictions: to politicians who experiment in short cuts: to intellectuals who, on entering the political arena, imagine that they manifest superiority by calling themselves independents: to those who seek in the applause of the ignorant compensation for their inability to acquire the esteem of them that know: to elderly gentlemen who lack the dignity to surrender in time to middle age: to those ill-balanced men and women who are unable to adjust their love of solitude to their desire for companionship: to those who keep diaries: to those who have not the sense to distinguish between vanity, conceit and pride: to those who try to escape from shyness by being daring: and to all those unhappy people who persuade themselves that intellectual brilliance can in some manner replace the

AUTHOR'S NOTE

essential virtues of unselfishness, probity, consistency and patience.

This book is intended for English readers. I have therefore, on almost every occasion, translated (and sometimes freely) the passages which I quote. Constant was a master of compact style; inevitably his remarks lose much in translation; it is impossible in another language to convey the skill with which he can insert a thousand stitches to the inch.

I trust that the English reader will not start, or finish, with a prejudice against Benjamin Constant. He violated many cherished human conventions; yet he remains an incomparable man. I beg the reader (when in doubt regarding this assertion) to recall the commentary of Sismondi, who knew him well: "Ce n'est que comparé à lui-même qu'on sent ce qui lui manque."

H. N.

Sissinghurst
September, 1948

CONTENTS

	AUTHOR'S NOTE	v
I	*The Constant Family* [1767]	1
II	*Boyhood and Education* [1774–1785]	19
III	*Madame de Charrière* [1785–1787]	38
IV	*England and Colombier* [1787]	57
V	*Brunswick* [1788–1791]	78
VI	*Minna and Charlotte* [1792–1794]	97
VII	*Madame de Staël* [1766–1794]	116
VIII	*The Directory* [1794–1796]	135
IX	*The Tribunate* [1797–1801]	154
X	*Escape and Recapture* [1801–1804]	174
XI	*Adolphe* [1807]	193
XII	*The God from the Machine* [1808–1811]	214
XIII	*Madame Récamier* [1814–1815]	235
XIV	*The Hundred Days* [1815]	255
XV	*Restoration* [1816–1830]	277
	LIST OF BOOKS	299
	NOTES	303
	INDEX	321

ILLUSTRATIONS

Benjamin Constant, Deputy for the Sarthe   *Frontispiece*

	FACING PAGE
Monsieur and Madame Charrière	49
Colombier in the Eighteenth Century	80
Charlotte Von Hardenberg	113
Madame De Staël	144
Madame Récamier in her old age	240

BENJAMIN CONSTANT

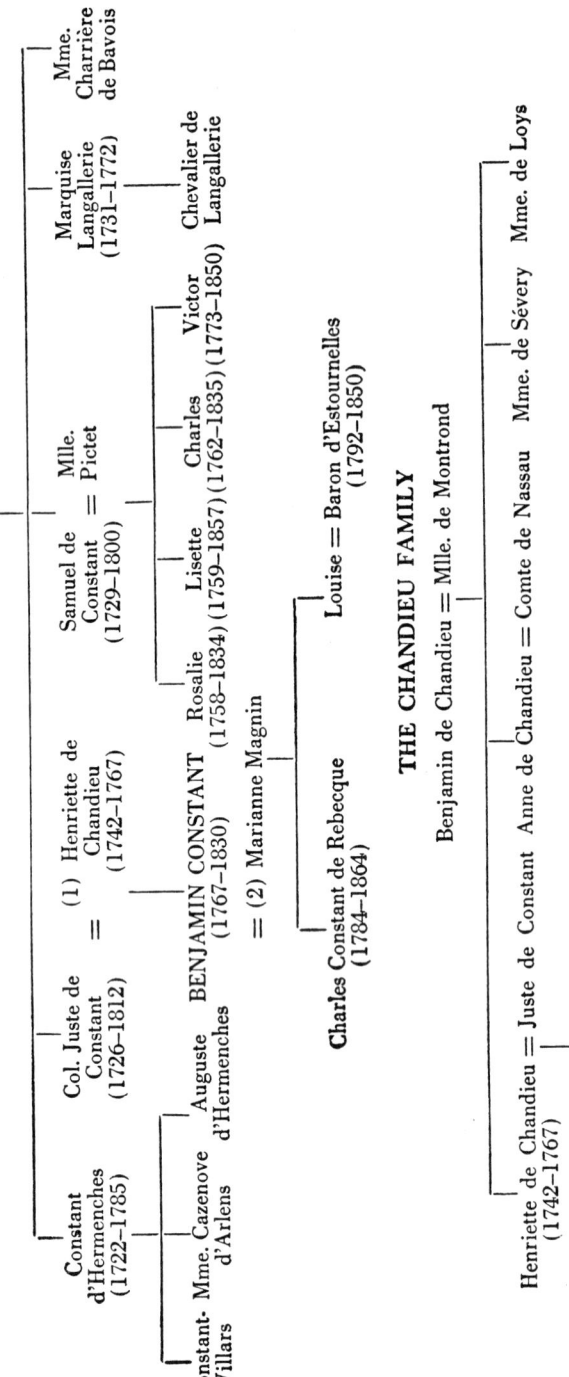

CHAPTER I

The Constant Family

[1767]

Benjamin Constant born at Lausanne, October 25, 1767—Origins of the Constant family—The aristocracy of Vaud and their relations with Berne—The Constant properties on the Lake of Geneva—The death of his mother—His father, Colonel Juste de Constant de Rebecque—His father's eccentricity of character—Description of in *Adolphe*—He decides to entrust Benjamin to Marianne Magnin—Indignation of the Constant family—The connection between Marianne and Juste de Constant—Other members of the family—His grandmother—His uncle, Baron Constant d'Hermenches—His uncle Samuel Constant de Rebecque—His cousin Charles de Constant—His cousin Lisette—His cousin Rosalie de Constant—Her affection for him—Her herbal—His aunt, Madame de Nassau.

1

THE life of Benjamin Constant is often represented as a classic example of the conflict between intellect and character. Yet the famous *dédoublement constantinien* is an oversimplified synthesis of gradually accumulating facts. Benjamin Constant was certainly not a case of split personality. Such duality as he possessed—and it has been much exaggerated—arose from the very ordinary circumstance that his compelling intelligence was not accompanied by an equally decisive will. If we are to understand the nature of Benjamin Constant's instability, it will be necessary to devote to his origins and upbringing more space than is customary in the biographies of intellectuals. Three very early factors combined to prevent the integration of his character. His mother died when he was born: he was never accorded any sense of home or country: and his normal development was dislocated by the intrusion of his father's impetuous eccentricity. These factors must be described and explained.

He was born in his mother's home in Lausanne on Sunday, October 25, 1767. The Maison Chandieu, as it was called, was at No. 6, Rue du Grand Chêne, opposite what is now the Hôtel Palace. It was a large two-storied building, with a row of high windows opening upon a neglected garden. The house was pulled down in 1912 and the site is now occupied by a block of flats. On one side of the front door is a hairdresser's establishment: on the other side, a shop which sells used postage stamps to the philatelists.

The Constant family (1) originated from the village of Aire in Artois, which became a province of the Spanish Netherlands. In order to escape the persecutions of the Duke of Alba, Augustin Constant in 1567 emigrated to Geneva: from there, in 1590, he moved to Lausanne. A certain Captain Constant, who may have been the son of this Augustin, saved the life of Henry IV at the battle of Coutras in 1587. The King's chaplain at the time was Antoine de Chandieu, who adopted the biblical surname of Sadael. Thus both on his father's and his mother's side, Benjamin Constant could claim to be descended from Protestant émigrés who had taken an active part in the third war of religion under Henry of Navarre. This circumstance became of importance to him when in later years he was seeking to establish French nationality.

The Canton of Vaud, in which the Constant family settled and prospered, had in 1536 thrown off its long allegiance to the House of Savoy, accepted the Reformation, and joined with the Canton of Berne. The Bernese oligarchy, instead of welcoming the Canton of Vaud as an equal federal associate, persisted in treating it as a conquered province. The Vaudois gentry, to whom the Constant family had quickly become assimilated, were denied any part in their own government; the Canton was administered by bailiffs sent from Berne. The bitterness engendered by the arrogance and exclusiveness of the Bernese patricians created among the Vaudois families a hereditary sense of injured pride. This congenital resentment played havoc with the life and career of Benjamin Constant's father. It deprived Benjamin himself of any corporate, local or patriotic identity. "I have always," he wrote when nearly thirty, "made it a point of vanity to detest my own country." Not the least among his initial misfortunes was the fact that he never thrust long roots into native soil.

Of Benjamin Constant's more remote forebears there is little to record. His great-grandfather, David Constant, is known to have written a compendium on political theory which attracted some attention at the time; the family as a whole were famed only for their remarkable longevity. Yet during those two hundred years this clan of Protestant refugees must by some means or other (the fruit-trade has been suggested) have amassed a considerable fortune. By 1767 the several branches of the clan owned a number of properties, strung out along the northern shore of the Lake of Geneva. They acquired feudal rights and territorial titles. Benjamin's eldest uncle was known as Baron Constant d'Hermenches; his father would occasionally sign himself "Baron Juste de Constant de Rebecque;" and Benjamin himself, although he dropped the particle at the time of the Revolution, was always careful when writing to his family to give them their proper local titles. The Constants regarded themselves, and with every reason, as belonging to the aristocracy of Vaud.

In 1767 Benjamin's father, Juste de Constant, owned as many as six properties in and around Lausanne. He had a house and an apartment in the Rue de Bourg, and, in the vicinity of the town, five separate villas, each with its patch of farm or vineyard. Lovely little houses they were, with ochre walls and green shutters, surrounded by cherry trees and limes. From their several hill-tops they looked down upon the level of the lake—now blue, now silver—and across to the dark mountains of Savoy. Some of these houses were rustic in character; there were barns and lofts with galleries supported upon posts; in their courtyards the water splashed all day and night through wooden runnels. One or two of these villas were of more elegant design; there was panelling and tapestry upon the walls, and parquet flooring, and chandeliers which tinkled as one walked. Fronting the view were small gravelled terraces, with a rose-bed or two, an arbour of acacia trees, and a carved central basin in which a fountain played. Beautiful names had been chosen for these houses: Saint Laurent, Le Désert, Valombreuse, Beausoleil and La Chablière.

Benjamin Constant, who had a deep distaste for Swiss (or any other) scenery, developed little affection for these properties. Four of them, together with the house in the Rue de Bourg, were sold at the time of his father's financial disasters. For a few years he himself retained La Chablière, which was let at a nominal rent to his uncle Samuel. In the end, La Chablière also was disposed of to a Swiss banker, and the last link severed with Lausanne.

2

The mother of Benjamin Constant was Henriette, daughter of Benjamin de Chandieu de l'Isle, a colonel in the French and Swiss armies. There was a tradition in the family that she had been for many years in love with Juste de Constant before she married him: she was twenty-five years old at the time of the marriage, and he was over forty. She died fourteen days after Benjamin was born; he was her only child; her funeral service in the church of St. François on November 11, 1767, was immediately followed by his own baptism.

There is a tendency in all biographies of Constant to dismiss his mother with no more than a passing sigh; it is contended that she bequeathed nothing to him except her delicate constitution and her soft red hair. It is true that her name thereafter was never mentioned between Benjamin and his father and that Constant makes no reference to her in any of his writings. It is true that he had sandy hair and the white skin and freckled hands and face which often accompany that complexion. Yet his constitution was certainly not delicate; it is in fact amazing, when one considers the constant strain he put upon his body, that he should have lived to sixty-three; and his nervous instability was derived, not from the Chandieus, but from the Constants themselves. Nor is it right to underestimate or to ignore the effect upon his character of the tremendous disaster of his mother's death. It removed the discerning watchfulness which might have enabled him to develop gradually, rather than by fits and starts; it gave him in childhood the disconcerting feeling that he did not belong to anybody, absolutely, anywhere; it rendered him ignorant of gentleness; it induced him throughout his life to confuse love with passion; it denied him maternal control, which alone could have curbed his wayward precocity; and above all perhaps it left him completely at the mercy of his capricious father.

Juste de Constant de Rebecque, the father of Benjamin Constant, was born in 1726 and at an early age entered the service of the States General in the Netherlands as an ensign in the

Swiss regiment. He became a Colonel in 1779 and a General in 1796. In circumstances which will be recounted later, he quarrelled with the officers of his regiment, was forced to send in his resignation, and became involved in a series of law-suits by which he was financially ruined. He retired to Brévans near Dôle in France and there died in 1812 at the age of eighty-six.

In his *La Jeunesse de Benjamin Constant*—a model of interpretative scholarship—Professor Gustave Rudler asserts that Juste de Constant was the evil genius of his son's life. Whether present or absent, the Colonel became for Benjamin an "exterior conscience," implacable and derisive, inconsequent and sneering, opinionated and unpredictable. He drove his son to take refuge inside himself, and thus created within him that egocentric individualism which, as Professor Rudler well remarks, is the "refinement of self-love."

Before considering the unfortunate pattern adopted for the early upbringing of Benjamin Constant, a more detailed account must be given of his father's eccentricity. It is always dangerous—and often a sign of conceit and selfishness—to indulge in wild experiments with one's own children. Juste de Constant's experiments with Benjamin were consistent only in their unwisdom. Yet he was not a stupid man. He was well read and had written much poetry; when young, he had been admitted to Voltaire's circle and had often taken part in the dramatic performances at Ferney. He possessed a fine presence; courteous eighteenth-century manners; considerable personal charm. "Nobody," recorded his niece Rosalie, "has more ways of making himself beloved, and even enthusiastically beloved. Yet nobody knows as well as my uncle how to mortify people by his bitter sarcasms." He was imperious and exacting; vain and tetchy; suspicious yet impulsive; obstinately self-opinionated, yet eternally variable. Such qualities and defects are often found in conjunction: what renders Juste de Constant so interesting a phenomenon is his really astonishing lack of common sense.

"My uncle," recorded Rosalie, "is a striking instance of inconsequence and of the unhappiness which results from it. The perpetual contradiction between his actions, his feelings and his opinions, has destroyed all his good qualities." Writing in 1796 his nephew, Charles de Constant, speaks of "a lack of ordinary prudence, inconceivable in a man of his age, experience and intelligence." Benjamin was never able to establish with his father relations of even averagely easy intercourse. "He is inarticulate," he writes to his aunt Madame de Nassau in July 1795, "and I am cold; each of us is dumb in his own manner; we love each other dearly, but often we have not a word to say." In a later letter to Madame de Nassau written on April 28, 1798, Benjamin gives an even more convincing glimpse of his father. "His opinions," he writes, "have always been in direct opposition to the circumstances in which he finds himself. A strain of eccentricity within him (and it increases daily) makes him stare in one direction while walking in another."

These incidental references to the strange temperament of Juste de Constant must be supplemented by the careful and accurate portrait of his father which Benjamin Constant inserted into his novel. On page 67 of *Adolphe* occurs the following illuminating passage:

> Unfortunately his conduct towards me was noble and generous rather than tender. I was extremely conscious of the claims he had upon my respect and gratitude; but never had there been any confidence between us. There was something ironical about his turn of mind which was unsuited to my character. All I asked at that date was to be allowed to surrender myself to those primitive and passionate impressions which take the soul away from the commonplace and which give one a contempt for

mundane things. In my father I found, not a censor exactly, but a cold and caustic observer. He would start by throwing me a pitying smile and then impatiently break off the conversation. I do not recall that ever in my first eighteen years did I have a whole hour's talk with him alone. His letters were affectionate, full of advice, sensible and sympathetic; but the moment we came face to face with each other, there was a sort of constraint about him which I was unable to explain to myself and by which I was much distressed.

In those days I did not yet understand the true nature of shyness—that inner suffering which pursues us even into advanced age, which represses our deepest feelings, which turns our words to ice, which falsifies upon our lips everything that we desire to say, and which allows us only to express ourselves in vague syllables, or in a tone of irony, as if we were anxious to revenge ourselves upon our feelings for the pain it causes us to be unable to express them. I did not then realize that my father was shy, even with his own son; and that often, having waited in vain for some show of affection on my part (which his own chilly bearing had inhibited) he would leave me with tears in his eyes and complain to others that I did not care for him.

The constraint which I felt in his presence had a great effect upon my character. Just as shy as he was, but more excitable on account of my youth, I acquired the habit of keeping all my thoughts and feelings to myself, of making solitary plans for the execution of which I relied on myself alone, and of considering the advice of others—the interest they took in me, the help they tried to give me, nay their very presence—as nothing more than an obstacle and an embarrassment.

Being a soldier, Juste de Constant was convinced that the aim of all education is the enforcement of discipline and that it is more important to instill obedience than to inspire affection or trust. As a child Benjamin was taught those strict rules of abstinence, that abhorrence of the sins of the flesh, which were traditional among Swiss Protestants. But his father, being absent minded in such matters, would by some indiscreet word or allusion destroy in his precociously observant son the effect of these admirable precepts. There is a revealing passage in *Adolphe* in which Benjamin Constant tells how shocked he was when he saw his father smile, as if in approval, at the profligate's motto: "It gives us so great a pleasure; it does them so little harm."

One scarcely realizes, [writes Benjamin Constant of this episode], how deep an impression such casual remarks leave upon the very young. At an age when opinions are still fluid and convictions vacillating, children are shocked to hear the precepts which they have been taught contradicted by some witticism which meets with general applause. Thereafter they come to regard the precepts as no more than empty formulas which their parents repeat in order to salve their own consciences: the witticisms, however, seem to contain for them the whole secret of life.

3

The plight of this motherless infant induced all the female members of the family to compete for possession. There was his grandmother, la Générale de Constant: there were his dead mother's sisters: there were his father's sisters-in-law and cousins. "To his family," writes Rosalie, "he was a frail and precious object which everyone wished to own." Juste de Constant's leave had expired; he was due to rejoin his regiment; it was absurd to suppose that an elderly officer would wish to return to Hertogenbosch accompanied by a baby of two weeks old.

The impulses and calculations of Juste de Constant were unrelated to any reasonable requirements. He informed his startled family that he had already made his own arrangements for the nurture and education of his little son. These arrangements were highly original in their inception and continued to be original for the next eighteen years.

In the year 1761 Juste de Constant had spent his summer

leave with his sister, Madame Charrière de Bavois, near the village of Bettens in the district of Lausanne. Madame de Bavois happened to mention that there was a girl of nine years old in the village who seemed to possess exceptional intelligence. Juste de Constant at once remarked that this was exactly what he had for long desired. He had always wished to train someone to become "the woman of his dreams." His remark was not taken seriously at the time, but when his leave expired he returned to Holland in a post-chaise with the child upon his knee. Protests reached him from the parents of the kidnapped girl as well as from his own relations. He replied that she was being educated in great comfort in some Dutch village, the name of which had escaped him. The parents received compensation; the girl herself was taught to read and write and play the spinnet; for the time the incident was forgotten. One is tempted to suppose that in executing this experiment Juste de Constant had been fired by the teaching of Jean Jacques Rousseau. *Emile,* however, was only published in the year following this abduction. It may be, of course, that Juste de Constant had obtained and studied an advance copy.

The name of this girl was Jeanne Suzanne Magnin, generally known as "Marianne." In the frequent and caustic references which Benjamin Constant made to her in later life he (perhaps deliberately) miswrote her name as "Mlle. Marin." Juste de Constant informed his mother that it was to this person that he intended to entrust his son. The united protests of the family induced him to postpone his decision for five years; Benjamin for that period was placed under the care of his grandmother; but in 1772, when Marianne was just twenty, she was transported from Holland to Lausanne and placed in charge of Benjamin. At first they lived in the house of Pasteur Pérey at Cornans, and thereafter at La Maladière, a farm attached to the La Chablière property. They had with them Jeanne Morand, an old maidservant of the Constant family, generally referred to as "Nanine."

For two years—between the ages of five and seven—Benjamin remained at La Maladière in the charge of Marianne. Being an exceptionally alert and sensitive child, he must soon have realized from the shrugs and silences of his aunts and grandmother that some mystery of disapproval surrounded the relationship between his father and his governess. A serious disturbance was thereby created in his lonely, precocious mind; his domestic affections were clouded at their source. His childhood's dislike of Marianne grew with the years into bitter hatred. "That harpy," he called her later, "who seeks to seize on everything." Before he was twenty we find him writing of "my father's mistress" in acid, self-wounding, shame.

It is probable that at some date Juste de Constant went through a form of marriage with Mlle. Magnin, although as late as 1800 we find Benjamin denying such a possibility. Two children, in any case, were born of this union—Charles in 1784 and Louise (who became Baroness D'Estournelles) in 1792. However regular the union may have become, Juste de Constant concealed it from Benjamin for some twenty-eight years. He seems to have sprung the whole story upon his son in the late summer of 1800. Benjamin accepted the revelation with his usual irony; but he was angry and hurt. "My new relations," he wrote to Rosalie on September 12, 1800, "continue to be a source of embarrassment. Having proclaimed myself to be an only son, I now find I have a little brother who tells the most fantastic tales about his childhood. It makes it look as if all this time I had been deliberately concealing his existence from the world."

Towards the end of his long life Juste de Constant fell completely under the domination of Marianne. She sought by every means to foment strife between Benjamin and his father and to induce the old man to disinherit his elder son in favour of her own children. But for the moment we are not discussing the erudite Benjamin Constant of forty-four, but the lonely little boy of six years old, interned at La Maladière under the guard of a woman whom he already much disliked. A perplexed, vivacious, clever little boy with red hair, whose disconcerting father was absent for months on end among the small garrison towns of the Low Countries.

4

The Constants, as has been indicated, were a numerous family: it is necessary to mention only those of Benjamin's relations who played a definite part in his life.

His grandmother, la Générale Constant de Rebecque, was an intelligent and dominating personality with an acute business sense. She never forgave her son Juste for having confided the baby Benjamin to the charge of Marianne Magnin. She took a warm interest in her grandson, and as a little boy he would write her long letters of such amazing precocity that Sainte-Beuve proclaimed them to be forgeries. They can be studied today in the Library at Geneva; they are written in a beautiful and adult script; they contain expressions, and indicate a power of observation and analysis, almost inconceivable in a boy of twelve; yet of their authenticity there can be no doubt whatsoever. La Générale, for whom he had a candid affection, died when he was fifteen years of age; she was unable to be of assistance to him in the troubles of his adolescence.

His father had two sisters, the Marquise Gentil de Langallerie and Madame de Charrière de Bavois. The latter is of importance only, since her house "La Chaumière" became the centre of the intellectual society of Lausanne. The former had a son, the Chevalier de Langallerie, who became the leader of a religious sect called "The Inner Souls." He was a tubby, greasy, greedy little man and Benjamin was wont to sneer at him as "The Pope of the Pietists." Yet at one stage in the long struggle to escape from Madame de Staël the unctuous assistance of the Chevalier de Langallerie was unexpectedly invoked. His help was transitory.

Of Juste's two brothers, the elder was Constant d'Hermenches who died when Benjamin was eighteen years of age. He exercised no direct influence upon his nephew, but his indirect influence was great. Handsome and profligate, extravagant and yet greedy about money, of extreme elegance and wide culture, Constant d'Hermenches became one of the most brilliant figures in the international society of the late eighteenth century. At his château at Bois de Vaud he would entertain the outstanding figures of the age. He also was in the service of the States General, and it was while he was with his regiment in Holland that he met the young Isabella van Serooskerken van Tuyll of Zuylen, with whom he conducted a long, amorous but platonic correspondence. Belle de Zuylen, having mismanaged all her matrimonial projects, having attracted even the complacent attention of James Boswell, finally married her brother's tutor. As Madame de Charrière in her later years she became the first truly formative influence in Benjamin Constant's life.

Samuel de Constant de Rebecque, Juste's younger brother, was a wholly different character. He was a small thin man with a diffident manner, a marked lack of gaiety, and prematurely greying hair. His three novels, *Le Mari Sentimental, Camille* and *Laure* were well spoken of. But he was incompetent in financial matters, speculated unwisely, and died impoverished. So long as he lived, Samuel Constant was a good friend to his nephew Benjamin. In his bewildered but comforting way, he was of assistance in many of the fantastic episodes in which they both were implicated owing to the vagaries of Juste. He died when Benjamin was thirty years of age.

Samuel de Constant had three sons and two daughters. Of the sons, the only one who need concern us is Charles de Constant, called "le Chinois" owing to his long residence in China in the service of the Compagnie des Indes. He remained a staunch, if critical, friend to his cousin Benjamin until the day of his death.

Of Samuel's two daughters, the younger, Lisette, was a shabby and inarticulate girl, who fell under the influence of her cousin the Chevalier de Langallerie and became an ardent pietist. The elder daughter, Rosalie de Constant, who has already been quoted, remained the most stable influence in Benjamin's disordered life. She analysed his faults with sharp lucidity; she deplored his inconsistencies with prim and often arid reproaches; she was never for one instant taken in by the elaborate devices with which he sought to conceal his own indecision; but she alone among his father's family realized the virtue which was in him and she alone was willing to forgive his lapses and to stimulate his pride. Rosalie was the first person in his life who gave him any conception of disinterested and dispassionate affection. The portrait of Rosalie, therefore, must at this stage be more sharply drawn.

Rosalie de Constant was nine years older than her cousin Benjamin and she survived him by four years. Hers was an unfulfilled life, devoted to the service of others. Her mother died when she was eight years of age and she was brought up by her Pictet grandmother who treated her with persistent harshness and occasional cruelty. When playing as a child in a hay-loft which had been declared out of bounds, she heard her grandmother approaching and tried to escape hurriedly down a ladder. The ladder broke and Rosalie fell, dislocating her shoulder; she remained a cripple all her life. She was also most short-sighted and would peek and peer into people's faces and at the books she read.

Her father at the time was living at St. Jean at Geneva, a house which possessed a splendid terrace and a famous view. As a child she remembered being taken to Ferney and playing with a stuffed leopard in Voltaire's library. At the age of fourteen she was brought to Paris in the hope that the great surgeon Tronchin would be able to cure her damaged limbs. She went to Versailles and stood there behind the barrier watching Louis XV, the Dauphin and Marie Antoinette, eat their meal in public. Then she returned to Switzerland, still short-sighted, still crippled on her left side, still doomed to spinsterhood.

Shortly afterwards they were obliged, owing to the failure of Samuel's speculations, to sell the house at St. Jean and to move to Lausanne. They established themselves at La Chablière, which Juste de Constant, and subsequently Benjamin, allowed them to lease for a nominal rent. Rosalie de Constant at this stage entered, under an assumed name, into a romantic correspondence with Bernadin de St. Pierre, whose *Études de la Nature* she had much admired. This correspondence petered out after 1793 when Bernadin de St. Pierre married Mlle. Didot. It was then that Rosalie invented an occupation which was to prove a solace to her throughout her life.

Until the end of the eighteenth century, the people of Vaud had been ashamed of their mountains which they considered to be rude and wild. It was M. de Saussure who, in 1780, first brought them into fashion. He encouraged Rosalie to make a botanical index of Alpine flora. This became the joy and occupation of her years. The shepherds and the cow-herds of the district were encouraged by small gifts to bring to La Chablière any new plants which might be found. With extreme precision, and with the use of a magnifying-glass, Rosalie would paint water-colour pictures of these flowers upon stiff sheets of paper. She would then add a careful, and it seems most accurate, description of their botanical names, lineage, habits and character. The sheets were then bound in rough boards of green cardboard. By 1801, she had collected as many as 3,000 descriptions and pictures of Alpine plants. They can be seen today in the Botanical Museum of the University of Lausanne. Beautiful they are in their delicate colouring, faced in each case with a technical description in Rosalie's neat and angular hand. There are fourteen folios of these pictures, each bound in the same tattered green cardboard, representing the careful assiduity of fifty spinster years.

In the intervals of composing her herbal, Rosalie was engaged in writing long and informative letters to her brother in China, helping her aunt Madame de Bavois to run her provincial salon at La Chaumière, and looking after her incompetent and melancholy father.

There exists a letter written by Samuel Constant to his daughters, at a date when Rosalie was thirty-five years of age. It provides a good example of the analytical unkindness which was the Constant mode:

> You have a free hand, my dear daughters, to do whatever you consider necessary. But I must beg you to be cautious in what you decide. Neither of you is the least good at sums; your concepts are vague, and unduly coloured by ethical considerations. Your intentions are excellent, your hearts of gold, but your capacities are those of your sex, in that they are directed by feeling and imagination rather than controlled by any sense of reality. . . . As for you, Rosalie, you impose unnecessary privations on yourself and thereafter put on an air of martyrdom: too often do you assume the pose of a victim.

Rosalie first met her cousin Benjamin when as a little boy he rode over to St. Jean upon his pony. She was entranced by his vivacity and by his cajoling manners. Throughout his life he would treat her as an elder sister, teasing her about Bernadin de St. Pierre, teasing her about her shyness, disarranging the Alpine flora upon her painting table, prying into the letters in her desk. Better than anyone else, better even than Madame de Charrière—far better than Madame de Staël—she appreciated the delight of his eternal childishness. It aroused within her nervous maternal longings.

The relations between them can best be illustrated by two separate extracts from their respective journals of a later date. "Benjamin," records Rosalie in her diary for 1802, "is much improved. He has the temperament of a spoilt but affable child. Always unreliable and at the mercy of every momentary impulse." "My Cousin Rosalie," records Benjamin in 1804, "is a good woman; a bit sour perhaps. She has a gift for saying unpleasant things in a cold, calm voice as if she did not notice what she was saying. A most unfortunate gift! But I suppose it is not easy to be agreeable, when one is a virgin of forty-five, and a hunchback to boot."

In the end, after many vicissitudes, her brother Charles returned to Switzerland and with the money he had acquired in the China trade was able to repurchase the old house at St. Jean. He married a Mlle. Achard but Rosalie, who was jealous of her sister-in-law, seldom went to St. Jean. When his wife died, Charles de Constant sold the big Villa at St. Jean and induced Rosalie to keep house for him in a small cottage called "La Sousterre" at the bottom of the garden. It was there that they were visited by Chateaubriand and there, on November 27, 1834, that she died.

So much for Benjamin Constant's uncles, aunts and cousins on his father's side. His mother had three sisters: Madame de Sévery, Madame de Loys, and the Comtesse de Nassau. The first two were colourless; the third was a woman of personality. She developed a disapproving but fascinated affection for her nephew Benjamin: with inquisitive horror she closely followed the intricate entanglements of his adult years.

The Comtesse de Nassau had married a German Graf by whom she had one son; the son died when he was young and she thereafter separated from her husband and settled at Lausanne. She was an alert woman, cynical and worldly; she was flattered and amused by her nephew, but remained convinced that his cajolery was exercised upon her in the hope of inheriting her fortune. This was an unfair assumption: whatever his faults, Benjamin Constant was never in quest of legacies. He sincerely liked Madame de Nassau; he confided to her many of his most intimate perplexities; he enjoyed both shocking and stimulating her elegant proprieties and her acute worldly sense. "She is a woman," he wrote in 1804, "of considerable intelligence and is much attached to me. But she has surrendered to the atmosphere in which she lives and has swallowed with relish all the prejudices of her small world. This creates a certain degree of constraint between us; but I manage to get round it by being extremely amusing."

At one stage Madame de Nassau indicated to her nephew that she would leave him her fortune if only he would break off all relations with Madame de Staël. He lied to her considerably on this subject, as he lied to everyone; but he was not a person to accept bribes. He refused to break with Madame de Staël at the time that his aunt demanded it; she was angered by his refusal and the accompanying deceptions; and when she died, she left her money to the two of Benjamin's cousins whom he most disliked.

Such was the Lausanne background against which Benjamin Constant spent his childhood, and some of his adolescent years.

It had far more effect upon him than he would ever have admitted; or indeed believed.

CHAPTER II

Boyhood and Education

[1774-1785]

Juste de Constant's experiments with his son's education—The tutor Stroelin—Benjamin is transplanted from Switzerland and taken to Brussels—The succession of tutors—Monsieur de la Grange—Monsieur Gobert—Monsieur Duplessis—Benjamin's precocity—His juvenilia and *Les Chevaliers*—His letters to his grandmother—Criticism of the method of education adopted—The expedition to Oxford—Mr. May—Benjamin is sent to the University at Erlangen—His relations with the Dowager Margravine of Anspach—He is sent to Edinburgh University—James Mackintosh and other undergraduate friends—The Speculative Society—Benjamin begins to gamble—He leaves Edinburgh under a cloud—Advantages which he derived from Edinburgh—He is housed with the Suards in Paris—He neglects his opportunities—He is removed to Brussels—Madame Johannot—He is sent back to Switzerland.

1

CONCEITED parents exploit and exhibit the talents of their children, ministering to their own self-esteem. Juste de Constant was determined that Benjamin should become, and be widely known as, an infant prodigy. He forced him to start learning Greek, Latin, counterpoint and mathematics at the age of five.

He employed for this purpose a German of the name of Stroelin. This tutor would belabour Benjamin when he was inattentive and thereafter fondle him in case he sneaked. Realizing the amazing precocity of his pupil, and having some intuitions regarding child psychology, Stroelin persuaded Benjamin that Greek was a secret language known only to themselves. Being by nature secretive, Benjamin was entranced by this device. His progress was rapid; but after a few months Marianne discovered that he was being beaten too often and too hard; she informed Juste de Constant and Stroelin was dismissed.

In the late autumn of 1774, when Benjamin was barely seven years of age, his father decided that the time had come to remove him from the guardianship of Marianne and the excessive affection of his female relations. He determined to launch him at once upon the world of men. Juste de Constant descended upon La Maladière and carried his son back with him to the Low Countries. For a few weeks he strove, in his regimental quarters, to educate the boy himself. But he soon became restive under an occupation requiring so much patience and entrusted Benjamin to the surgeon of his own regiment, a Monsieur de la Grange. In the company of this, his second tutor, Benjamin left Hertogenbosch and went to Brussels. Monsieur de la Grange, as a tutor, was ill chosen. He was atheistic, illiterate and vain. He lived a dissipated life and on reaching Brussels he established himself and his pupil in a house of ill fame. A rumour of this reached the ears of Juste de Constant who rushed enraged to Brussels and to the rescue of his son.

Benjamin thereafter was lodged with the family of a teacher of music, where he received much musical education but little else. He was allowed to frequent a neighbouring library, the shelves of which were stocked with novels and the irreligious literature fashionable at the time. He records in the *Cahier Rouge* that he would pour over these books for eight or ten hours a day; and he ascribes to this immoderate and ill-directed occupation the weakness of the eyes from which he suffered all his life.

Early in 1776, when Benjamin was nine years of age, Juste de Constant met a certain Monsieur Gobert, who undertook to educate his son for him "for a large fee." Impulsive as always, Juste de Constant failed to make any enquiries regarding Monsieur Gobert's antecedents or capacities. Had he done so, he would have discovered that Monsieur Gobert had been involved in some scandal in Paris, had been obliged to escape to Brussels and that he was living there in the company of several mistresses. He would also have discovered that he lacked education. Monsieur Gobert knew little Latin and employed Benjamin to copy out, in his beautifully clear script, an historical work of no value upon which he had been engaged. After two years of such tuition, it was suddenly discovered at Hertogenbosch that Monsieur Gobert was a man of dissolute habits and defective knowledge. Again Juste de Constant hurried to Brussels and a violent scene occurred. "I left this my third tutor," records Benjamin Constant in the *Cahier Rouge* "convinced for the third time that those who were entrusted with the task of instructing and disciplining me were themselves most ignorant and immoral men." Monsieur Gobert was dismissed with objurgations and Benjamin for a while was sent back to the gentler atmosphere of La Chablière and Lausanne.

Early in 1779 Juste de Constant discovered a fourth tutor for his son. This was Monsieur Duplessis, a defrocked monk, a man of fifty years of age, who was witty and kind and weak. With him Benjamin returned to the Low Countries. Juste de Constant, who loathed weakness in any form, could not conceal from Benjamin his dislike of this fourth tutor. Benjamin himself was fond of Monsieur Duplessis and was sorry when he left them to become tutor to a young Count d'Aumale. The end of M. Duplessis was unfortunate. The Count d'Aumale had a sister who amused herself by flirting with her brother's elderly tutor; with the result that Monsieur Duplessis became madly enamoured and blew out his brains.

It was at this period, when Benjamin was twelve years of age, that his precocious talents and nervous excitability first made themselves apparent. Among his family and the officers of his father's regiment he was at that time regarded as a musical prodigy. He had already started to write poetry in imitation of Horace and Voltaire. He could read Homer with ease. He turned Livy into Alexandrines; he began a tragedy in verse on the subject of Dido Queen of Carthage; and he composed five long cantos of a prose poem or "heroic romance" entitled *Les Chevaliers* which was published by Professor Rudler in 1927.

It cannot be said that *Les Chevaliers* is any better than other school-boy fantasies. It is little more than a wordy echo of Ariosto and the *Chanson de Roland,* indicating considerable reading and a boyish love of resounding names. What is more interesting is the dedicatory epistle to his father, written in that uncanny adult hand. This epistle is worth quoting in its entirety, since it shows us that at the age of twelve Benjamin Constant had already developed a crust of irony with which to protect his unrequited yearning for affection:

Dear author of my days,

I have been told that fathers always regard the productions of their children as works of surpassing merit, even though they are often no more than a bundle of reminiscences strung together without literary art. In order to demonstrate the falsity of this rumour I have the honour herewith to offer you this work, being quite certain that, although I wrote it, you will not find it good; and that in fact you will not have the patience to read it.

BOYHOOD AND EDUCATION

Juste de Constant, as might have been foreseen, was delighted by this proof of his son's precocious sarcasm. He had the manuscript and dedication beautifully bound between morocco boards.

Even more illustrative of Benjamin Constant's development at this period are the letters which he addressed from Brussels to his grandmother. It is these letters which Sainte-Beuve pronounced to be too adult to be authentic, and the originals of which can be seen today at Geneva.

> I wish [he wrote to her on November 19, 1779] I could find some means to prevent my blood circulating so rapidly and could give it a more regular rhythm. I have been trying to see whether music could produce this effect and have been playing adagios and largos which would put thirty cardinals to sleep. The first bars go all right, but by some magic these slow airs always end by becoming prestissimo. It is the same with my dancing. The minuet always ends in a skip and a jump. I fear, my dear grandmother, that this evil is incurable and will prove impervious to reason itself. I ought by now to have some spark of reason since I am now twelve years old plus a few days. . . . But if the dawn of reason is so wan and feeble, what on earth will it all be like when I am twenty-five?

Juste de Constant was imprudently ostentatious of his gifted son, whose ways were so ingratiating, whose manners so pert. He took him out and showed him off.

> Do you know [writes Benjamin to his grandmother] that I am now going out into society at least twice a week? I have a smart suit, a sword, my hat under my arm, one hand on my chest, the other on my hip. I can hold myself upright and play the big boy as well as I can. I watch, I listen and up to now I do not envy society its pleasures. People do not appear to care for each other very much. But I do get a certain amount of emotion from watching the gaming tables and seeing the gold coins spin. I should like to make money for a thousand reasons; they tell me that these reasons are foolish.

I have dealt in some detail with the system of education imposed upon Benjamin Constant in his earliest years since it provides a clue to his character. It is no excuse for Juste de Constant to say that this system of cosmopolitan cramming was traditional with the Vaudois aristocracy. It was his fault that Benjamin's tutors were so carelessly selected; it was his fault that the boy was alternately snubbed and shown off. By nature Benjamin Constant was affectionate, generous, expansive and sociable. His education—being at one and the same time intensive and intermittent, solitary and mundane—developed his critical faculties at the expense of moral and social values. Even as a child his precocious, over-heated, intellect was capable of analysing his actions and emotions; it never managed to establish control.

"Benjamin's childhood," writes Professor Rudler, "was bathed in self-love." He himself in after years was fully aware of the harm that had been done:

> Consider my education [he wrote to Madame de Nassau on May 24, 1794], my vagabond and haphazard way of life, the objects of vanity with which my childhood was nourished, that tone of irony which is our family habit, the pose of ridiculing all sentiment, of attributing value only to success and brilliance—is it surprising that my young head was turned?

On his thirty-seventh birthday, on October 25, 1804, he made the following confession in his diary:

> I realize that until the age of fourteen (adored by my father, who at one moment would treat me with excessive severity and at the other egg me on to bouts of vanity) I lived surrounded by universal admiration of my precocious talents, accompanied by a universal mistrust of my violent, quarrelsome and sly character.

Benjamin Constant, from the day of his birth, was never given a chance.

BOYHOOD AND EDUCATION

2

In October 1780, Benjamin Constant reached the age of thirteen; his father decided that the time had come to send him to the university. Without making the slightest preliminary enquiries he hurried across to England and presented the boy at Oxford; he was enraged when the authorities informed him that Benjamin was too young to be admitted. For two and a half months they remained in lodgings at Oxford, making occasional excursions into the surrounding country and visiting Blenheim. Eventually Juste de Constant discovered a young English tutor, a Mr. May. He engaged this man to teach his boy the English language and then they all three returned to Geertruydenberg, in the Low Countries, where Juste's regiment was then stationed.

Mr. May appears to have been an estimable man, but he got on Juste's nerves. Such authority as Mr. May might have established over his pupil was quickly destroyed by the outspoken contempt with which Juste regarded him. Mr. May was sent home to England and his place taken by a Monsieur Bridel. Juste could not conceal his impatience at the slow and precise enunciation with which Monsieur Bridel spoke the French language. He also was dismissed and, on the advice of the Margraf of Anspach, Juste decided to send his son to the small German university of Erlangen all by himself. He matriculated there on February 6, 1782 at the age of fourteen. He remained there a year and a half.

Erlangen at that date was a small Residenzstadt of some 8,000 inhabitants. It contained a young but serious university of some 250 students. Professor Rudler, with his accustomed energy of research, has unearthed the curriculum which obtained at the time when Constant was a student. It comprised philosophy, history, logic, law, rhetoric, the Greek and Latin classics and even heraldry. Although in his *Cahier Rouge* Constant was more interested in recalling his escapades than his studies, it is evident that, during his first year at least, he worked hard and acquired much solid information. Prosper de Barante in later years contended that Erlangen had exercised more influence upon Constant than Edinburgh or Paris and that as a young, and even an older, man there was always something about him which suggested the *Privatdozent* of a small German university.

The Margraf of Anspach-Bayreuth was an eccentric but cultivated man; his education and outlook were French rather than German. Although married to a Princess of Saxe-Coburg, he had for seventeen years been under the domination of Mlle. Clairon. She ran his court, she ran his principality, she managed all his affairs. But when the Margravine died in 1791 he suddenly emancipated himself from Mlle. Clairon, sold his principality to Prussia, abdicated, and married Lady Craven.

The Dowager Margravine, who had met Juste de Constant in Brussels, took an immediate fancy to Benjamin. She was amused by his gay precocious manner; she may have been sorry for him in his lonely exile; she made a favourite of him from the start. Night after night he would attend her court, pay attention to the ladies, and indulge in games of faro with the gentlemen. Before long he was obliged to confess to his father that he had contracted gambling debts; Juste de Constant was amused by such spirited behaviour on the part of his stripling son; he paid the debts without a murmur.

There is no evidence that Benjamin Constant was precocious in his sexual development. I have in fact a suspicion that it was much retarded. When at Brussels, he had met an English girl of his own age, whom as he confessed to his grandmother, he "infinitely preferred to Cicero and Seneca." At Geertruydenberg he believed himself to be in love with the daughter of one of the officers, but this affair never advanced beyond the stage of passionate love letters which were never delivered. After he had been at Erlangen a few months he seems to have decided that his intellectual and social precocity should be accompanied by an equal physical maturity. He has described the episode with his accustomed astringency:

> I wanted [he confesses in the *Cahier Rouge*] the glamour of possessing a mistress. I chose a girl of shady reputation whose mother in some way had got herself into the bad books of the Margravine. The odd thing about this affair is that neither did I care for the girl nor did she surrender herself to me. I was perhaps the only male she had ever resisted. But the delight I experienced from pretending to have a mistress, and from hearing other people say so, consoled me for having to spend my time with a person for whom I had no affection and for not sleeping with a woman with whom I was supposed to have an affair.

At the instigation of this girl and her mother Constant began to exercise his nimble wit at the expense of the Dowager Margravine. His jokes were repeated. The Margravine was so incensed that she forbade him the court. "The Dowager's protests," he wrote, "suited my purpose perfectly. I wanted to be talked about." The Margravine went further. She wrote to Juste de Constant informing him that his son was doing himself no good at Erlangen. A furious summons was despatched ordering Benjamin to return at once to Geertruydenberg. On arrival, he was informed that they were both leaving immediately for Edinburgh. They reached the Scottish capital on July 8, 1783. Benjamin was then fifteen years of age.

3

We do not know what circumstances induced Juste de Constant to decide on Edinburgh. It is probable that he possessed friends in the Scottish Regiment then serving under the States General in Holland. It was from them that he must have learnt of the high repute which Edinburgh University already enjoyed. Juste arrived armed with useful letters of introduction. Within three weeks he was able to return to Holland, having deposited his son in the family of Dr. Andrew Duncan, Professor of Medicine. Benjamin remained under Dr. Duncan's roof for a period of twelve months. "The most agreeable year," he recorded later, "of my whole life." He thereafter, in August 1784, lodged with "an excellent family" on the outskirts of the town.

The Edinburgh students in those days were given considerable liberty; for the first time Benjamin Constant was able to mix on equal terms with boys of his own age. He studied history under Professor Alexander Fraser and Greek with Professor Dalziel. He tells us that it was the fashion at Edinburgh to work hard and that it was during the eighteen months which he spent at that university that he acquired the habit of serious study which became such a solace to him in the troubles of his later life.

The high seriousness of the Edinburgh of 1783 has been defined in more portentous terms in the memoirs of Constant's contemporary, Sir James Mackintosh (1), then known as "Jemmy the Poet." "It is not easy," writes Mackintosh, "to conceive a university where industry was more general, where reading was more fashionable, where ignorance and indolence were more disreputable. Every mind was in a state of fermentation. . . ." Sir James, looking back upon his long and useful life, was inclined to feel that the atmosphere of his old university had been a shade too metaphysical. "Accurate and applicable knowledge," he writes, "was deserted for speculations not susceptible of certainty, nor of any immediate reference to the purposes of life. Strength was exhausted in vain leaps to catch what is too high for our reach. Youth—the season of humble diligence—was often wasted in vast and fruitless projects. . . . Docility is thus often extinguished, when education is scarcely begun."

Sir James, for all these strictures, agrees that the Edinburgh undergraduates of 1784 were a very brilliant lot. He admits that he himself was "speculative, lazy and factious," and that he possessed "the tumultuary mind of a disputatious boy." "Yet on the whole," he writes, "we were a combination of young men more distinguished than is usually found in one university at the same time."

The centre of this group of ardent boys was the "Speculative Society" (2) which had been founded twenty years before for the discussion of literary and social subjects. Sir James Mackintosh in his memoirs recalls the names of some of the more striking or distinguished members of this Society. There was Charles Hope, subsequently Lord President of the Court of Sessions; there was Malcolm Laing, the historian (3); there were Adam Gillies and John Wilde, James Grant and Richard Kentish; there was Thomas Addis Emmet, the United Irishman; and there was "Baron Constant de Rebecque, a Swiss of singular manners and powerful talents, who made a transient appearance in the tempestuous atmosphere of the French Revolution."

Benjamin himself, although he established firm friendships with most of the leading members of the Speculative Society, appears to have been most intimate with Kentish and John Wilde. The latter was the son of a tobacconist and possessed a fervent imagination and a dominant character. He thereafter became assistant Professor of Civil Law, in which capacity he gave a few tutorials to Walter Scott. His mind became clouded and he ended his days in an asylum. Benjamin Constant was for long haunted by the spectre of his boyhood friend mouthing demented in a mad-house; it was a spectre which accorded well with the morbid despondency of his middle years.

Professor Rudler, when preparing his admirable work upon the youth of Benjamin Constant, managed to obtain in Edinburgh the minutes of the Speculative Society. He found that during the period of Constant's membership the following subjects were among those discussed. Ought there to be universal religious tolerance? Is duelling justifiable? Ought the existing Marriage Act to be repealed? Should Members of Parliament act as the delegates of their constituents or as their representatives? Is the character of a nation determined by moral or physical causes? Have the nations of Europe any reason to fear the effect upon the Balance of Power of an increase in the strength of Russia? And is a militia preferable to a standing army? It is interesting to note that on the last issue Benjamin Constant voted against a standing army. It is also curious that the only subject upon which he himself read a paper to the Society was "The influence of pagan mythology upon modern ethics." That was the subject which he studied with fascination all his life.

"I spent," he writes in the *Cahier Rouge,* "some eighteen months at Edinburgh. I enjoyed myself immensely, I studied sufficiently and I behaved in such a way that everyone spoke highly of me. Unfortunately a little Italian, from whom I was taking music lessons, introduced me to a faro bank which was run by his brother. I played; I lost; I made debts to right and left, with the result that my sojourn in Edinburgh was marred."

It is not easy for those who have never become victims to the vice of gambling to understand the hold which this passion can obtain upon the minds of men. We have seen how Benjamin Constant as a child of twelve was fascinated by the glamour of the gaming tables "and seeing the gold coins spin." We have seen how at Erlangen he first began, at the age of fourteen, himself to indulge in faro and already to contract gambling debts. It may be that this vice is congenital and due to some defect of blood or glands. It may be that it afflicts people of extreme nervous impatience who find therein an excitement more immediate and intensive than that provided by the more prolonged struggles of ordinary life. Or it may be that a temperament which combines a burning desire for success with insufficient will-power and endurance, is fascinated by this simulacrum of activity, in which decision is provided, not by inner volition, but by the external intervention of chance. Constant always saw with absolute clarity the misery which his gambling habits brought upon himself and others. He was never able to subdue them. As an old man, when he might have been content to remain a respected leader of the Liberal Opposition, he would quite consciously destroy his own repute and influence by limping, when the Chamber closed, into one of the gambling dens of the Palais Royal.

It was this, the eternal curse of his life, which came to mar his last months at Edinburgh. "The moment having arrived," he writes, "which my father had fixed for my departure, I left Edinburgh promising to pay my gambling debts, but leaving my creditors in a state of intense indignation and thus a most unfavourable impression behind me."

It is too much to say that Constant slipped away from Edinburgh in order to avoid paying his debts at cards. It is not too much to say that he left the university under a cloud. Yet those eighteen months remained of durable value to him. He had acquired the precious habit of solitary study, a habit which once acquired remains a delight in after life. He had learnt to speak English with fluency, although with a Franco-Scottish accent. He had made many friends who, in spite of his conduct, remained loyal to him for many years. And above all he had achieved a real understanding of British institutions, of the true meaning of constitutional monarchy, and of what was meant by liberal democracy.

Speaking of his own days at Edinburgh, Sir James Mackintosh confessed that it was there that he himself had imbibed "the strong spirit of liberty, which, of all moral sentiments, in my opinion tends most to swell the heart with an animating and delightful consciousness of our own dignity; which again inspires moral heroism and creates the exquisite enjoyments of self-honour and self-reverence."

Constant himself conceived of liberty in more analytical terms. Yet it is assuredly true that it was at Edinburgh that he learnt to regard liberty, not merely as a political formula, but as the only ethical purpose in which he unwaveringly believed. Benjamin was a very inconsistent man; but to this conception of liberty he adhered consistently throughout his life.

4

On leaving Edinburgh, Benjamin Constant spent three "useless" weeks in London and thereafter crossed to Paris where his father had made arrangements for his further education. These arrangements were for once sensibly conceived. Juste de Constant had induced Monsieur and Madame Suard (4) to receive Benjamin into their house in the Rue Louis le Grand. Here was a valuable opportunity which Benjamin, with egoistic levity, cast aside.

It is customary for young men, finding themselves upon the

very verge of emancipated life, to resent the continuance of supervision and control. Benjamin Constant, at the age of seventeen, was prematurely adult. The liberties of his Edinburgh days, the self-conceit engendered by the flattery he had received in childhood and the reputation for "power-ful talents" which he had acquired at the university, his satirical disrespect for every established convention, his justifiable mistrust of his father's managements—all these combined to render him rebellious to implicit disapproval. He approached the Suards in a mood of sneering antagonism and thereby overlooked one of the few valuable occasions which his father's errant solicitude had provided. Twenty-six years later, when writing the *Cahier Rouge,* he admitted, with his habitual acumen of self-reproach, the folly of his attitude. "My father," he wrote, "had made an arrangement for me which could have provided me with all manner of advantages and opportunities, had I known how to profit by them, or even wished to do so."

Jean Baptiste Suard was a distinguished man of letters who in 1785 had been a member of the French Academy for eleven years. He had written several erudite books of literary criticism and was one of the few Frenchmen of his age who possessed a real knowledge of English letters. He had been the friend of Wilkes and Hume; he was at the time fulfilling with general approval the delicate function of Chief Censor of Plays; he was a constitutional monarchist of progressive opinions. His wife was a woman of intelligence and beauty; she was the sister of the publisher Panckoucke and her salon in the Rue Louis le Grand was generally admitted to be rivalled only by that of Madame Geoffrin. Had Benjamin discovered the Suard circle for himself, he would have been delighted to find there in a quiet harmony with his own political and literary opinions: since it was imposed upon him by his father, he noticed only the discords struck by the conventions of an older age. This was doubly unfortunate. He missed the opportunity to train himself modestly in the difficult elegance of the pre-revolution world. And in subsequent years, when Suard had become a man of influence under the Empire and Restoration, the memory of his adolescent rudeness and intemperance created between them a barrier of constraint.

Benjamin Constant arrived in Paris in the spring of 1785. The room which had been set aside for him in the house of Madame Suard was not at the moment available. He was lodged for four weeks in a neighbouring hotel. By one of those mischances which seem always to have entangled Constant's footsteps, there was living in this hotel at the time a young Englishman of dissolute habits and considerable wealth. This unidentified Englishman appears to have been amused by the precocious red-haired undergraduate whose conversation and accent he found most entertaining. He encouraged Benjamin to accompany him to the brothels and gaming tables of Paris with the result that by the end of the month there were physical dilapidations and considerable gambling debts. On transferring to the Suard house in the Rue Louis le Grand, Constant asserts that his "behaviour became less extravagant." But once again his father, with his amazing capacity for never letting well alone, intervened to create a diversion.

Fearing that the venerable Suard and the cultured Madame Suard would not exercise sufficient vigilance, Juste de Constant thought it wise to arrange for more direct supervision. He consulted the chaplain to the Dutch Embassy in Paris who recommended a man of the name of Baumier, who represented himself as a Protestant abjured by his family on account of his religion. Baumier was in fact a dissolute and ignorant man. Benjamin Constant (who was seldom acid about weaknesses other than his own) describes him as being completely devoid of morals and in addition "dull and insolent." Baumier began by aiding, abetting and sharing his pupil's habits of profligacy; but when the relations between them had become strained to breaking point, he wrote to Juste de Constant stating that his son's way of life in Paris had passed beyond human control. The Colonel made one of his abrupt and fulminating appearances; Baumier was dismissed and Benjamin was snatched away from the Suard circle, the potential benefits of which he had, during this first visit, only enjoyed for some four months.

5

He was deposited in Brussels and Juste de Constant returned to Geertruydenberg. During the three months that Benjamin then spent in Brussels he frequented two distinct circles. There was a section of local Belgian society, represented by the d'Anets and the d'Arembergs. And there was a smaller group of Genevese residents with whom he became more intimate.

Among the latter was a Madame Johannot (5), who was living separated from her husband and who was a person of intelligence and charm. Benjamin, who was always attracted by women older than himself, established with this lady relations of affectionate friendship. She told him of her unhappy marriage and how her husband had brutally deserted her in favour of his mistress. Benjamin's sympathies were aroused. Then abruptly one day she confessed to Benjamin that she had fallen in love with him. He was deeply moved by this the first disinterested affection which he had ever inspired. There is a passage in the *Cahier Rouge* in which he records his gratitude to Madame Johannot:

> As I write these words, twenty-five years have passed since I discovered that she loved me. Yet I still experience a feeling of gratitude when I recall the delight which her confession caused me. . . . She retains a place in my memory which is wholly different from that occupied by all the other women I have known. My affair with her was very short and reduced itself to mighty little. Yet she did not force me to pay for the sweet sensations she brought me by any admixture of suffering or agitation. At the age of forty-four I am still grateful to her for the happiness she gave me when I was eighteen.

Monsieur Johannot, according to the *Cahier Rouge*, was a despicable creature who caused long suffering to his charming wife. In the end she moved from Brussels to Paris where some years later she committed suicide. Benjamin Constant happened to be in Paris at the moment and living, although he did not know it, only a few doors from the house where his first benefactress was dying miserably and in the belief that she had been deserted by all the world.

The affair with Madame Johannot—the only absolutely calm relationship which Constant ever experienced—lasted only some four weeks. In November 1785 Juste de Constant appeared in Brussels and instructed Benjamin to return to Switzerland immediately.

He got back to Le Désert after an absence of four years. His family did not find that he had improved in the interval. They thought him contemptuous, flippant and conceited. Rosalie de Constant regretted to have to tell her brother that Benjamin, although as childish as ever, had started to give himself airs. Always, on returning to Lausanne, did he meet with this glum disapproval. "And yet," Rosalie would write, "he is so gay—so amusing—so very amusing."

Such was the inconsequent prelude to Benjamin Constant's inconsequent life. A feverish desire for success can only strengthen into ambition if directed and controlled by will. Even with the stoutest of us, will-power is a root of gradual growth; it cannot harden if continually transplanted. Juste always handled his son as a pot-plant, shifting him impetuously from one greenhouse to the other, each one of which possessed a different temperature.

CHAPTER III

Madame de Charrière

[1785–1787]

Constant returns to Lausanne—His work on the history of religion—His conception of love—His affair with Mrs. Trevor—His return to Paris—His gambling debts—Madame Saurin—His first meeting with Madame de Charrière—The early life and adventures of Isabella van Tuyll—Constant d'Hermenches and James Boswell—The Marquis de Bellegarde—She marries Monsieur de Charrière—Her character and early married life—Her novels—She comes to Paris and meets Constant—the nature of their friendship—The episode of Jenny Pourrat—He is summoned to join his father.

1

HOWEVER much we may resent Juste de Constant's habit of playing tricks with his son's education, there is one fact at least which must be entered to his credit. He never tried to induce Benjamin to adopt a military career; he never insisted that he should follow the family tradition and take service with the Swiss Regiment in Holland. Juste had always been convinced that Benjamin was destined to achieve fame and fortune as a writer; he was indulgent to his evasions during the prolonged periods when, in practice if not in theory, he was doing nothing at all.

From November 1785 to November 1786 Benjamin remained at Le Désert, paying occasional visits to his friends and relations at Lausanne and Geneva. He resumed the theme which a year previously he had discussed at the Speculative Society at Edinburgh and started working on a book about pagan mythology. He soon discovered that he did not as yet possess the necessary scholarship to contribute any fresh value to such a subject. For the moment the polytheism of the Romans was laid aside. He was glad in later years that he had not persisted in his original intention. He might with application have produced a book of sorts within two years; but his vanity would, he admitted, not have allowed him thereafter to alter opinions or repudiate statements which, in the then state of his information, would assuredly have been incorrect. At a later date this study became merged in the vaster enterprise of a comparative history of religions. Upon this enterprise Benjamin Constant was engaged for more than forty years. The five volumes of his *Religion considered in its sources, forms and development* only appeared in print between 1824 and 1834, the last two volumes being published after his death. The book which deals specifically with *Roman Polytheism in its relation to Greek philosophy and the Christian Religion* was also published posthumously in 1833. It is sad to reflect that the works to which Benjamin Constant devoted so many years of research and industry, and upon which he hoped to base his reputation as a historian and a man of letters, had, by the time of their eventual publication, been rendered almost completely out of date.

Having wisely abandoned, for the time at least, his study of Roman mythology, Benjamin decided to translate into French the first three volumes of Gibbon's *Decline and Fall*. He found however that the cadences and antitheses of that masterpiece did not accord conveniently with the structure of the French language. He therefore fell back upon translating John Gillies' more outright *History of Greece* which had been published that year in London. He had only just set to work upon this translation, when his industry was distracted by one of those emotional disturbances which he mistook for love.

Benjamin Constant was the cerebral type of libertine—a type which often inflicts, and sometimes suffers, more misery than any other. For him, love was not so much an emotion kindled by the personality of someone else: it was an ecstasy generated within his own imagination and projected outwards, until, almost fortuitously, it encountered some solid object. No other intoxicant could render his perceptions so sensitive or the motions of his brain so rapid and acute: he resorted to it as a drug. Those who fall in love with love, rather than with the object of their desire, discover that their adoration comes to centre upon the quality of their own emotion; it is the tension of pursuit, the intensity of expectation, which stimulates their excitement; but when the quarry is captured or escapes, they fall to earth, overcome with lassitude and disillusion. Constant was always saddened by the suddenness of his satiety. Had he been, as some averred, an entirely heartless man, he could have passed his victims by with a sardonic smile. Yet with him the desire to escape was always restrained by tenderness; reaction and repulsion were arrested by pity. He was never strong enough to reject the error of being in love with love; but always, and sometimes at the cost of much personal suffering, he endeavoured to redeem it.

In the summer of 1786, while he was busily engaged upon Gillies' *History of Greece*, his labours were, as I have said, dislocated by what was perhaps the most artificial of all his cerebral passions. He imagined that he had fallen in love with Mrs. Trevor. The episode which followed was so fantastic that it would not be worth mentioning but for the fact that it provides a key to the pattern of his later loves. Benjamin, bored by Gillies and Le Désert, may well have felt that the moment had come to revive the agreeable sensations which Madame Johannot had inspired. He generated within himself the expectation of romance; but instead of going out in search of an object worthy of his adoration, he waited until chance should have taken the initiative and brought some object (whether adorable or not) within the orbit of his readiness. The conjunction of expectation and opportunity caused an explosion. In the end Benjamin managed to convince himself that he was in fact seriously in love; upon Mrs. Trevor, fortunately, he produced no more than a momentary sense of embarrassed amusement.

Harriot Burton, only child of the Rev. Daniel Burton, canon of Christ Church, had been born in 1751. At the time of her meeting with Constant she was thirty-five years of age and he eighteen. In 1771 she had married John Hampden Trevor. He was the second son of the first Viscount Hampden, to which title he himself eventually succeeded. By 1786 John Trevor, having served for a while at Munich, was Minister to the Court of Sardinia and resident at Turin. His wife, hoping to avoid the summer heats of Piedmont, rented a villa near Lausanne. Her arrival caused a certain stir in the district. She was a hospitable woman and her house was soon filled with the gayer members of the Vaudois aristocracy and the many Englishmen and foreigners who had either accompanied her, or who were completing their studies in Switzerland. Even Gibbon, then within exactly eleven months of completing his great history, became inquisitive. "By the by," he wrote to Lord Sheffield on July 22, 1786, "Mrs. Trevor is now here, without her husband. I am just going to see her, about a mile out of the town. She is judged elegant and amiable."

2

In the *Cahier Rouge*, written at Hardenberg some twenty-five years later, Benjamin Constant tells the story of his affair with Mrs. Trevor in that tone of affectionate malice with which he always treated the follies of his youth. His account is not wholly convincing. Mrs. Trevor was in no sense a novice, and Benjamin himself was not, at the age of eighteen, quite as bashful or as innocent as he makes out. But the central theme is true enough. He was not in love with Mrs. Trevor; he was in love with love; and the resultant disparity between his passion and its object landed him in a situation which was both disconcerting and false.

"Mrs. Trevor," writes Constant, "had once been very beautiful; she still retained a lovely expression, magnificent teeth and a charming smile. I much enjoyed going to her house; there was a great deal of gambling, so that I was able when there to indulge a taste more vivid perhaps than that which the lady herself inspired. She was a tremendous flirt. She had an affected manner and that light alacrity of mind which the desire to attract imparts to women who have no other form of intelligence. She did not get on with her husband from whom she was almost always separated; she was surrounded by five or six young Englishmen who formed her escort."

He then recounts how he first began to visit the house, partly because he found there a society less glum than that of his Lausanne relations, and partly of course because they gambled for high stakes. He soon discovered that all the young men pretended to be in love with Mrs. Trevor and he decided to imitate their pose. He wrote her "a beautiful letter" in which he declared his passion. He returned next morning to receive her reply. "The agitation," he writes, "generated within me by the uncertainty of the result threw me into a fever, not unlike the passion which at first I had only simulated." Mrs. Trevor replied in a short note in which she reminded him of her conjugal loyalties and offered him her most tender friendship. The passage which follows in the *Cahier Rouge* is an excellent example of the *dédoublement constantinien*, of the duality of participant and observer:

> I ought not, of course, to have taken this as the last word. I ought to have investigated further to see how far this "tender friendship" would lead us. Instead of this, I thought it more subtle to demonstrate the most violent despair at being offered only friendship in place of the passion which I had tendered. Picture me therefore rolling upon the floor, banging my head against the walls, at the mere mention of that cursed word "friendship." The poor woman, who had so far only had to deal with lovers more expert than I was, did not know how to conduct herself during this scene. It was rendered all the more embarrassing, since I did not make a single gesture which could have helped her to bring it to an end in a manner which would have been agreeable to each of us. The whole time, I kept myself at a distance of three yards; when she approached me, in order to comfort and console, I drew away from her, saying again and again that since friendship was all that she could offer, it only remained for me to die.

This difficult scene was prolonged for four hours. "I left her," records Constant, "considerably irritated with a lover who could thus dispute about synonyms."

Having been denied his expectation (and we may be sure that Mrs. Trevor kept it continuously alive) Constant ended by generating within himself a state of nerves which was almost indistinguishable from being in love. His passion lasted for some three or four months. Mrs. Trevor continued to manifest the tenderness of her friendship. "Neither she nor I," he writes, "ever got anything out of it. I was at one and the same time wildly excited and terrifically bashful. I did not then know that one ought to take rather than ask; I asked all the time; I never took."

At one stage in the proceedings Constant considered it suitable to become jealous of one of the young Englishmen who formed part of Mrs. Trevor's train. He accused this young man of paying indelicate attentions to Mrs. Trevor and challenged him to a duel. The Englishman (it may well have been the Mr. Edmund Lascelles who recurs later in this story) replied that, so far from being in love with Mrs. Trevor, he had come to the conclusion that he disliked her very much indeed. Constant then again challenged him to another duel on the ground that he had insulted the woman he loved. The Englishman, we may suppose, told Constant not to be an ass.

In November 1786 Juste de Constant arrived at Lausanne and announced that Benjamin must now accompany him back to Paris. There followed a tear-stained parting from Mrs. Trevor. "I took her in my arms; my tears splashed upon her hands; I spent nights weeping upon a bench on which I had once seen her seated; she cried also; had I stopped arguing about the meaning of words, I might have achieved a more definite result. But all that happened was a chaste kiss upon lips that were already somewhat faded. Finally I left her in inexpressible misery. She promised to write to me; they carried me off."

Juste de Constant and his sobbing son left Lausanne for Paris on November 16, 1786. They were accompanied by Benjamin's cousin, Charles de Constant, who happened to be on leave from China. The latter, who was five years older than Benjamin, wrote to his sisters a detailed description of this journey. His letters have been preserved. Benjamin, it seems, was so heart-broken, that at one moment they thought of turning back. He continued to weep throughout the journey, exclaiming upon the cruelty of human nature. "So I started," writes Charles, "to sing a little song. Benjamin said that I had a coarse and narrow mind. . . . Although he is amusing enough, he does not say one word which it does not pay him to say. . . . I am not enjoying their company. My uncle makes difficulties about everything and pays attention only to Benjamin, who has never ceased to have a tear in his eye and an epigram upon his lips." They spent the night of Monday, November 20 at Genlis. In the carriage next morning Charles listened to Benjamin reciting to his father "in a tender voice," a poem which he had written to Mrs. Trevor during the night:

> "Vous qui empoisonnez ma vie
> N'augmentez pas ma douleur.
> Mon sort n'est pas digne d'envie:
> Pourquoi me ravir mon maheur?"

Benjamin was always an atrocious poet; but the sentiment, at the moment, was sincere enough. On reaching Paris he seems immediately to have forgotten all about Mrs. Trevor. He met her there three months later and experienced no emotion at all; and when he was in England in the following summer, he did not trouble to visit her, although he must have known that she was then taking the waters at Tunbridge Wells. Mrs. Trevor thereafter passed completely out of his life. In her later years she lost her reason and died in 1829.

3

On reaching Paris the three Constants took rooms in the Hôtel des États Unis in the Rue Gaillon; all they could obtain was a small entresol which was expensive and uncomfortable. Juste insisted upon the hotel servants addressing Benjamin as "Monsieur le Baron" and was (perhaps justifiably) fastidious about the pocket money which he allowed his son. He was continually urging Benjamin to return to the Suard household, where he would find renewed opportunities for establishing useful relations with the literary and social world. Benjamin, somewhat unwillingly—in view of his past conduct towards the Suards—agreed to this proposition. Charles regarded his uncle's ambition as misplaced. "I would take a bet," he wrote to Rosalie, "that Benjamin will never become famous." Nor did Charles, although a tolerant and experienced man, succeed in establishing easy relations with Juste. "I must tell you," he wrote to Rosalie on December 4, "about my uncle. First, he gets on my nerves. Secondly, he bores me. Thirdly, he is not to my taste. . . . His suspicious, restless, arrogant, cross-grained and sardonic character is ill-attuned to a temperament such as mine. How warmly do I sympathize with Benjamin's despair!"

It was in the first fortnight of that December 1786 that Benjamin left his father and cousin and returned to the Suards. Juste and Charles moved from the Hôtel des États Unis and established themselves in the Hôtel Ventadour. Charles went out into society. He sends a description of a supper given at the Swedish Embassy by Madame de Staël. He knew nobody, and was embarrassed and bored. People came up to him and said: "Is it you, Sir, who are just back from China?" They did not wait for his answer. There exists no evidence at all to suggest that Benjamin at this date (although the Suards were intimate with the Necker family) ever met Madame de Staël. That baleful encounter was postponed for eight years.

In this, the second period of his residence with the Suards, Benjamin Constant began to develop and exploit his social gifts. The mode at the time was anglo-mania and religious scepticism; Benjamin had much to say on each of these two subjects. The audacity of his opinions and the brilliance of his epigrams arrested attention while they inspired distrust. "When I recall," he writes in the *Cahier Rouge* "the sort of things I used to say and the reasoned disdain that I displayed for everybody and everything, it remains a marvel to me that anybody ever stood me at all." Yet it was in the salon of Madame Suard that he caught the last gleams of an expiring epoch, and met men—such as Condorcet and La Fayette—who played a leading part in the drama so soon to open.

When at Lausanne he had known a Madame de Bourbonne, whose passion for gambling was as obsessive as his own. At her house in Paris, he had, within a few weeks, lost far more money than he could pay. He did not dare to ask his father for further assistance, and in his despair he decided to appeal to Madame Saurin, the benevolent widow of the author of *Spartacus,* and an intimate friend of the Suard family. He wrote her a tactfully worded letter, begging for a loan, and stating that he would call next day to receive her answer. Madame Saurin at the time was sixty-five years of age; she had in her youth been extremely beautiful—"a fact," writes Benjamin, "which she remembered ever afterwards, and all to herself." When Benjamin arrived next morning he discovered to his horror that Madame Saurin had never received his letter and that he would be obliged to explain verbally the nature of his embarrassing request. Stuttering with shyness he mumbled out a few phrases such as "I may have presumed too much upon the kindness that you have always shown me. There are moments when a man loses his head. . . ." "Go on," panted Madame Saurin, "Go on!" Benjamin's protestations became more and more involved. Suddenly, Madame Saurin covered her face with her hands and started to tremble violently. He became aware that she had interpreted his demand for money as a declaration of passion. "The misunderstanding which had arisen," he records, "the emotion which overcame her, and a huge red damask bed which stood two feet away, plunged me into indescribable terror." In the end he had to make it clear to Madame Saurin that he had come only to ask for cash. Without a word, she left the room, and returned with the exact sum that he had suggested. They parted in silence.

It is to the credit of Madame Saurin that she bore no resentment for this humiliating episode. We find her in 1792 writing to a friend and asking for the latest news of Benjamin. "However eccentric he may be," she wrote, "one should always remember his excellent qualities and the brilliance of his intellect." It was seldom that Benjamin remained for long unpardoned.

Juste de Constant, in March 1787, left Paris and returned to his regiment. It must have been in that month that Benjamin Constant first met Madame de Charrière.

4

Isabella van Serooskerken van Tuyll was born in 1740 at the castle of Zuylen in Holland. She was forty-seven years old when she first met Constant and he was nineteen. The story of her disappointed but not uncomplaining, life, the story of her writings and her friendships, has been told with respectful detail in the two large volumes which Monsieur Philippe Godet published in Geneva in 1906. An elegant variation upon Monsieur Godet's *Madame de Charrière et ses amis* was written by the late Mr. Geoffrey Scott in 1925, under the title *The Portrait of Zélide*.

Belle de Zuylen, as she was called, was the most industri-

MONSIEUR AND MADAME CHARRIÈRE

From the miniatures by L. A. Arlaud (1781) in the University Library at Geneva. Reproduced by kind permission of the University authorities

ous and gifted of all the Dutch girls of her time. She would rise at six in the morning and drive into Utrecht in order to take lessons in conic sections. She was not a rich girl; she was not either submissive or modest; she was not even pretty. She possessed a beautiful neck and splendid teeth; but she had ugly hands and her complexion, even in her youth, was all too florid. Her eyes were bright blue, disparate and protruding; one of them, it was said, suggested malice and the other gentleness. She had a slight but agreeable impediment in her speech and a habit, when engaged in conversation, of tilting her chair backwards. It is clear from her rapid alternations between excitability and moroseness, from the bulbous appearance of her eyeballs, and from the glandular swelling which later developed in her neck, that she suffered from Graves' disease. But she survived, in comparatively good health, until she was sixty-six.

From her earliest years Belle de Zuylen had set out in search of an illustrious marriage. When she was nineteen years of age she attracted the attention of Constant d'Hermenches, Benjamin's uncle, who was universally regarded as one of the most seductive profligates in Europe. For fifteen years she maintained with him a correspondence which was affectionate rather than passionate, cynical rather than enraptured. Constant d'Hermenches decided that it would be an excellent thing if he married off Mademoiselle de Tuyll to his old and complacent friend the Marquis de Bellegarde. Negotiations were opened and dragged on for four weary years. At a party in Utrecht she met James Boswell, "A young Scotsman, who is full of good sense, intelligence and naïveté." She formed with him a frank and reasonable friendship. He explained to her that he would not think of marrying her, even if she possessed the wealth of seven of the United Provinces. "I should make a bad wife for you," she answered. "I have no subaltern qualities."

Other suitors were also considered, among them old Lord Wemyss, who had been attainted for his conduct during the '45 rebellion and was not regarded at Zuylen as in any sense a desirable husband. In the end Monsieur de Bellegarde, who had been kept in the offing in case nothing better turned up, decided that Belle possessed too sharp an intelligence and too small a dowry. He retired from the scene. "Don't mention a husband to me again," she wrote to Constant d'Hermenches, "if I want one, I shall know how to find him myself."

In 1766, when Belle was twenty-six years of age, there appeared at the castle of Zuylen a modest little Swiss gentleman of thirty-four, who had been engaged to teach arithmetic to her younger brother Ditie. The name of this tutor was Monsieur de Charrière. He was very small, he was very shy, he was calm and pompous, and he suffered from what Belle called "a certain clumsiness of mind and manners." As the other suitors melted away one by one, Belle decided that she might do worse than marry this quiet, honourable little man. For two years he resisted her assaults, but in the end he capitulated. "Mlle. de Zuylen," he wrote to his sisters at Colombier, "has been a friend of mine for seven years; for the last two years she has occupied herself with the project of marrying me." "He loves me," wrote Belle to Constant d'Hermenches, "without illusion or enthusiasm; he is sincere and just to the point, sometimes, of causing me pain." They were married at Zuylen on February 17, 1773. On the night of their wedding, Monsieur de Charrière made himself sick by drinking rum punch; his bride was suffering from neuralgia which she sought to assuage by drinking opium. Thereafter they left for Switzerland.

He brought his proud but not undutiful bride back with him to his little manor house at Colombier, near the lake of Neuchâtel. He introduced her to his two maiden sisters and to the domestic tasks which she was expected to perform. He introduced her to lakeside society. She was kindly to her humble husband; but never tender, either to him or to his two sisters. She filled the neighbours with acute alarm. Hers was a character, as Geoffrey Scott remarks, "so avid of living, so sceptical of life, which could find no harmony within itself nor acquiesce in the discord." During the first years of their married life, as Benjamin Constant informs us, she sought by every means to torment her husband "in the hope of imparting to him some of her own vivacity." She failed in this experiment. Monsieur de Charrière, as Constant also records, was "an intelligent man, a man of noble and refined character, but the coldest and most phlegmatic person that it is possible to conceive." And thus, after eleven years of strained but uneventful marriage, she started to write novels.

Already, at the age of twenty-three, she had published a short satire entitled *Le Noble,* which had caused much scandal in Dutch society, in that the central portrait was recognizable as that of her own father. The irritated apprehension with which she was regarded at Utrecht was thereby much increased.

In 1783, Samuel de Constant, Rosalie's melancholy father, had published a novel entitled *Le Mari Sentimental,* in which the hero, Monsieur Bompré, marries a young wife and is driven to suicide by her interference with his personal habits. Madame de Charrière was enraged by this attack upon a noble woman and replied by writing *Mistriss Henley*. The theme of her novel is that of a too well-meaning husband who makes life intolerable for his wife by his own excess of virtue, by the awful reasonableness with which he coped with her hysterics. "I have," she wrote in this novel, "no serious complaints to make. Nobody will recognize my portrait of Mister Henley. Probably, he himself will never read what I have written. But if he read it, if he happened to recognize himself? What then?" She instructed Monsieur de Charrière to make a fair copy of this manuscript. Although he was suffering from writer's cramp at the time, he submitted obediently. *Mistriss Henley* was followed the next year by *Lettres neuchâteloises*, which were resented at the time as containing satirical comments upon local Swiss society. At this stage there occurred a mysterious but lamentable episode in the life of Madame de Charrière. While spending the winter of 1785 at Geneva she met a handsome young man with whom she fell desperately in love. Her affection was not returned, and indeed the young man appears to have been engaged to someone else. Madame de Charrière went back to Colombier in a mood of deep despondency and immediately wrote her most successful novel, *Caliste*. Her husband, worried as he always was by her prolonged fits of melancholia, decided that what she needed was a thorough change. In February 1785 he brought her to Paris, where they rented an apartment in the Hôtel Chinois at No. 5, Rue Thérèse. They went into society and eventually became members of the Suard circle. It was there, more than a year later, that she met Benjamin Constant.

5

They had much in common. Madame de Charrière, even as Benjamin Constant, despised all conventional doctrines and prejudices; she believed, perhaps unduly, that the only true integrity was that of her own reason and conscience. She enjoyed analysing her own character with self-torturing lucidity; what she treasured most in life was intellectual courage, intrepidity of statement, reality of intercourse. At the same time she had an avid taste for sentimental complications, for the twisted bypaths of human character, for tortuous psychological refinements. She was a profoundly despondent woman. "I have within me," she once wrote to her brother, "a relentless enemy—black imagination. It poisons all my pleasure." Yet even at the age of forty-seven Madame de Charrière was avid of mental adventure, reckless in her intellectual indulgence and escapades. She combined in her morbid nature that unfortunate mixture of exaltation and gloom, of excitement and scepticism, of impulse and calculation, which was exactly attuned to Benjamin's own temperament at the time. Each of them was egoistic, self-centred, conceited; each of them was a natural cosmopolitan. "You and I," she wrote to him later, "when we are together, belong to no country." They were both convinced that the world had failed to appreciate the wonder of their own brilliance and that by the fools who surrounded them they were equally misprised and misunderstood. Above all, perhaps, each of them possessed an insatiable passion for conversation. Far into the night he would sit by her bedside, absorbing opium and discussing his life and her life, his adventures and her adventures, his character and her character. "Her conversation," he recorded in the *Cahier Rouge* "was for me a delight hitherto unknown. I surrendered to it entranced."

Speculation has been aroused as to whether, at least during those few months in Paris, they were actually lovers. It would in any case have been a matter of small importance to either of them; the bond between them—and it was a potent bond—was wholly cerebral. Madame de Charrière in such matters was unexpectedly prim. "She wanted," as Geoffrey Scott has shrewdly remarked, "the prize for goodness as well as the forbidden fruit."

Meanwhile Juste de Constant, at Hertogenbosch, was beginning to get anxious about Benjamin's future. His gambling debts had begun to exceed the limit which even he considered reasonable in a young man of good family launched upon the great world of Paris. A friend of his had written suggesting that it would be an excellent thing if Benjamin could marry the young Pourrat girl, an heiress reputed to be worth a dowry of ninety thousand francs a year. Moreover she was only sixteen years of age and extremely pretty. Benjamin, when consulted, agreed to do whatever was required. The father of Jenny Pourrat was a prosperous banker and her mother was one of the leading hostesses in the business and literary world. They owned an apartment in Paris and a fine estate at Louveciennes.

Benjamin opened the proceedings by writing to the mother. He confessed his passion for Jenny Pourrat and asked for her hand. Madame Pourrat replied that Jenny's hand was already pledged to someone else, but since she continued to invite Benjamin to her house, and since he learnt that she had been making enquiries in Switzerland regarding the extent of the Constant fortune, he did not regard this as a final refusal.

Had he continued to conduct himself conventionally, all might have been well. But the uncertainty of the position, the exciting equilibrium between acceptance and denial, set up an agitation of the nerves. "I behaved," he confesses, "like a lunatic." He continued to visit the Pourrat apartment, and when in the presence of Jenny he talked only of indifferent things. But every day he would send her passionate letters in which he constructed for himself, and her, a whole fabric of unreal romance. He assured her that she was being forced by her parents into marrying a man she did not love; that it was intolerable for him to see a being to whom he was devoted exposed to such parental cruelty; and that the only solution of the problem was that they should elope. She replied that her future was entirely in the hands of her father and mother and that it was not proper for a girl of sixteen to receive such letters from a young man. Benjamin continued to write to her, insisting that elopement was the only solution. "But," he adds in recording this episode, "when I found myself alone with Mlle. Pourrat, I became overwhelmed with embarrassment. I only spoke to her of trivial matters, and I never made any allusion at all to the letters which I had been writing to her every morning, or to the feelings by which they were inspired."

In the end Benjamin, who by then had worked himself into the state of love, decided to take Madame Pourrat into his confidence. His interviews with Madame Pourrat were so intimate and so prolonged that they aroused the jealousy of her lover, a certain Monsieur Louis Claude Bigot de Sainte-Croix. One evening, when Madame Pourrat and Benjamin were closeted together (it was the evening of June 8, 1787) Monsieur de Sainte-Croix entered the room and made a scene. Madame Pourrat rose with dignity and taking Benjamin by the hand led him up to Monsieur de Sainte-Croix and asked him to explain that he was not in love with Madame Pourrat, but with her daughter Jenny, who had rejected his advances.

"I saw myself," writes Benjamin in the *Cahier Rouge* "being dragged in front of a perfect stranger in order to confess to him that I was an unsuccessful lover, a man rejected both by the mother and the daughter. This wound to my self-esteem drove me suddenly insane." He decided that death would be preferable to so humiliating an explanation; drawing a phial of opium from his pocket he began (but only began) to swallow its contents. Monsieur de Sainte-Croix dashed the phial from his lips; Madame Pourrat rushed for antidotes; and Benjamin recovered with such dignity as he could muster.

"This," he remarked to his journal, "was not the only occasion in my life when, having staged a dramatic situation, I have suddenly become bored by the solemnity entailed by sustaining the action, and have reacted by myself destroying the situation which I had planned."

Benjamin quickly recovered from the small amount of opium which he had swallowed and went off to the Opera with Jenny Pourrat to see the *Tarare* of Beaumarchais.

By Madame Pourrat, however, he was not forgiven; she wrote next day to say that he had abused her hospitality and must not come again. Monsieur de Charrière was despatched in vain to make the peace. Jenny before long married the Comte de Turtot and lived till 1851. When Benjamin met her again in later years he was delighted that the affair had miscarried; he found that Jenny laid down the law.

This farcical episode brought him ever closer to Madame de Charrière. She at least did not laugh at him; she at least treated him, not as an hysterical infant, but as a man of deep culture and high intelligence. Night after night, after he had finished with the gaming tables, he would go to the Rue Thérèse. They would sit up drinking tea and opium together until the dawn glimmered through the blinds.

On learning that the marriage arranged between Mlle. Pourrat and Benjamin had unfortunately miscarried, Juste de Constant became enraged. He despatched Lieutenant de Benay of his regiment with instructions to proceed to Paris, to seek out Benjamin, and to bring him immediately to Hertogenbosch.

CHAPTER IV

England and Colombier

[1787]

Benjamin escapes to England—He reaches London—He meets Richard Kentish and goes with him to Brighton—He leaves Kentish abruptly and decides to ride to Edinburgh—The effect upon him of this solitary journey—His impressions of England—His strange appearance causes consternation—On his return journey he is almost drowned in Windermere—He reaches Dover in a penniless condition and has to pawn his watch at Calais—He goes on to Hertogenbosch—His reception from his father—He is sent back to Switzerland—His duel and illness—He spends two months at Colombier—Description of Colombier and the de Charrière household—Benjamin remains there for eight weeks—He leaves for Brunswick February 1788.

1

JUSTE DE CONSTANT had assured Lieutenant de Benay that for the return journey he would be able to use the commodious carriage in which they had all, the previous November, travelled from Lausanne to Paris. De Benay had therefore driven from Hertogenbosch in a cabriolet which only held one person. He discovered on arrival that Benjamin had sold the travelling carriage in order to raise money. It was not easy to find another. They decided to squeeze into the cabriolet as best they could.

De Benay had not been in Paris before; Benjamin persuaded him to spend the day there and only to start on the road to Hertogenbosch after dark. De Benay devoted his afternoon to visiting the sights of the city while Benjamin returned to his rooms to change into a travelling suit and to pack his things. He found there a "dry cold letter from the prudent Jenny." The ultimate denial which this letter implied, the agitation always aroused in him by any rejection, the dreaded prospect of a scene with his father, all these combined to create in him a mood of nervous recklessness. As he packed his belongings the idea of escape began to weave its patterns in his mind. He would emigrate to the United States; he would borrow capital from his aunts; he would become a farmer in Virginia. He rushed round to the Rue Thérèse to say goodbye to Madame de Charrière and obtained from her the sum of thirty louis in gold. He then joined de Benay at the Palais Royal, where they dined.

Seated at the next table was a man who had been one of the intimates of Madame de Bourbonne. Benjamin explained the miserable position in which he found himself and hinted at his desire to run away. The difficulty was that he had not enough money for a passage to America. "Why not go to England?" suggested his neighbour. The proposal flashed upon Benjamin as the perfect solution.

After dinner he and Lieutenant de Benay packed themselves into the cabriolet. Benjamin sat upon the seat and de Benay (who was a very stout young man) sat on a stool wedged in between Benjamin's knees. The stool shook and rattled as the cabriolet bumped over the cobbles and they had not got beyond the barrier before de Benay refused to go any further in such discomfort. They must stay the night in Paris and at any cost next morning they must find a proper carriage.

Benjamin returned to his rooms, deposited there his heavy luggage, and taking only one shirt and his thirty louis slipped downstairs. "Le cordon, s'il vous plait," he shouted to the concierge, and stepped out into the street. He spent that night in a brothel and took the post-chaise early next morning to Calais. It took him twenty-two hours to reach Calais, there was a boat waiting, and on the evening of June 26 he found himself in Dover. He sat down and wrote to Madame de Charrière a long and excited letter in which he described his adventures. He also wrote to his father, begging forgiveness for his escapade, expressing his loathing of society and his longing for solitude, and asking for permission to remain in England for three months. There was only one thing, he said, that he desired in life; it was to make a sensible marriage and to live quietly thereafter with his wife and father. Having despatched these letters he set out for London. In order to ease his solitude, he bought a monkey and two dogs. The monkey was a nuisance and he therefore exchanged it for another dog. The three dogs were also a nuisance, so he sold two of them at considerable loss and continued his journey with the third dog, an affectionate animal who accompanied him throughout his pilgrimage.

On reaching London he discovered that of his thirty louis he had only thirteen left. His lodging cost him 10s. 6d. a week; his food 3s. a day; allowing for an extra 3s. for incidental daily expenses, he calculated that he could maintain himself for a period of four weeks. He then remembered the address of his father's banker in London and managed to obtain an advance of £25. He also approached Mr. Edmund Lascelles, one of the young men whom he had known when he was courting Mrs. Trevor. Mr. Lascelles was a Member of Parliament, a man of fashion, and a person of such exquisite elegance that he would spend three hours a day with his hairdresser, holding a hand mirror in front of his face and giving instructions as to the disposal of each separate curl.

Benjamin asked Mr. Lascelles for a loan of £50. Mr. Lascelles refused. Benjamin and his dog walked onwards regretting the hollowness of all human friendship.

But it was not as bad as that. He met his old Edinburgh friend, John Mackay, who assured him that the little matter of his card debts had now been forgotten and urged him to visit his old university. He wrote to John Wilde who replied affectionately, begging him to come to Edinburgh. He also met Richard Kentish, another former member of the Speculative Society. Kentish was now established as a doctor and urged Benjamin to accompany him and his wife to Brighton. He went there for a few days, was thoroughly bored, and departed suddenly leaving a note of farewell for Kentish. It was thus that he started upon his nine weeks' rural ride to Edinburgh and back.

2

The events of this wild journey (1) are of interest only in so far as they illustrate the fecklessness of Benjamin Constant's character and his variations between egoism and remorse. In a young man of twenty years of age such fluctuations of feeling and intention are customary and understandable; the charm of Benjamin Constant derives from the fact that, although intellectually mature at thirteen, he remained temperamentally adolescent to the day of his death. This English escapade, moreover, is isolated from the main current of his past and future life. For the first time, and the last time, we catch Constant alone. Until then, his life had been dominated, either in terms of obedience or reaction, by the "external conscience" which his father represented. Thereafter, his thoughts, his actions and his ambitions were determined, not by his own volition, but by the presence of some other personality or some outside circumstance. During his nine weeks in England he discovered the delights of solitary rumination—a mental exercise for which his splendid intellect was always yearning but which his parasitic temperament rendered him all too often unable to enjoy.

On leaving Brighton he had the vague intention of obtaining hospitality from the Reverend Bridges, vicar of Wadenhoe in Northamptonshire. It has been suggested that he had known Mr. Bridges during those three months which he spent at Oxford when a boy of thirteen. I can find no confirmation of this suggestion: Mr. Bridges remains a mystery. Benjamin first went to Newmarket in the hope of being able to increase his meagre resources by betting at the races; there were no races, and he walked on foot to Thrapston. At the inn at Thrapston he hired an old white horse, stating that he intended to ride to Wadenhoe. He also bought a little bitch to whom he gave the name of "Flora." On reaching the vicarage he found that Mr. Bridges was absent and he decided therefore to take the horse on to Edinburgh. He did not realize, it seems, that this was a breach of the law and that, had the owner of the horse taken action, he might have been sentenced to imprisonment or deportation. Unconscious of his danger, he rode on through Leicester, Derby and Kendal and arrived at Edinburgh at 6 P.M. on August 12, with some ten shillings in his pocket. Within two hours he made contact with John Wilde and those other friends who were still at the University. "They were grateful to me," he recorded in the *Cahier Rouge*, "for the eccentricity of my escapade. The English are always attracted by eccentricity." After a fortnight of uproarious entertainment at Edinburgh, he borrowed £10 from Wilde and started, via the Lake District, upon his homeward journey. Mr. Bridges had by then returned to Wadenhoe and he spent two days at the vicarage, attending family prayers before breakfast; they lasted for a whole hour. He then returned the old white horse to the inn at Thrapston, hired another horse with the meagre money which Mr. Bridges had advanced him, and arrived almost penniless in London.

The effect upon him of this solitary journey can be judged by the frequent references which he made to it in after life. "It was then," he recorded in his diary many years later, "that for the first time I experienced the inestimable happiness of being alone." In the *Cahier Rouge* we find the following evocation of the days when, *laetus et errabundus*, he rode on his white horse, his dogs trotting beside him, through the English lanes:

> England is the country of all others in which the rights of the individual are most carefully safeguarded and in which class distinctions are most scrupulously observed. I travelled for almost nothing. My total expenses, including the keep of my horse, did not exceed 10s. a day. The loveliness of the countryside, especially at that time of year, the magnificent roads, the cleanliness of the inns, the impression of happiness, good-sense and orderliness which the natives convey—all these are a source of continuous enjoyment for any observant traveller. I could speak the language well enough to be mistaken for an Englishman, or rather for a Scotsman, since I had retained my Scottish accent from the time of my earlier studies at Edinburgh University.

In spite of this, it seems that Benjamin Constant was regarded as an object of curiosity as he passed on his old white horse from inn to inn. He was a lanky young man, with untidy clothes, a freckled face, and long red curls which fell in a loose cluster over his collar. Owing to the weakness of his eyes he wore green spectacles which, in spite of the Vicar of Wakefield, appear at that date to have been a novelty upon the road. We find him on July 22 writing to Madame de Charrière from Chesterford:

I would give—no, not ten louis—(since that would clear me out completely)—but let us say a smile from Mlle. Pourrat—to be able to do without my beastly spectacles. They give me such an odd look, with the result that when I want to enter into casual conversation with people (the only sort of contact I care for) they are put off by the oddity of my glasses. They are so diverted by staring at me that they fail to answer my questions. . . . I should like to assume a more ordinary appearance, but my spectacles make that impossible. They and my coat, which is of too fine a cut, give me the appearance of "a broken gentleman" (*sic. In English in the original*) which does me a great deal of harm. The lower classes here hate poverty and loathe the aristocracy. Thus when they see a gentleman who seems impoverished, they either avoid him or insult him. The only way to get out of this is to convey the impression that I am a commercial traveller on his way back to London.

He had intended, when he landed at Dover, to occupy his time by writing a novel. This project was abandoned. In a letter to Madame de Charrière written from Patterdale on his return journey, he admitted that his passion for conversation interfered with the zest needed for writing fiction. "I have," he wrote to her, "given up the idea of writing a regular novel. I am by nature too much of a chatterbox not to become irritated when my characters insist on saying things when I want to talk myself." He decided therefore to compose an intimate diary or confession which would be entitled *Letters from Patterdale to Paris*. But this project, as so many of Constant's projects, never got beyond the stage of an idea.

He did not care for the English lakes, since they reminded him of his own detested Switzerland. Moreover, when boating on Windermere, he was caught in a squall and nearly drowned. On returning to his inn that evening he composed an epitaph for himself couched in atrocious verse. He sent it to Madame de Charrière, asking her, if need arose, to erect a stone to his memory, "underneath the four limes which you will find on the path from Le Désert to La Chablière." This escape from sudden death induced in him a reflective mood. His father had written to say that the treacherous conduct of his son was bringing white hairs in sorrow to the grave. Benjamin was overcome with remorse and at Market Harborough, six days after leaving the Lake District, he added to his epitaph the following pathetic dirge:

> Mais d'un père chéri la déchirante image
> Me suit au delà du tombeau;
> De ce père accablé par l'âge
> J'ai doublé le pesant fardeau;
> Et moins son fils que son bourreau
> J'ai répandu sur sa tête blanche
> Tous les maux que le ciel vengeur
> Dans son implacable furie
> Envoie au criminel que poursuit sa rigueur.

Madame de Charrière who had some sense of rhythm, must have been revolted by these ungainly lines.

On reaching London he went once again to see his friend Kentish whom he had left so brusquely at Brighton two months before. Kentish does not appear to have been over enthusiastic, but Benjamin managed to extract from him a loan of ten pounds with which he made his way to Dover. The older dog, who had followed him all that way, collapsed when just outside Dover and Benjamin put the animal in charge of a postilion with instructions to return it to London and to present it to Kentish. He wrote to the latter expressing the hope that, having treated his friend as a dog he would be willing to treat the dog as a friend (2). Constant landed at Calais accompanied by Flora but without a penny in his pocket. "England," he wrote afterwards in the *Cahier Rouge*, "asylum of all that is noble! Home of happiness, liberty and wisdom! But not a place where one can count unreservedly on the good intentions of undergraduate friends. But I am being ungrateful; for one who behaved badly, there were twenty who behaved well."

At Calais he was able to raise three louis by pawning his watch; at Antwerp he managed to persuade the proprietor of the *Le Laboureur* inn to lend him a further three louis. With leaden feet he cadged his way onwards towards Hertogenbosch and the dreaded interview with his father. "I know exactly," he had written to Madame de Charrière in July, "how my father will receive me. He has written to say I am forgiven, but none the less he will be furious with me for my escapade. Whatever he may do or say, I am resolved not to quarrel with him. Frank, I shall be, and gay and ever so amusing; I shall force him to laugh and to make friends." As the moment approached he was filled with apprehension. On reaching Hertogenbosch, he sought out his father's lodgings. He found him playing whist with three brother officers. "Ah there you are!" exclaimed Juste and continued to deal the cards. Finally the officers left them and they were alone. "You must be tired," his father said. "Let me show you to your room." As they went up the staircase Juste noticed that Benjamin's coat was torn. "That is the sort of thing that *would* happen," he said, "on a mad journey such as yours." Such was the only reference Juste de Constant ever made to the episode. Affectionately he kissed his son good night.

Benjamin remained three days at Hertogenbosch. He was then ordered to go back to Switzerland. Madame de Charrière had now left the Rue Thérèse and had returned to Colombier. Benjamin travelled post with a Bernese officer as far as the Swiss capital and thence by diligence to Neuchâtel. From there he drove out to Colombier. He arrived there at 8 P.M. on October 3, 1787. "I was welcomed," he records, "with transports of delight. We resumed the conversation we had begun in Paris."

3

On this, his first visit to his beloved Colombier, Benjamin Constant remained for only one or two nights. He sat up till the early hours of the morning, describing to Madame de Charrière the incidents of his visit to England, telling her of the strange silent scene which had occurred at Hertogenbosch, discussing the eternal themes of the relation between reason and sensibility, between egoism and duty. He was grateful for his father's restraint and forgivingness; he was anxious to obey instructions. He therefore left Colombier and walked on foot to Lausanne. He established himself, as ordered, in his father's property at Beausoleil, where he received a conventional welcome from Marianne ("my father's mistress, although I did not know this at the time") and from the other members of his disapproving family. He toyed somewhat indolently with his books upon polytheism; he played with his little dog Flora; and from time to time he would sample such back-street pleasures as Lausanne could supply.

He had only been at Beausoleil a fortnight when he received from his father a letter which caused him perturbation. Juste de Constant had been presented to the Duke of Brunswick (3) at that time in command of the Prussian army in Holland. He had discussed with this distinguished soldier the future of his problem child, who, being unable to enter the service of the detested oligarchy of Berne, being unsuited to a military career, having as yet not justified the expectations of literary eminence which his father had for so long cherished, would be obliged to find some respectable civilian employment in a foreign land. The Duke of Brunswick had little sympathy for young men who were unsuited to serve in regiments; but in order to please Colonel de Constant he agreed to give Benjamin a post as one of his minor chamberlains. It was decided that Benjamin should leave for Brunswick before Christmas.

Early in December he set out on his journey, having arranged to spend a few days at Colombier in order to say goodbye to Madame de Charrière. Two incidents occurred to impede his further progress. He was obliged by these incidents to prolong his sojourn at or near Colombier for eight happy and important weeks.

Accompanied by the little dog Flora, and sending his heavier luggage on by diligence, he rode on horseback across the hills which separate Lausanne from Neuchâtel. As they were passing a country house near Yverdon some sporting dogs dashed out of the gateway and set upon Flora. Benjamin tried to drive them off by lashing out with his riding crop. The owner of the dogs then emerged and an altercation ensued. He was the chevalier Duplessis d'Ependes, an officer in the service of France. High words were exchanged, a challenge was delivered, and Benjamin then rode back to Lausanne in order to obtain a second for the duel. Two days later, he returned to the appointed spot, accompanied by one of his cousins who was to act as his second. They found there a Captain Pillichody of Yverdon, who represented M. Duplessis. The latter, much to his second's embarrassment, failed for some reason to put in an appearance. While they were waiting at the inn Uncle Samuel appeared, despatched by Rosalie, and anxious to stop the duel. All day they waited in vain for M. Duplessis, and in the end they rode back to Lausanne. The duel did however take place some days later on January 8; Benjamin in his *Journal Intime* records that he acquitted himself excellently on that occasion. That, so far as is known, was the first of the many duels in which he became engaged.

The existing manuscript of the *Cahier Rouge* ends abruptly with this account of the Duplessis incident of January 8, 1788; it may be that there exists somewhere a continuation of this fascinating human document; if so, it has remained undiscovered. On the last page of the extant manuscript, Constant made same reflections upon the quality of his own courage. He had been interested to observe that on his way out to the duel he had been infected by a mood of uproarious gaiety; he and his cousin had sung and shouted all the time. "It is not," he wrote, "that I regard myself as possessing more physical courage than other people; it is rather that I have been gifted by nature with an utter contempt for life, even with some secret longing to escape from life and thereby to avoid all the tiresome knocks that may be in store for me. I am liable enough to be frightened by some unexpected event which upsets my nerves; but danger, if I am allowed fifteen minutes reflection, leaves me completely calm." This was no vain statement; it was demonstrably true.

The second incident which delayed his departure for Brunswick was that on arriving at Colombier he found that he was suffering from a malady which he had contracted at Lausanne. He was obliged to postpone his departure for Germany and meanwhile to place himself in the hands of Dr. Leschaux of Neuchâtel. His illness was complicated by acute ophthalmia. He was obliged to spend some nights in Dr. Leschaux's own house at Neuchâtel, writing almost hourly letters to Madame de Charrière, and trying with difficulty to read the salacious works of Rétif de la Bretonne, by which he was profoundly disgusted. So soon as he was convalescent, he returned to Madame de Charrière's house at Colombier. It was during these weeks that she imposed upon him the dominance of her lucid and astringent intellectualism; it was during those weeks that he acquired feelings of deep pity for the heavy intensity of the domestic atmosphere by which she was surrounded.

4

The village of Colombier is situated some four miles to the south-west of Neuchâtel and is separated from the lake by the fields and woods which cover the delta of the Areuse. The houses are grouped upon a sharp little hill crowned by a pinnacled castle, the foundations of which date back to Roman times. The castle had been used as his headquarters by Marshal Keith but was then inhabited by the collector of tithes; it is now a military barracks. Upon a small square outside the castle gate stand the church and presbytery; the inside of the church is whitewashed with evangelical austerity; there is no altar and the wide wooden pulpit makes a brown splash against the chalky walls. There is a campanile beside the church, constructed of yellow brick; a bare white clock under the short eaves strikes the hours with a sharp scrannel sound. On clear days one can look out from the castle terrace, down upon the avenues which run to the lake, and across to where, beyond the mountains of Fribourg, the Alps, from the Diablerets to the Jungfrau, hang their far white sails.

The de Charrière house, known locally as Le Pontet, is situated in an abrupt hollow between the castle mound and the rising ground behind. The view towards the lake is blocked by the sharp hill on which the village stands; the view to the north is immediately cut off by trees and vine-yards; only to the west is there a gap in this enclosure, with a view between the Boudry and the La Tourne towards the "trou de Bourgogne" which marks the gorge of the Areuse and the road to Pontarlier. There is but little sunshine in the hollow.

From the church one can reach the house by a sharp descent, called "Les Egralets," composed of long steps and cobbled inclines. To the right before one reaches the main door, is a kitchen garden, enclosed by a rough crenellated wall, and containing in the centre a stone basin shaped like a four-leaved shamrock. In one corner of the kitchen garden stands a shed, containing the pressoir for making wine.

The house itself is a typical Swiss manor-house of the early seventeenth century. One enters through a round and hooded arch and finds oneself in a small courtyard surrounded by buildings on three sides. To the right is a wooden arcade, supported by a heavy kingpost. Underneath this arcade there is a stone trough, oblong and large, into which a thin stream of water pours continuously from a pipe set in a stone pillar. The terminal of this pillar is roughly shaped into a pomegranate. The sound of water echoing under the arcade, the sound of the church clock rasping out the hours, became the undertone to Madame de Charrière's thirty-four years of unsatisfied and self-pitying married life. It was in that trough that, in her early days, she washed the family linen, "like Nausicaa" as she informed, defiantly, her friends of the great world.

When she first arrived at Colombier in September 1771 the house was divided into two superimposed flats, approached by a stone stairway in the turret. Each of the two floors is based upon the same mean plan. A narrow passage runs down the centre, lit by a single window at the end. Doors open to right and left of this passage, leading into ill-proportioned rooms. The windows are small and lifeless. The place suggests a village hospital of ancient design or a dormitory in a Victorian boarding school. The rooms are warmed by oval stoves, decorated with the blue and green tiles of the district which are called *catelles*. The only large room in the building is that which Madame de Charrière herself constructed out of the loft above the arcade and washing trough. She called it her "salon d'été"; and would use it for the musical parties which she sometimes gave. It was infested with mice; there were stains upon the ceiling and the walls. It was at best a bleak ramshackle room with a thin Aubusson carpet and a lonely chandelier. At a later date she had the room redecorated with frescoes and emblems in the Directoire style. But it remained an inhospitable room; it was rarely used.

On the first floor, when she reached Colombier as a bride—intimidating but determined to be gracious—lived her father-in-law (then in his dotage) and her husband's two maiden sisters. There was Mlle. Louise, aged forty, who would spend her days working in the kitchen garden and who would peer about the house making sharp ejaculations of surprise. There was Mlle. Henriette, who was of the same age as Madame de Charrière herself, and who failed to conceal her resentment at the intrusion of this proud Dutch woman with her brittle laugh and her Parisian airs. Mlle. Henriette had tight lips and a long disapproving face. Her speech was precise; her silence a reproach.

Madame de Charrière was not popular with her neighbours or with the society of Neuchâtel. She had never been popular. It was not so much that she lacked condescension; it was rather that her condescension was so marked. After the publication of the *Lettres Neuchâteloises,* in which she had accused her neighbours of being unable to read or even spell correctly, only a few, less sensitive, citizens drove out to Colombier. There was Monsieur de Peyrou, whose fine house in the town is still standing. There was François Chaillet the botanist. There was Mlle. Moula, known as "Muson," a prim and modest little lady, who cut silhouette portraits of the Colombier circle. Madame de Charrière, whose didactic instincts were ill-controlled, insisted upon Mlle. Moula studying logic and reading Locke. There was Mlle. Moula's sister, who had married an Englishman of the name of Cooper, and who went off to Windsor to be French governess to the daughters of George III. There was the Pastor Chaillet, the local vicar, a fat spongy man, who wrote an acid diary in a microscopic hand and who would play piquet for hours with Monsieur de Charrière. And there was her personal maid Henriette Monachan, who twice produced illegitimate babies, and to whom her mistress would give lessons in calligraphy and Latin.

Such was the narrow circle within which Madame de Charriére spent her days. She employed her time writing long letters to distant friends or composing her novels upon enormous sheets of paper in her bedroom. In summer she would sit in the small flower garden, beside the large *perruquier* or Rhus which still untidily survives. Outside her bedroom window, facing the insistent clock upon the hill (so close it seemed to her, only a hundred yards away) she had a board placed on which she would in winter strew crumbs for the birds; the stanchions which supported this board are still in place. She would spend hours at her harpsichord composing operas. At one time she decided to set to music the *Zadig* of Voltaire and summoned an Italian musician, Zingarelli, to assist her. The composition was a failure and Zingarelli left.

In the earlier years of her marriage she had been glad to escape from Colombier and to mingle again with her own wider world. In 1774 she had revisited Zuylen and during successive winters she and her husband would take a fine apartment in Geneva in the De Tournes-Rilliet house at No. 6 Rue Beauregard. After the episode of her infatuation for the beautiful but nameless young man of 1784 she refused ever to set foot in Geneva again; Monsieur de Charrière was sent alone to the Rue Beauregard to collect her belongings.

At one period, being distressed by the state of her nerves, she made an expedition to Strasbourg to consult Cagliostro (4) a man for whom she retained an obstinate affection. Occasionally she would spend a week or two alone at Chèxbres. And in 1786, as we have seen, Monsieur de Charrière, in a desperate attempt to cure her melancholy, rented a flat for her in the Rue Thérèse in Paris. That was the last time she left Colombier. It may have been that she found these absences rendered her return more unendurable. She remained in her dark and ill-placed manor-house for the next seventeen years until she died.

Monsieur de Charrière was a punctilious, silent, bewildered and considerate man. Her attitude towards him is fully demonstrated in her novel *Mistriss Henley.* "I would rather," exclaimed the self-pitying heroine of this novel, "that Mister Henley struck me in the face with his fists than that he should surround me with this atmosphere of interminable reasonableness." He was fond of her in his reserved way and when she was absent he would write her pathetic and respectful letters. "I have made it a rule," he writes, "not to talk to you about my own feelings. But, in spite of all that you have made me suffer for some time, I cannot refrain from telling you that your departure has left me with a feeling of sad solitude which I am unable to master." Conscientiously, but dully, he sought to fathom the secret of her irritability and depression. "I forgot," he wrote to her when she was staying at Chèxbres, "to mention something which I have been meaning to tell you for some time. I recognize in my sister Henriette many of the faults with which you have so often reproached me. I now begin to understand what was in your mind. I cannot stand the *sustained* voice she puts on when she reads aloud, or makes a remark about something which interests her. This explains what you meant when you told me that 'I read aloud too well.'

Henriette reduces everything to a general maxim; special cases only interest her in their relation to some general orderliness; she has no simple or spontaneous reactions; in fact I seem to recognize in her a caricature of myself."

5

Into this tense and opaque atmosphere burst Benjamin Constant—gay, admiring, adventurous, voluble, and twenty years of age. They would retire together to the "Cabinet de l'angle," her corner sitting room, with its two tables covered with papers and music scores, its sofa and its china stove. At midnight she would move next door into her high scarlet bed and he would sit on talking to her until the church clock outside struck two or three or four. Sometimes, but only rarely, she would pause in her conversation and there would be a momentary silence. He would glance up slyly—"Eh bien, Madame?" he would ask her. "Eh bien, Madame?" and then the torrent of their talk would again be unloosed. All else was silent in the house, except for the sound of water under the arcade and the church clock striking the hours of approaching dawn. Benjamin, at his own table, was supposed to be taking notes for his history of religion. He would make these notes (not on playing cards as Sainte-Beuve imagined) but on stiff small sheets of paper which he strung together with a string. The lamp between them would throw her shadow upon the wall. Months later, when he was in Brunswick, she sent him one of the silhouettes which Mlle. Moula had cut. He replied indignantly: "She has given you the outline and appearance of a stout Dutch peasant. She ought to have done better than that! I know few profiles more expressive than yours. I used to watch it upon the wall when we were talking together; your smile is a happy blend of vivacity and tenderness." On winter nights sometimes, when the wind howled round the house, they would steal into the kitchen. It is a small room with a large hooded fire-place and one window looking upon the courtyard. They would make themselves tisanes from the lime blossom drying in the corner. The hum of the kettle provided an undertone to their talk. Finally he would leave her and creep down the rickety staircase which led from her bedroom to his own little hutch, with the cracked ceiling, on the floor below. They would all meet together for the midday meal. Mlle. Henriette would stare in front of her in disapproving silence; Mlle. Louise would utter her little exclamations of surprise; Monsieur de Charrière would silently fondle Jaman, his dog. The newspaper would arrive from Neuchâtel. Monsieur de Charrière, in his "sustained" voice, would read it aloud.

Benjamin's family meanwhile had become uneasy regarding this prolonged and mysterious sojourn at Colombier. Gossip had reached Lausanne of the strange intimacy which had sprung up between this man of twenty and this proud restless woman of forty-eight. Rosalie went so far as to hint that he was exposing himself to ridicule. It was said (and this was true) that he would often call her "Barbet," or "little spaniel," to her face. It was said (and this was also true) that she would call him "my white devil." Benjamin, as always, was enraged by the hinted reproaches of his family. "How saddened and indignant do I feel," he wrote, "at all this harshness, this unceasing tyranny, this acerbity, this clenching of the teeth. All because of what? Merely that for once in my life I have been completely happy."

The time had come none the less when he must leave Colombier. Now that there were no duels in the offing and that he had recovered his health, he must fulfil his promise to his father and his father's promise to the Duke of Brunswick. Benjamin Constant started for Germany in the first week of February 1788.

He carried with him a new, a precious possession. For the first time he had met someone who made an equal appeal to mind and heart; someone whose interest in the subtleties of his character and adventures was as passionate as his own; someone who did not seek to change or to reform his temperament but who examined it delightedly as an object of intricate natural beauty; someone who by her understanding and sharp sympathy could provide him with a sense of security and calm; someone to whom he felt that he belonged.

His intellectual integrity, his emotional taste, even his literary style, were enhanced by this astringent companionship. She taught him to eschew all second-hand ideas or feelings and to avoid the showy phrase. "You clear my ideas," he wrote to her, "you lighten my work, you simplify my style." It is often said that Constant possessed a genius for self-criticism; he possessed nothing of the sort; what he did possess was a remarkable gift for self-analysis. Madame de Charrière, with her rigid eighteenth-century standards, did much to improve the symmetry of this analysis. Yet I agree with Professor Rudler that she did not improve his character.

She confirmed him in his opinion that all human conventions were either unintelligent or harsh; that the only sure rule is to cherish and exploit the capacities, even the defects, with which "nature" had endowed one. To that extent she increased his egoism, while at the same time diminishing his self-reliance. In her bitter disappointment with life, in her dread lest he might escape her, she discouraged his ambition. Her disillusion came from experience: his from self-distrust. She revenged herself for her own failure by persuading him that he could never succeed.

In Paris she had been a stimulant; at Colombier she

became a sedative; in the years that followed she allowed herself to be an irritant. She was at heart an insensitive woman, and did not know that one cannot retain the affections of the young if one continues to teach and preach. It was true that she understood Benjamin Constant as no human being had ever understood him before: it was also true, as Geoffrey Scott has said, that she failed to realize in time that he might weary of being understood.

CHAPTER V

Brunswick

[1788–1791]

The journey to Brunswick—His homesickness for Colombier—Nature of Constant's egoism—The Maurice Barrès legend—His arrival at Brunswick—The Court Circle—His duties as Kammerherr—The Duke and Princess Caroline—Féronce and Mauvillon—Coldness of Madame de Charrière—Did he ask her to elope with him?—Juste de Constant's misfortunes—His disappearance—The sentences passed against him by the Standrecht—Wilhelmina von Cramm—Benjamin's engagement and marriage—Their visit to Lausanne—Quarrel with Madame de Charrière—He goes to the Hague—His return to Brunswick—His depression and lassitude—The French Revolution.

1

THE journey to Brunswick was hard and cold. For the first few hours, for the first few days, the sounds and voices of Colombier still moved within his brain. As the post-chaise jolted along the icy roads, his thoughts revolved around "the calm and happy things which I now miss." He wrote to her from every inn.

"Only fourteen days ago," he wrote on February 18, 1788, "at this very hour (ten minutes past ten at night) we were sitting by the fire in the kitchen. Rose had not yet gone to bed and from time to time she would get up from her stool in the corner and throw some sticks upon the fire; she would snap the sticks in her hands. And you and I, we were discussing the relation between genius and insanity. How happy we were! Or at least how happy I was!"

What he wondered, would she be doing when she received his letter? It would reach her at midday when the postman came out from Neuchâtel with the newspaper. "Monsieur de Charrière will be stroking Jaman. He will read the gazette aloud. And Mlle. Louise will exclaim 'But! But! But! . . .' "

"The roads are ghastly," he wrote, "the wind is of ice and I am sad. Sadder today than I was yesterday, even as I was sadder yesterday than the day before, even as I shall be sadder tomorrow than I am today." "I would give ten years of health at Brunswick," he wrote from Rastadt on February 23, "for one year's illness at Colombier." He was sick and wretched; he had caught a cold and was suffering from eczema. Brunswick loomed ahead of him in colours which were sombre and absurd:

> Certainly I owe my health to you, perhaps even my life. But I owe you much more than that. Life on this earth, whatever the Pasteur Chaillet may say, is for most of the time a gloomy thing. You made it sweet for me. For two months you consoled me for the wretchedness of existence.
>
> As long as I live, as long as you live, in whatever situation I may find myself, I shall be able to say, "There is Colombier in the world." Before I knew you I used to say: "If they persecute me beyond endurance, I can always kill myself." Now I say: "If life becomes unendurable, I can always escape to Colombier."

These letters reflect something more than the momentary homesickness of a childish young man when condemned to leave a protective atmosphere for an environment and a function which inspired him with dread. They are an expression of the spiritual loneliness which afflicted Constant all his life. It is not possible to understand him unless we are able to appreciate and remember this soft, spontaneous side. If we regard him merely as an egoist and a cad—even with admirable instincts—we may fall into the error of Maurice Barrès and come to regard him as the precursor, or "intercessor," in the *Culte du moi*. In his ironical self-depreciation Benjamin asserted that he might be selfish but was not self-centred. "I did not possess," he confessed in *Adolphe,* "the depth of egoism which my character may have led some people to assume. Although I was interested in nothing but myself, I only took a mild interest in my ego."

It may be, as Faguet has remarked, "that he was more personal than a gentleman should be." But we have only to confront the reality with the portrait which Barrès has introduced into *Un Homme Libre* to realize that such virtu as Benjamin possessed was not of the Renaissance model. For Barrès, Constant was at one and the same time a fanatic and a dilettante; a man who beneath a contemptuous manner concealed "the insane bohemianism of his imagination"; a man who possessed so vivid a conception of the precarious in life that he was never able wholly to surrender himself either to his ambition or his passions; a man who "took an agonizing delight in bitterness" and who derived an intellectual pleasure (the pleasure of pride) in feeling that his life was exhausting itself in indulgences which he despised and who thus achieved in the end the supreme intoxication of despising himself. It is from this false analysis that Barrès proceeds to his, I admit grandiose, evocation of the spirit of Benjamin Constant:

> Superb among the saints, I salute you with love unequalled! You who are among the most illustrious of those who, in pride of their true selves, can bruise, sully and eternally deny all that they possess in common with the mass of humanity. The dignity of men such as you is concerned exclusively with certain exquisite emotions, which you are able to multiply within yourselves, and which the world knows not and cannot see!

COLOMBIER IN THE EIGHTEENTH CENTURY

The Charrière house is to the left of the picture below the clock tower and the castle mound

BRUNSWICK

"Beyond anyone," writes Barrès, "I admire Benjamin Constant, because he lived amid the dust of his own illusions; because he never surrendered himself to the beauties of nature; and because he found fulfilment in the sardonic contemplation of his own soul—that subtle miserable soul of his."

All this perhaps is a magnificent overture to existentialism. But it bears but slight relation to the homesick young man with eczema, jolting across winter roads on the way to Brunswick with Flora shivering upon his knees.

2

Benjamin Constant arrived in Brunswick on March 2, 1788. Ten days later his appointment was gazetted as "Gentleman of the Chamber to his Serene Highness the Duke of Brunswick." He retained this appointment for five years. His salary amounted to 66 louis a year; his father accorded him an allowance of 115 louis; his lodging cost him no more than 10 louis a year, his Swiss valet Crouzat was not expensive, and he calculated that, with the free meals at court, he would have an ample income for incidental luxuries. He promised his father that he would renounce his gambling habits, and in fact upon the back of a Knave of Hearts he drafted and signed a solemn pledge, dated March 19, 1788, not to touch a card for a period of five years (1). He appears to have abided by this pledge for several weeks.

The city of Brunswick in those days was of circular design, enclosed by high ramparts upon which the citizens would ride and walk. There was an ancient *Rathaus* and narrow mudded streets with projecting eaves. The old palace, the *Graue Hof* (2), was large and inconvenient. Benjamin received his instructions from the Lord Chamberlain, Baron von Münchausen. His task, it seemed, would be to see that at the court dinners the men and women were seated according to their correct precedence. He would wear a Court uniform and a sword. The women would be seated on soft chairs at one side of the table and the men would be placed opposite to them on chairs which were hard. Every Sunday at six there would be a full Court drawing-room. On Fridays in the winter months there would be a masked ball. In the intervals there would be concerts and dramatic performances. He must also join the ducal club which dined every Thursday at the Hotel d'Angleterre and at which the Duke himself would preside. As for the rest, the Vice-Chamberlain would be instructed to take him round from house to house to pay the necessary calls.

Constant followed these instructions obediently. He was disgusted by the squalor and stupidity of the Court officials. The gentlemen of the Court only allowed themselves a clean shirt once a month and a clean handkerchief once a fortnight. The ladies of the Court appeared to him to be "Vermin." The food at the ducal dinners was very bad indeed.

There were in fact three separate Courts at that time in existence at Brunswick. There was the Court of the Dowager Duchess, sister of Frederick the Great. She was aloof and serious and seventy-six years of age; she drove through the town in a coach drawn by eight Hanoverian creams; she spoke beautiful French; her relations with Benjamin Constant were rare and distant. There was the Court of the reigning Duchess, the Princess Augusta, daughter of Frederick, Prince of Wales and sister of George III. She was vivacious, unconventional, and sometimes malignant. At the time of Benjamin's conjugal troubles she took the side of his wife and treated him with venomous disdain.

In the third, and central place, came the Court of the reigning Duke, Charles William Ferdinand, Duke of Brunswick-Lüneburg. Although universally regarded, especially in England, as one of the most romantic soldiers of his age, he was a man of small stature and considerable obesity. He was much impressed with his own dignity; he spoke in French, very slowly and weighing every word; he adopted a tone of elaborate, even affected, politeness which did not diminish the alarm which his presence inspired. He treated Constant with courteous consideration under which could be detected his contempt for all civilians, and especially for those who bemeaned themselves by becoming functionaries at his Court.

The Duke and Duchess had four sons and two daughters, who were all either delicate, eccentric or insane. The Crown Prince Charles was stupid and extremely short-sighted; Constant describes him "as fat and greasy as a barrel of oil." He married Princess Louise, daughter of William IV, Stadholder of the Netherlands. Of the other sons, Prince George was a nitwit and Prince Augustus was almost totally blind. Prince Frederick William, who succeeded his father in 1806, was killed at the Battle of Quatre-Bras in 1815. The Princess Caroline, the second daughter, was at that time, twenty years of age; she was described by Mirabeau as "amiable, witty, pretty, lively and effervescent." Constant unfortunately makes no references in his diary to Caroline of Brunswick. He can scarcely have spoken to this small vivacious girl with the fair hair (3).

During the first few weeks he was almost amused by the novelty of his functions. As the months passed he found that that unreality of these small German Courts was almost more than he could bear. "The position," he wrote, "of royalty is so contrary to nature, that it renders ordinary men stupid and gifted men insane." He was by habit inelegant, by nature physically clumsy; he discovered that the ladies of the court tittered when he made his bows. On one occasion the Lord Chamberlain and the Vice-Chamberlain were both absent from illness, Benjamin had to take their place. "It will be amusing," said the Duchess, "to watch Constant performing." He was hurt by this remark. "Why," he wrote to Madame de Charrière, "should it be so amusing?" He began to shirk his duties and to spend long hours alone, riding round the ramparts or reading in the ducal library. Flora produced five puppies, one of which bore an unmistakable resemblance to Jaman. "I shall," he wrote to Colombier, "call him Jaman after his father and I intend to give him a liberal education!" He was not attracted by Germany—"Even the fir trees," he said, "are twisted, dwarfed and ugly."

> The Germans [he wrote to Madame de Charrière on March 9, 1788] are heavy. Heavy when they try to reason, heavy when they try to be funny, heavy when they get sentimental, heavy when they are amusing themselves, heavy when they're bored. Their vivacity resembles the caracoling of the cream horses of the dowager Duchess. "They are ever puffing and blowing when they laugh" (*in English in the original*). They seem to imagine that if one wants to be gay one must be out of breath; that to be polite one must lose one's balance.

3

There seems no reason to ascribe to "temperamental pessimism," or even to the *maladie du siècle*, the natural unhappiness which overwhelmed Benjamin Constant during those months of 1788. He had exchanged a delightful companionship for the society of people by whom he was misprised. It is irksome to be tied to a function far removed from one's own tastes and abilities; it is galling to realize that one performs that function clumsily. To him the ladies and gentlemen of the Courts of Brunswick were an obnoxious company; for them the young Kammerherr of twenty, with his slipshod habits and his freckled face, became the object of that shallow derisiveness with which courtiers are apt to relieve their boredom and to protect their self-esteem. He reacted to their tittering, with quick satirical snarls; his unpopularity was thereby much increased.

Two friends only did he make during that period. The first was Jean Baptiste Féronce von Rosenkrantz, the Duke's prime minister. He was an educated man of Genevese origin; nervous, retiring, bashful, almost blind. He remained a compassionate friend to Constant through the troubles to come. The second was Jacob Mauvillon (4), whose calm stoicism and liberal opinions provided some sedative at least for Constant's sense of inefficiency and jangled nerves. Anxious as he was to redeem himself in the eyes of his father, he might well with their friendly guidance have come to accept his surroundings and have built up a studious private life detached from his Court functions. Circumstances then arose to destroy such equanimity as he might have achieved.

In the first place the letters from Madame de Charrière assumed a querulous and didactic tone. It may be, as has been suggested, that Mlle. Louise and Mlle. Henriette instilled into the saturnine thoughts of their sister-in-law the suspicion that Constant's affection for her could not possibly be sincere. He had only remained those two months at Colombier because he was ill and needed protection; it was absurd to imagine that a woman of her age could permanently hold the affection of a boy of twenty. How could she suppose either that a man of his gifts and ambitions could possibly sacrifice to her his youth and his career? It may be also that Constant's family, anxious to create discord, repeated to her some of the witticisms in which, even at the expense of those he truly loved, he was apt to indulge. More probably the whole unhappy misunderstanding was due to Madame de Charrière's restless and destructive character; her inability to leave things alone; her habit of digging up every plant in order to examine the roots; her deep suspicion of happiness.

For him, the letters from Colombier, with the small neat head of Perseus upon the seal, were the bright moments of his Brunswick life. In a letter of March 13, 1788 he told her how at some court function he had felt at the back of his mind that somebody extremely agreeable was waiting for him outside. He had a warm inner feeling of expectation. Who was that person? It was Barbet; the memory of Barbet; perhaps even a letter, a little Perseus, when he got back to his rooms. One evening he had been playing loto with the Duchess. "Why is it," he said to himself, "that the Duchess seems so agreeable this evening?" And then he realized that his mind was far away from Brunswick and in the little corner room at Colombier with Barbet's entrancing silhouette dancing upon the wall.

The letters he received in response to his affection were fussy and disbelieving. He recognized in them the same note of doubting constraint, the same tone of distrust, which was always ruining his relations with his father. "And yet," he wrote to her, "the relations between you and me are utterly different from those between a father and a son." Again and again in her letters he found rasping sentences asserting that she was not deceived by his protestations, that she was too lucid and had known too much of life's eternal treachery to surrender herself to such illusions, that she knew full well that after a few weeks at Brunswick the memory of Colombier would fade from his mind. "Why Madame," he protested, "should you adopt towards me a tone so wounding and so harsh?" These suspicions of his integrity were destroying the sweetness of their friendship; Colombier, instead of being the asylum of his hopes and dreams, had become a place from which he received tart letters of suspicion and complaint. Nothing remained to him that really mattered; if this continued he would go mad or take his life.

BRUNSWICK

There exists a torn portion of a letter from Constant to Madame de Charrière, dated April 4, 1788. From all that remains of this letter it might seem as if Constant were breaking to her some project of his to escape from Brunswick, to elope with a married woman, and to settle in London or Paris. There is no evidence at all that any such woman had at that period entered into Constant's life. I agree with Professor Rudler that, in order to put an end to her nagging suspicions, he had suggested that she should leave Monsieur de Charrière and live with him. The conclusion of the letter tends to confirm this assumption:

> Good night! I love you more than any man has loved you, or ever loved! You are in your scarlet bed; you are holding out your hand to me! Goodbye my angel, you who are worth more than all the angels whom they tell us about. Goodbye! May you be very very happy!

Thereafter occurs a sudden gap in the correspondence. And almost immediately Constant's whole heart and mind were distracted by the disasters in which his father became involved.

4

The origins of this distressing affair, which brought ruin on Juste de Constant and his son, can be related shortly.

In 1784 Juste de Constant had been appointed Colonel in command of the Swiss Regiment in Holland, known as the "Regiment of General May." It contained a number of younger officers from the patrician families of Berne; they resented a despised Vaudois being placed in command. In 1785 there had arisen a severe clash of wills between Colonel de Constant and his officers, with the result that Juste had been granted eighteen months leave of absence. In March 1787 he had returned to his regiment.

The rivalry between the political parties in the Low Countries had by then reached the verge of civil war. The Conservatives, or Orange Party, aimed at restoring to the Stadholder the privileges which had been taken from him. They were supported by the British Government in the person of their astute and resolute envoy, Sir James Harris, first Earl of Malmesbury. The Patriots, or democratic party, aimed at establishing a Dutch Republic; they were supported by the French who were in fact bound by treaty to come to the assistance of the Dutch if they were attacked from outside. The situation was serious since it might well have led to war between France and England.

In July 1787 the Princess of Orange, a woman of strong will and impulsive actions, was detained by the Republicans when trying to make her way to the Hague. She called upon her brother, the King of Prussia, to avenge this insult. On September 13, 1787 the Prussian army, under the command of Benjamin Constant's employer, the Duke of Brunswick, invaded the Low Countries. No serious resistance was offered, the French failed to fulfil their treaty obligations, the danger of war was averted, and the Stadholder entered the Hague in triumph. The republicans were completely routed, and the House of Orange restored to all the privileges which it had lost.

Colonel Juste de Constant had during this campaign received orders to take his regiment from Hertogenbosch to Antwerp, which had surrendered to the Duke of Brunswick on October 10. He reached the city on October 16, 1787. As there was some looting going on in the town, he gave instructions that the men should be confined to barracks. Owing to some misunderstanding, the first battalion was duly confined, but the second was allowed to roam the streets. The men of the free battalion shouted rude remarks at the men of the battalion which had been confined; trouble broke out between them, and a sergeant was killed. This incident was followed by further acts of insubordination. The officers of the May Regiment then complained to Berne that Juste de Constant was an incompetent and indeed intolerable Colonel; they refused any longer to serve under his command. The matter was referred to the Standrecht, or Swiss High Council, at Berne. After taking several months to examine the evidence, they decided, in August 1788, that Juste de Constant had been responsible for the incidents, reprimanded him severely, and suspended him from his command for a period of six months.

Juste de Constant obtained advance notice of this sentence. Unable to face the derisive looks of his officers, blinded by wounded pride, he bolted from his regiment and disappeared. This happened on the night of August 17, 1788. Under that date, twenty-six years later, Benjamin noted in his diary: "It was on this day that my poor father committed the insane action which proved the ruin of his life."

On learning of his father's disappearance, Benjamin Constant left Brunswick immediately and in three days, pausing neither to eat nor sleep, he reached Amsterdam. He was joined there by his uncle Samuel, who in spite of his age and infirmities had made an equally rapid journey from Lausanne. Together they had an audience with the Stadholder. They found that Juste had left enormous debts behind him at Hertogenbosch. Benjamin, who was convinced that his father had drowned himself in one of the canals, assured his uncle that he would sell all the Swiss properties and satisfy the creditors. "He hates Switzerland," wrote Uncle Samuel to his daughters, "he does not want to retain any property there at all; he wants to leave it for good." But Juste had not committed suicide. He had hidden himself at the inn of the Couronne Impériale at Bruges. And on the day that Samuel reached Holland from

Switzerland, Juste was in a post-chaise on the way to Lausanne. Benjamin, having been unable to find his father's body, returned to Brunswick; it was there that he learnt that his father was alive and well at Beausoleil.

The Duke of Brunswick had at first been sympathetic to Juste de Constant, feeling that the junior officers had no right to allow their Bernese prejudices to affect their loyalty to their commanding officer. But when he learnt that Juste had bolted from his regiment, thereby exposing himself to a charge of desertion, his military conscience was outraged. It was with the greatest difficulty that Benjamin managed to persuade the Duke to write to the Stadholder and to ask him to intervene. Fortunately the latter was annoyed by the action of the Standrecht in Berne in passing sentence upon a matter which had occurred in his own dominions and in one of the regiments of his own service. He ordered Juste de Constant to return to Hertogenbosch. On arrival there the Colonel was presented with authenticated copies of the fourteen sentences which had been pronounced against him. Apart from the main sentence regarding his action at Antwerp, there were thirteen other cases brought by him, or against him, which concerned disputes with individual officers. He submitted these papers to the lawyers at the Hague. They advised an appeal. On March 12, 1789 this appeal was rejected by the Standrecht in Berne. Juste then published a pamphlet denouncing the Berne Government and all its ways. Fearing that he might then be arrested for desertion, he again went into hiding and eventually returned to Switzerland. He did not, however, abandon the controversy. The legal proceedings which he thereafter instituted dragged on for nine years. The costs of these appeals and counter-appeals ran away with all that remained of Juste's fortune. He transferred La Chablière and the house in the Rue de Bourg to Benjamin; he presented Beausoleil to

Marianne; but the rest of his properties were sold below their value and in the end Juste abandoned Switzerland in anger and established himself for the rest of his life at Brévans, near Dôle in France(5).

5

In the midst of these disturbances Constant became involved in an affair which was to cause him much distress. One evening, in November 1788, in the ante-room reserved for ladies in waiting and the maids of honour, he noticed a young woman sitting on a sofa in floods of tears. He went up to her and enquired the cause of her misery. She said it was because she was unwanted and unloved. They became engaged upon the spot.

Wilhelmina von Cramm was the daughter of Captain Karl von Cramm of the Brunswick army and of Anna von Bülow his wife. She was nine years older than Benjamin and possessed neither dowry nor looks. With some difficulty he persuaded his father to consent to this union. Juste transferred to him what remained of the Chandieu property and gave him a present of plate and furniture, including two beds, two carpets and thirty pair of sheets. The Duke, whose consent had also been obtained, promoted him to be a Legationsrat, increased his salary from 66 to 100 louis a year, and allowed him a house with free fuel from the ducal forests.

Benjamin looked forward to a life of quiet domesticity. "Oh for £300 a year!" he wrote to Madame de Charrière in English, "a cottage and my Minna to keep me company!"

They were married on May 8, 1789 and within a few weeks he took her to Lausanne to be introduced to his family. The first impression was unfavourable. "We were astonished," wrote Rosalie, "to find her very ugly, her face pitted with smallpox, very thin with red eyes." On second thought Rosalie modified this opinion. "She is tall," she wrote, "not ill-made, has gentle and agreeable manners, pretty hands, lovely hair, and a nice tone of voice. She is gay and intelligent without the usual German stiffness." In a very short time Minna had gained the affections of the whole family. "Benjamin," Rosalie records, "worships her as if she were a woman of beauty. She has certainly rendered him more sensible; his character has improved."

Benjamin rode alone to Colombier to visit Madame de Charrière. The interview, which only lasted for two hours, was unhappy. He left without even asking to see her husband. It would be an error to suppose that Madame de Charrière's ill-temper on that occasion was due to any jealousy of Minna von Cramm: she was too self-complacent a woman to be jealous of anyone who did not threaten her intellectual ascendancy. It seems rather, if we are to judge from the correspondence that ensued, that the quarrel arose over his father's misfortunes. Benjamin had tried to convince Madame de Charrière that Juste had behaved with dignity and wisdom; she asserted that such a contention was unworthy of his intelligence; the whole business was evidently not as simple as he tried to make out.

> Your cryptic utterances [he answered] bore and bother me; I have no use for Sibyls. I retract not one word of what I said. My father's conduct in every one of his cases has been strictly in accordance with the law. In spite of all this I pray to God that he will keep you in His heavenly care and beg you earnestly to burn all my letters. I burnt all yours before I left Switzerland. I insist on this as a right. It is for you to decide whether to relieve me from a source of embarrassment or whether to punish me for all the confidence I have given you in the past.

Madame de Charrière was angered by this undisciplined letter. She scrawled across the top: "Send me a note—and sign it in full—saying that you have burnt *all* my letters. I shall then at once burn yours." She signed this minute in full: "I. A. E. van Tuyll van Serooskerken de Charrière. Wednesday, September 23, 1789."

Having read this peremptory note a second time, she added a further paragraph. "If you have recovered your senses by the time this reaches you, then do not worry any more about your rude and cruel outburst. I shall forget it sooner than you will."

She then took a fresh sheet of paper and wrote another, perfectly ordinary letter. Or was it so ordinary? The sting was contained in the last sentence. In this she reminded him of certain sums which he had borrowed from Monsieur de Charrière. His delay in paying this debt would expose him to unpleasant criticism: "I can well believe it," she added. "It has left a disagreeable impression even on me." She asked him at the same time if she might preserve from the burning at least some of his little notes—"indifferent scraps of wit and friendship"—and "one other letter." Having sent her envelope down to the post office, she despatched her coachman to get it back. The letter was found among her papers after she was dead. Silence thereafter descended between them.

Benjamin left Switzerland for the Hague, accompanied by his wife, the younger Jaman and a goat. He hoped to be able to put some order into his father's affairs and he therefore, with the Duke's permission, remained in the Low Countries throughout the winter.

This, the first serious quarrel with Madame de Charrière, only lasted for three and a half months. By May of 1790 he was writing to her again. "You will always remain," he assured her, "the dearest, as well as the strangest, of my memories." On his return to Brunswick, he was overwhelmed with melancholy. "I feel more than ever before," he wrote on June

4, 1790, "the utter emptiness of things. . . . I am nothing but a pinch of dust." He had lost his ambition, he had lost his faith, even his philosophy seemed no more to him than a string of words. It was evident that God had been called away before he had time to finish creating the universe. Human beings, he wrote, reminded him of a row of identical watches, each without a dial; every watch said to the other watches, "I go round and round; therefore I must have some meaning."

> Goodbye [he wrote to Madame de Charrière], Goodbye you dear and amusing piece of mechanism. You who have the misfortune to be so far superior to the clock of which you form a part —and therefore always cause the clock to go wrong. I don't want to boast, but it is more or less the same thing with me, isn't it?

She was touched by these confessions. She wrote urging him to take care of his health and to read Tacitus. Urging him to be patient and not to mind so dreadfully if the works went wrong; all works, to her mind, went wrong, always, everywhere.

He remained on at Brunswick with his wife, his dogs, and his valet; playing loto with the Duchess; attending the Club dinners with the Duke; discussing politics with Monsieur Mauvillon and Monsieur Féronce; working in a desultory fashion at his studies on comparative religion; fulfilling with dumb dissatisfaction his functions as a Kammerherr at the Court; feeling that his youth and promise were slipping away from him, while he remained, disliked and forgotten, in this German backwater of the river of the world.

In September 1791 he paid a visit to Switzerland in order to assist in the liquidation of his father's estates. Rosalie wrote to her brother in China: "Benjamin has been here with us for three months. His character is amiable; but there is little that is really interesting about him." In November he left la Chablière on his way back to Brunswick. He stopped two nights at

Colombier. They sat up talking late into the night. Something of his old gaiety had momentarily returned to him; after he had said good night to her she heard him dancing round and round his bedroom with an enormous dog which he had bought at Lausanne to keep him company on the journey.

On his way back from Switzerland to Germany, he passed through the ranks of the army which Condé was recruiting among the French émigrés. He described this army as "an organized rabble." On returning to Brunswick he was greeted by Minna. He found her "cold, hard and dry."

His depression during this period was not due solely to the increasing unpleasantness of his relations with his wife. He had at first greeted the French Revolution with spontaneous enthusiasm. The liberal sentiments which he had acquired at Edinburgh had not been diminished by his experiences at the court of Brunswick, or by what he believed to be the persecution of his father at the hands of the Bernese aristocracy. Jacob Mauvillon, with his high expectations of Mirabeau, increased his excitement and his faith. It was intolerable, when such events were happening in Paris, to be forced to serve as a flunkey in a German Court. He read Burke's *Reflections* the moment they appeared in 1790; he was loud in asserting that both in their premises and conclusions they were ignorant and false. He became known at the Court as "The Swiss Jacobin." He was not at that stage a Jacobin; he would have wished to be a Girondin, a follower of Roland; the only thing he believed in was liberalism and the rule of law.

As the Revolution became more and more uncontrolled, this early enthusiasm was clouded with perplexity. Even Mauvillon began to shake his head in doubt. In a few months Marat and Robespierre appeared as "two Parisian vipers." As the years passed, it became indeed bitter to watch, from such a distance, and in an atmosphere of such sneering, the sacred cause of liberty being increasingly debauched. It was galling to admit (even to oneself) that, not Burke only, but even the dull courtiers of Brunswick may have been right after all. Horrible it was for him to listen to the ponderous affirmations of Baron von Münchausen, to the giggling sallies of the Duchess and her ladies. The wise men had been made to look foolish, and the idiots wise. He began to lose faith even in his own enlightenment. And the years passed.

CHAPTER VI

Minna and Charlotte

[1792–1794]

His relations with his wife become embittered—He meets Charlotte—Their short love affair—He separates from both his wife and Charlotte within the same week—His return to Switzerland on leave of absence—Lausanne society—He spends three months at Colombier—He returns to Brunswick—A cold reception—He starts on a biography of Mauvillon and works hard at his history of religion—He modifies his attitude towards the French Revolution—He resigns his appointment at the Court of Brunswick and comes back to Switzerland—Madame de Charrière reproves him for his German ways of thought—Madame de Staël visits Colombier.

1

BY THE summer of 1792, Benjamin Constant's relations with his wife had degenerated into hostility, morose on his part, shrewish on hers. He could not forgive the thin levity of her ways, her failure to respect his intellectual tastes or even his personal dignity, her indifference to his desires for serious study and scholarly conversation. She could not forgive his habits of solitary retirement, his moods of melancholy, the brooding, and sometimes astringent, quality of his egoism. "I know, I know," he wrote to Madame de Charrière on September 17, 1792, "that for the happiness of others I ought to live alone. I am capable of fine and generous actions;

but I am no good at all at pretty little ways. Solitude and literature—these are my true elements."

Minna meanwhile had fallen in love with someone else. She did not try to conceal her attachment either from Constant or the world. As a distraction (perhaps as a revenge) he also embarked upon an affair with an actress of the name of Caroline. She was able in her simple way to salve his wounded pride. "My great consolation," he called her, "the consolation which now makes my life happy." This short, and perhaps silly, interlude did certainly enable him to shake off the lethargy, the alarming apathy, to which he had succumbed. Caroline proved no more than an episode; but it was an episode which he remembered with gratitude all his life.

By January 1793 the situation had become unbearable. "My wife," he wrote to Madame de Charrière, "has a thousand good qualities, but she no longer loves me. She loves someone else. She is without the capacity, or even the desire to amuse herself. I live surrounded by hordes of cats, birds, dogs and casual acquaintances. There is also her lover. Such is the company in which I pass my days."

Already he had come to the conclusion that his marriage must in some manner be dissolved. He consulted lawyers about a separation. Delicately he sounded the Duke himself. And then, in January 1793, he met Charlotte.

Georgina Charlotte Augusta, Countess of Hardenberg, was the wife of Wilhelm, Baron von Marenholtz. She had been born on November 29, 1769 in London, where her father, Graf Hans Ernst von Hardenberg, was at the time counsellor to the Hanoverian Legation. Hers was a stupendous christening. King George III and Queen Charlotte were present at the ceremony; she was held at the font by the Dowager Princess of Wales. She had been married while still a girl to Baron von Marenholtz, a man much older than herself, by whom she had one son. At the time of her first meeting with Constant she was a full-blown young woman of twenty-four. She had fair skin and hair, a plump friendly face, large white hands, a highly romantic disposition and a profound capacity for devotion. She fell in love with Constant from the first moment and remained in love with him for thirty-seven years.

In the fragment of a diary which Constant on his deathbed presented to his secretary (and which has since disappeared) there was a short entry which Sainte-Beuve copied down. It ran as follows: "Charlotte, January 11, 1793. Discovery of correspondence March 25. Rupture. Separation." Constant, being fascinated, as well as alarmed, by the passage of time, had a passion for dates and anniversaries; he did not always record them accurately; there is no need however to doubt this particular sequence of events.

For two months they lived together openly at Brunswick. Baron von Marenholtz was a generous man; so soon as he realized that Charlotte was unhappy with him, he gave her full liberty and a substantial allowance. The difficulty, when it arose, came, not from the husband, but from Charlotte's father, who was then sixty-five years of age.

It does not appear that Constant, at that time, was seriously in love with Baroness von Marenholtz. He was bored by her romanticism; he underestimated her intelligence; he was irritated by the general atmosphere of pink ribbons and *Schwärmerei*. His acute (perhaps too acute) awareness of emotional proportions caused him to despise her efforts to combine the status of a distinguished German aristocrat with the rapturous surrender of a woman willing to lose the whole world for the man she loved. Yet her gentleness, her uncomplaining acceptance of his own egoism, her calm self-sacrifice —all these rendered her manner a welcome contrast to the shrill asperities of Minna, even as fourteen years later he again found in her a soft asylum from the despotism of Madame de Staël.

This affair, as was to be expected, caused a sensation in the Court of Brunswick. Minna was incensed by the fact that Benjamin should have found so rapid and so patrician a compensation. She revenged herself by communicating to the Duchess some letters written from the Hague in which Benjamin had made fun of the Prince of Orange. "Charlotte," wrote Benjamin to Madame de Charrière, "may be a little mad, but Madame de Constant is a monster—a vile and treacherous monster."

At this stage Charlotte's father decided to put an end to the scandal. On March 25, 1793 he insisted that she should return to her parents and hold no further communication with her paramour. On the very same day Constant learnt that the deed of separation from Minna had been completed. "My troubles," he wrote to Madame de Charrière, "will shortly be over. Hymen! Hymen! Hymen! What a monster you are!" The deed was signed on March 30, 1793. In this document Minna admitted that the fault was hers, and that Benjamin's conduct had been correct throughout; she did not ask for alimony, since she had been given a pension by the Duchess. It was not until January 31, 1794 that the formalities were completed and full legal separation became a fact. He did not at the moment sue for divorce, mainly perhaps because the Duke did not desire a Court scandal. Nor did he allow mention to be made of Minna's adultery, on the ground, as he alleged, that he did not wish to accuse a woman who could not defend herself. It is more probable that he was deterred from making such an accusation owing to his own sexual vanity; which was abnormal.

In any case, within the space of that same week of March 1793, Benjamin found himself liberated both from Minna and

Charlotte. This double liberation left him with an ache of loneliness by which he was appalled.

"What strange and utter weakness!" he wrote to Colombier on March 31, 1793. "For a whole year I have been longing for this moment, for complete freedom and independence. The moment has come, and I shudder in my bones. I am actually terrified by the loneliness which now surrounds me. It frightens me—I who used to groan at having any connection with anyone—to cease suddenly to belong to anyone or anything at all." "An object which escapes us," he comments, "is of course totally different from one by which we are pursued."

He decided to stay on for two or three months at Brunswick, in case it might be said that he had been dismissed from Court. It would be a trying ordeal, but in the end would come the quiet satisfactions of Colombier. "How odd that I, who have always made it a point of vanity to detest my own country, should now be assailed with homesickness for Switzerland! . . . I shall see again that white table, and that other table, the black one, on which everything is heaped. Once again will come the night, once again we shall make our infusion of limes." Could she find him some rooms in the village? All he wanted would be a bedroom, a writing-room and a room for his books. One or two rooms for his servants and a stable for his horses. What remained of his life would, he assured her, be spent at Colombier. "Always," he wrote, "one comes back to you."

He had learnt much from the bitter experiences of the last eighteen months:

> One year of torture at the hands of the most offensive and cruel woman that has ever existed has altered my character. For eighteen months I have been as a stranger in my own home; slighted, despised, insulted. I have learnt to appreciate even the slightest consideration. I no longer regard myself as the centre around

which all else must turn. This long and tragic experience [he writes on May 17] has convinced me that only good conduct can evoke good conduct in return. All deviations from good conduct create harm. With all my strength I am fighting against indifference to vice or virtue; against that form of indifference which resulted from my strange upbringing and my even stranger adolescence and which has been the cause of all my misfortunes. I shall win this fight, since indifference in such matters is opposed to my true character.

As always with Constant, his bitterness and his new sense of freedom were checked by an imaginative pity. "My feeling of liberty is poisoned by the thought of what Minna must be suffering and what she will suffer; by the idea of the gentle life she used to lead, and of the pleasures which will now be denied her. But why was she so contemptuous towards me? I was far more intelligent than she was; she trod me underfoot. Intelligence is not a weapon; character, good conduct, these are the only true weapons of defence."

Constant left Brunswick at the end of May 1793. He still retained his appointment as Kammerherr. It was announced that he had been granted leave of absence.

2

Although Madame de Charrière had secured rooms for him in the castle at Colombier, he stayed at Lausanne, waiting for his "dear, dear library" to arrive from Brunswick. He continued to occupy himself with his father's unending lawsuits and with the liquidation of the estates. He thought at one moment of establishing himself definitively at La Chablière but doubted whether there was a room there large enough to house the 4,000 books which he amassed while in Germany. He therefore hung on somewhat fecklessly at Beausoleil, acquiring from Geneva certain works of reference which he required, asking Monsieur de Charrière to obtain others for him at Neuchâtel and Zurich, and mingling occasionally with such society as Lausanne could offer.

The social world of Lausanne was at that period dominated by Benjamin's two aunts, the Countess de Nassau and Madame de Bavois. The former, as has already been recorded, was a woman of character and gifts. But she lived with a companion, a Mlle. Rieu, who got upon Benjamin's nerves. "I will confess to you," he wrote to Colombier in October, "that in spite of Madame de Nassau's real intelligence I have had more than enough of her company, especially when Mlle. Rieu is present. The way that woman grunts and clears her throat, the sententious little nods that she gives when she makes some peculiarly idiotic remark; these things make me want to bang her on the head."

Madame de Bavois lived in a little house, called La Chaumière, on the road which runs down from Lausanne to Ouchy and the lake. Every Saturday she gave an afternoon party which was attended by the social and intellectual world of Lausanne. Rosalie, on these occasions, would act as the daughter of the house. Madame de Charrière for some reason had a sharp dislike of Madame de Bavois. Benjamin defended her. "Yes," replied Madame de Charrière, "quite a clever little woman, if you like—perhaps too much so. Personally I find her singularly unattractive. I can understand that those who enjoy vivacity at any cost can put up with her better than I can. One day she builds a new house, next day she writes a foolish play, the day after she gives an ingenious little supper party, which must cost her very little. She has a way of shrinking back into her tiny little frame, of extracting something from it; exhorting, flattering, cajoling left and right;—young and old, wits and swells."

In addition to the two salons of Madame de Nassau and

Madame de Bavois, there was a literary society, founded by Deyverdun, the companion of Gibbon, which his uncle Samuel would sometimes persuade him to attend. At this period, moreover, he made friends with Thérèse Forster and her lover, Louis Ferdinand Huber (1). This friendship was not wholly approved of by Madame de Charrière. She suspected Benjamin of concealing pro-Jacobism sympathies and she regarded Huber and Thérèse as dangerous revolutionaries. This friendship—and it ripened into an intimacy—was a great solace to Constant during those dull autumn days. Huber, or "Hüberchen" as he called him, was one of the few men friends with whom he was able to establish relations of easy confidence.

On December 2, 1793 Constant transported himself, his belongings, and a new dog "Muset," to Colombier. A flat had been prepared for him in the old castle on the hill, at that time tenanted by Monsieur Borel, the collector of tithes. He spent his days and took his meals at the Charrière house in the hollow below the castle hill; it would take him with his long legs, no more than three minutes to run down the slope and steps of Les Egralets and to reach the arch of the manor house. He remained at Colombier for three months, working at his history of religion, on occasions visiting Neuchâtel and even Berne in order to discover new works of reference, and spending long hours talking to Madame de Charrière in the corner room. She had by that time given up the long struggle against middle age. Thérèse Forster, who saw her at this date, records that she had completely lost her figure, had become "large and shapeless" with dull red cheeks and blue protruding eyes. He enjoyed opening her correspondence, fiddling with her private papers, upsetting the arrangement of her sheets of music. Their intimacy during those three months was once again fresh and completely unruffled. She would sit in her covered bath, with damp cloths draped around her, and they would talk for hours. "We were," he recorded, "as happy as kings."

Madame de Charrière was at this time managing a whole colony of French émigrés, notably Camille de Rousillon and his brother Pierre. Madame Achard was also at Colombier during this period with her daughter Ninette. Constant did not at all relish this intrusion upon the private calm of Colombier. He was not at this time in a good state of health; he suffered from palpitations which he sought to cure by taking two cold showers a day; and his melancholia would come back to him in a dark cloud. He was saddened also by the death of his Brunswick friend, Jacob Mauvillon.

In March 1794 the final formalities regularizing his separation from Minna were signed, sealed, and deposited. He received from the Duke an amiable letter, inviting him to return to Brunswick. His family at Lausanne had been whispering that he had been dismissed from the Court for disgraceful behaviour. He was anxious to disprove this calumny. On April 3, 1794, he left Colombier suddenly, without daring to inform Madame de Charrière of the date or hour of his departure.

On his way to Germany he stopped for two nights at Göttingen. He had been given by Huber letters of introduction to some of the university professors and was stimulated by their scholarship and encouragement. Why not, during this final Brunswick period, also become a scholar and produce a work of serious importance which would establish his fame and compensate for all those wasted years? He might start with a biography of Mauvillon and an examination of the nature of liberty and the theory of constitutional monarchy. Yes, he would begin by writing the life and thoughts of Jacob Mauvillon.

3

He reached Brunswick on the night of April 20, 1794. The next morning he paid a call on the Lord Chamberlain, who was courteous but cold. He then went on to see Féronce, who warned him that his jokes at the expense of the Prince of Orange had been widely circulated and done him much harm at Court. He must not expect a friendly reception.

During these his last months of service as Kammerherr he absented himself as much as possible from all Court functions. His distaste for them was increased by the fact that whenever he came face to face with his late wife (who was now in close attendance on the Duchess) she would burst into peals of artificial but disturbing laughter. From Charlotte, who was being very obedient to her father, he heard not a word.

Before leaving Switzerland he had written to her announcing his impending return. Knowing that her father intercepted all her correspondence, he was careful to adopt a disguise which Charlotte could penetrate without difficulty. He sent her a note, purporting to come from a Swiss bookseller, and asking for payment of a bill of thirty-two pounds. The titles of the books listed, most of which contained the names of Charlotte or Henri (2), made marked allusions to their common experiences; even the dates on which the books were said to have been despatched were the key dates in their own love affair. The letter bore the address, in English, "Dove House." It was signed Bécé and announced that the writer was about to leave Switzerland and hoped to be in Brunswick before the end of April.

Charlotte was puzzled by this unexpected communication and showed it to all her friends, asking them if they had ever heard of a place called "Dove House" or of a bookseller of that strange name. In the end someone had the ingenuity to suggest to her that "Dove House" might stand for "Colombier" and Bécé for B.C.

Being practically debarred from Court, having but few friends who remained faithful to him in the town, he flung himself into his biography of Mauvillon. He spent long hours with Madame Mauvillon discussing the plan of the book and accumulating material. He now realized (and it is amazing that he should not have seen it earlier) that sooner or later he would have to resign his position as chamberlain. The sense of irresponsibility which this gave him, the resentment he felt at what he imagined to be harsh treatment, above all perhaps the renewal of contact with Mauvillon's ideas, turned his mind again to the tragedy of the French Revolution. He had been revolted by the Terror and shocked by the execution of the King and Queen. But he now began to feel that things had gone so far in France that only a despot, perhaps only a blood-stained despot, could restore order and preserve peace. He persuaded himself that some form of tyranny, even the tyranny of a Robespierre, was essential before liberty could be reborn. The hostile atmosphere of Brunswick thrust him even further to the left. He came almost to believe that Jacobinism had become necessary and that it was no longer possible or intelligent to pursue the Girondin path:

> We live in times of storm [he wrote to Madame de Charrière on June 7, 1794] and it is poor fun, when a hurricane blows as it is now blowing, to be a reed. On the other hand it is most unsafe to be a lonely oak; and in any case I am not the stuff that oaks are made of. I have given up therefore taking an individual point of view; I no longer want to be "myself"; I want to be with those who on the whole think as I do and who are working towards the same direction. In a time such as this, centre parties are no use whatsoever; the middle path becomes hopeless.

He plunged himself into his work, and found therein a new self-confidence and a renewal of pride and hope. "I am not bored," he wrote to Madame de Charrière subsequently. "Were it not that I hate being parted from you, I should congratulate myself upon my present way of life. The habit of industry has now been recaptured. I can sit down and work whenever I wish to; it does no harm to my health and infinite good to my mind. Even the phantom of literary success (that phantom which you have been at such pains to exorcize) has returned to me and embellishes my love."

Studious as he had become, anxious as he was to get clear of Brunswick, to resign his functions, to transform his legal separation from Minna into complete divorce, he kept himself aloof from all society. Even when Charlotte relented and asked him to come and see her, he refused on the ground that it would only open old wounds. He must finish his book on Mauvillon (it was never finished), he must complete his material for his great work on religion, he must obtain absolute liberty from all conjugal or ducal bonds, he must leave Brunswick as soon as possible. More important than anything, perhaps, he must reform his own character. Madame de Nassau had accused him of being devoid of true feeling. On May 24, 1794 he replied to her as follows:

> Indifference has caused me too much suffering; I abjure it. One may flatter oneself that one can rise above the emotional side of life, and see therein only what is absurd; but I have learnt all too well that this leads one to miss the depths. The trick of irony may afford some satisfaction to one's self-esteem; yet it is not worth one minute of real feeling. I am bored by my own attitude of derision; I am tired of hiding my heart within a covering of indifference and so depriving myself of the gentler sensations. Since the luxury of disdain has not brought me happiness, to hell with the conceit of supposing myself superior to those who really feel. I prefer the folly of enthusiasm (if anything that makes one happy

can be a folly) to this my terrible wisdom. As a calculating egoist
I wish no longer to be a calculating egoist. Come back to me, oh
trustfulness which I was once so pleased to discard! Come back
to me passion which I have so often stultified! Oh come back, you
simple sweet pleasures, which I have so long rejected! You hidden
day-to-day virtues which I was proud to despise: love, friendship,
kindness, happy credulity—all those virtues which were snatched
from me by the extravagant precocity of my childhood's education.

Constant, abandoning the biography of Mauvillon, resigned his appointment and left Brunswick at the end of July 1794. It was not however until November 18, 1795 that he obtained his divorce. He was enraged in later years to learn that Minna still called herself Madame de Constant. She continued to reside in Brunswick under the protection of the Duchess. Towards the end of her life her passion for animals assumed eccentric proportions. She lived in a little house which the Duchess had left her, surrounded by birds, monkeys, lizards, snakes and all the stray cats and dogs of the city. Benjamin also was fond of animals; but he never cared for menageries. With Minna the thing developed into an obsession; her house became insanitary and she lost many of her friends. She died in 1823.

4

On his return to Switzerland that August, Constant spent a few days at Colombier and then proceeded to Lausanne, where he took rooms at the Lion d'Or. His family, after all his misfortunes, were more than ever irritating. "For two hours," he wrote to his confidante at Colombier, "I had to listen to them assuring me that I am intolerably conceited, that I only refer to myself or human nature in general in order to show off, that my wit is purely imitative, the sort which induces young men to parade startling opinions, and that this manner of speaking (which is incidentally the only one that I possess) is now entirely out of date."

It was at this stage that Madame de Charrière made a fatal, and indeed final, mistake. She should have realized that Benjamin was feeling unhappy because unsuccessful, and that the reflections made by his family upon his wasteful life and unfulfilled promise were galling because he felt them to be true. Now was the moment of all others for her to lay aside the high analytical manner, to provide comfort, confidence and above all encouragement and esteem. Yet her reply to his appeal was not a maternal reply; it was matriarchal.

All her life she had vaunted and gloried in her own reason, believing that intellectual integrity—the recognition of naked fact—were the supreme virtues. To these deities she would sacrifice herself and others in an orgy of laceration. Such was her pride that she preferred to accept defeat with defiant dignity rather than to make one motion of compromise or withdrawal by which it might have been averted. For her, lucidity of thought and expression had become an inner conscience; she was too conceited, as well as too proud, to pause for a moment to consider whether there might not be occasions when feeling was more valuable than thought; she was too embittered by her own failure in life to have the generosity to welcome or stimulate the success of others. She should have realized that Benjamin Constant, after all the suffering and humiliation of the last year, was passing through a crisis in self-esteem; that the moment had come for her to be tender rather than acute.

She answered his appeal in her old didactic manner. Might it not be true that his epigrams, his double ironies, really did obscure for some people the good sense which was in him? She herself of course knew that he put on this manner—half serious, half mocking—in order to disconcert those with whom he conversed. "In a way," she wrote, "it is not a bad thing, since it amuses you, it amuses those who admire you, it imposes upon silly people and throws even the most logical out of their stride. Yet in another way, it is not a good thing, since it leads people to misjudge and to misunderstand you, and since, by creating suspicion and boring those whom it does not amuse, it precludes people from listening to the serious and sensible things which you have to say."

Benjamin, who had asked for sympathy, had been met, if not exactly by reproof, then at least with an analytical diagnosis. He was hurt and angry. He replied in words which were different from the tone of affectionate respect with which he usually addressed Madame de Charrière. "What does it matter to you," he wrote, "whether I have one fault or another? The greatest fault I can have is that I should ever hold any opinions which are not identical with your own." How differently, he thought, would Charlotte—poor silly, romantic, devoted Charlotte—have responded to his appeal! And that reminded him. Would Madame de Charrière please burn any letters in which he might have made fun of Charlotte? "You have a habit," he wrote, "of leaving my letters drifting about your room. If they fall into the hands of strangers they would deal a death blow to my moribund repute." He ended with the words, "Well, goodbye, my aristocratic and laconic friend, always so full of excellent advice."

Madame de Charrière appears for once to have detected a note of sincere irritation, even perhaps to have had some premonition of the danger to come. She replied quite amicably: "If you write me any more letters as sharp as the last one, I shall cease to be your laconic friend and shall become a friend who has ceased to utter a single word."

Benjamin was all contrition. On September 20, 1794 he

sent an abject apology. "I need you," he wrote, "I need your friendship; do not allow the folly of one after-dinner mood to deprive me of it. I shall come back to you without any reservation, without a single menace. I humiliate myself. I love you and ask your pardon."

She waited seven important days before answering this apology. "Very well," she wrote on September 27, "come here when you want. The vaunting son will be welcomed as a prodigal." The fatal governess side could not, even at so tense a moment, be suppressed. "When you return from Germany," she wrote, "it always seems to me that your sentences get longer and your style less clear-cut. I fear that under this German influence your thoughts may come to present themselves in less direct, lucid or luminous form."

On September 16 she had written a note to her friend Mlle. L'Hardy: "What a curious, what an amiable, man is this Benjamin Constant! When he is here at Colombier with me we get on splendidly together. But the moment he returns to Lausanne he begins to assume airs of independence and intractability which almost provoke a quarrel between us."

One's dislike of Madame de Charrière begins at this stage to be clouded with pity.

5

On September 24, two days before her letter to Mlle. L'Hardy, three days before her reply to Benjamin's apology, an enormous yellow travelling carriage, driven by postillions in green livery, stopped at the humble door of the Charrière manor-house at Colombier. Swathed in scarves and feathers Madame de Staël descended and climbed up the stone turret staircase to the corner drawing-room. She had come to pay homage to the author of *Mistriss Henley* and *Caliste*.

CHARLOTTE VON HARDENBERG, subsequently BARONESS VON MARENHOLZ, subsequently MADAME DU TERTRE, subsequently MADAME BENJAMIN CONSTANT

This was not the first meeting between Madame de Charrière and Madame de Staël. The conjunction which during those September days formed, and then suddenly shattered, that tragic triangle had begun some six years before.

In 1788, when *Caliste* was published, Madame de Staël had written five long letters to its author couched in her accustomed style of exaggerated eulogy, lauding its theme and prose. When in Paris during the year following Madame de Charrière had not, so far as we know, attended the receptions at the Swedish Embassy. During that year she had published a defence of Thérèse Lavasseur in which she had had some acid things to say about Madame de Staël who had attacked that lady in her *Lettres sur Rousseau*. This may well have been the reason why they did not meet.

Madame de Staël was the most forgiving woman that ever lived. She never kept an enemy or forgot a friend. On Sunday, August 11, 1793, believing (quite wrongly) that Madame de Charrière possessed indirect means of approaching both the King of Prussia and the Duke of Brunswick, she had paid a visit to Colombier. She begged Madame de Charrière to intercede on behalf of La Fayette (3). Madame de Charrière was flattered by the visit of this famous woman and by the request for assistance. She admitted that the brilliance of Madame de Staël's personality and conversation enabled one to forget her physical ugliness. "How I wish," she had written to Benjamin four days before, "that you were going to be here on Sunday. Madame de Staël is coming here that day. Monsieur de Charrière met her the other day at Coppet and she told him that she was anxious to meet the author of *Caliste*. Gladly would I dispense with such a wish on her part. If you were going to be here, it would be all right. But I loathe the idea of being scrutinized all alone. It is not the results of the scrutiny which alarm me, but the scrutiny itself. It is tiresome to be obliged to listen and to make replies, which, given my mood, are sure to be different from the replies I should want to make."

This first visit, none the less, was a success. On September 12, 1793 Madame de Staël wrote from Coppet to say that she had been rereading *Caliste* and come to the conclusion that only in Holland can one learn how to write perfect French. A month later there came another letter. Did Madame de Charrière know of any house in the vicinity of Colombier which she could rent for the winter? "I have come to believe that only the sight of you, only the sound of your voice, can save my life." Madame de Charrière, who never cared for gush, and hated women of greater intelligence than her own, was appalled by such a prospect. There appeared to be no house in the district suitable for a woman of such eminence.

In March 1794 Madame de Charrière received a copy of *Zulma* and replied that she thought it very bad indeed. She was at the time annoyed with Madame de Staël for failing to return some books which she had lent her. Madame de Staël, who was always lavish about her personal possessions, did not realize that she had committed any crime. She noticed that Madame de Charrière's letter was a cold letter, but imagined that she was hurt because, the previous winter, her plan for wintering near Colombier had not been brought to fruition.

Early in September 1794 Madame de Staël left Coppet for Berne, hoping to induce the Bernese Government to adopt a more generous attitude to the French émigrés. She was accompanied by her old friend Count Louis de Narbonne (4). She reached Berne on September 13 only to find that Their Excellencies were obdurate. On her return journey she stopped for a few nights at the Chateau de Greng, near Morat, where its owner, Monsieur de Garville, kept open house for all the scattered émigrés. Leaving de Narbonne at Greng she drove back to Coppet stopping at Colombier on the way.

On this, her second visit of September 24, 1794, she remained two hours in the house of Madame de Charrière. She made a bad impression. "I was able," wrote Madame de Charrière to Benjamin, "to get some insight into all the variations of her silliness. She boasted of her wit, as if she did not possess any. She boasted about her titled friends, as if her husband had picked her up the day before in a milliner's shop. She showed off to me about the great world of Paris, as if she had been a girl from the provinces who had only been there six weeks.

"There was," concluded Madame de Charrière, "nothing authentic about her. What fun we shall have discussing her together! I simply long for you to meet her!"

This longing was quickly satisfied. Five days later, on September 28, 1794, Benjamin Constant and Madame de Staël met for the first time on the road between Coppet and Nyon.

CHAPTER VII

Madame de Staël

[1766–1794]

Origins of the Necker family—Jacques Necker—Suzanne Curchod—The birth and education of Germaine Necker—Her precocity—Her visit to London—Her first visit to Switzerland—Gibbon's estimate of her at the age of eighteen—Projects of marriage—William Pitt—Baron de Staël—She marries the latter January 14, 1786—Her salon in the Rue du Bac—Her interference in French politics—She falls in love with Narbonne—The attack upon the Tuileries—She assists Narbonne to escape to England—The September massacres—She is in mortal danger but is rescued by Manuel and Tallien—She escapes to Switzerland—Birth of Albert—She rejoins Narbonne at Juniper Hall—Meeting with Fanny Burney—She returns to Switzerland—Death of her mother—She meets Benjamin Constant September 28, 1794—Constant falls a victim to her personality—He confesses this to Madame de Charrière—The latter's resentment at this new attachment—Their quarrel—The end of Madame de Charrière.

1

ANNE LOUISE GERMAINE NECKER, Baroness de Staël-Holstein, was born in Paris at 6 P.M. on April 22, 1766. She was thus twenty-eight years old at the time she first met Benjamin Constant and he was twenty-six.

The Necker family originated from the little town of Pyritz in Pomerania. Madame de Staël's grandfather, Karl Friedrich Necker, had moved from Pyritz to Cüstrin and had in 1724 obtained an appointment as lecturer in German law at the Academy of Geneva. In 1726 he became a Genevese citizen and thereafter married Jeanne-Marie Gautier, by whom he had two sons. The first was Louis Necker who in later life assumed the surname of de Germany. The second was Jacques Necker, who was born on September 30, 1732.

Jacques Necker, the father of Madame de Staël, had at the age of fifteen been sent to Paris as a clerk in the banking house of Vernet. He had an excellent head for figures and prospered exceedingly. Within a few years he became a partner in the firm of Vernet and shortly afterwards, with a fellow Genevese, he founded the famous bank of Thélusson and Necker. M. Thélusson managed the London branch, whereas Jacques Necker remained in Paris. By speculating in grain and making loans to the Treasury he amassed an enormous fortune. In 1763 Jacques Necker fell in love with the widow of a French officer, a certain Madame Verménoux. In the following year Madame Verménoux, being on a visit to Geneva, was impressed by the intelligence, and touched by the penury of the orphaned daughter of a Swiss pastor, Suzanne Curchod (1). She engaged the girl as a paid companion and brought her back to Paris. Mlle. Curchod was a young woman of resolution, beauty, astuteness and grim culture. She had not been many months in Paris before she was able to detach Jacques Necker's affections from Madame Verménoux and marry him herself. Germaine, subsequently Baroness de Staël-Holstein, was their only child.

Madame Necker had social and political ambitions. Her salon in the Hôtel Leblanc, Rue de Cléry, became the centre of the literary, artistic and financial world of Paris; it also became a focus for the liberal intellectuals. She induced her husband to accept the post of Genevese Minister in Paris and to become a director of the French East India Company. These appointments gave him the entrée to Versailles. In

1775 Jacques Necker published an important pamphlet in which he attacked the free-trade policy of Turgot and suggested remedies for the chaotic condition of French public finance. In the following year he was appointed Director of the Treasury, a title which, in 1777, he himself changed to Director-General of Finances. He redistributed the poll-tax, established credit banks and started to fund the French debt. In 1781 he published his *Compte Rendu* of the French financial situation in which for the first time the state of the French exchequer was divulged to the world. A few weeks later he was dismissed.

In 1784 he purchased the Château de Coppet near Geneva together with the feudal rights attached to it (2). In 1787 he was banished by *lettre de cachet* to within forty leagues of Paris owing to his criticisms of Calonne. Public opinion, urged on by the intellectuals of Madame Necker's salon, insisted on his recall; in 1788 he was again appointed Director-General of Finances. He secured the summoning of the States General, the double representation of the third estate, and the system by which the three orders should deliberate and vote in common. He was thus regarded by the Court, as well as by the Estates General, as the father of the revolution. His dismissal on July 11, 1789 was the signal for the attack upon the Bastille. In sudden panic Louis XVI recalled him immediately; his return to Paris was a triumphal progress. But the situation quickly developed beyond his capacities and in 1790 he resigned and retired again to Coppet, where he lived on in luxurious and self-satisfied retirement until his death in 1804.

Jacques Necker was a heavy, slow-moving, slow-speaking man, with an expression which was simultaneously pompous and surprised. He possessed great integrity, a fine tolerance, considerable ability, a fund of common sense and a convic-

MADAME DE STAËL

tion of his own superior qualities; a conviction which was much enhanced by the incessant adulation of his wife and daughter. Fundamentally however he was an indecisive man; "afloat," as Gouverneur Morris remarked, "upon the wide ocean of incidents." Mirabeau at the time (and Bonaparte subsequently), dismissed him as "a fool"; that was an overstatement; yet it is difficult for us to appreciate the enraptured worship which his wife and daughter lavished upon him, or to understand the awe which to the day of his death he was regarded by the whole Coppet circle. He lacked imagination even as he lacked alacrity of mind; his ponderous self-complacency proved utterly unable to cope with the fierce and mobile forces which he had helped to unleash.

2

There exists at Coppet a drawing of Germaine Necker as a child of nine or ten. She is seated upon a footstool, her hair is dressed in the Court manner, and her clothes are too elaborate for a little girl. Her face is ill-shaped, her teeth protruding, her nose unfortunate; yet from her eyes there flashes a fire of vivacity which redeems all these defects; one realizes that she is not merely taking in the intellectual conversation around her; she is also taking part. When she was only two months old her mother had written that she was "very impatient to start talking"; it was an impatience that developed rapidly and remained.

Madame Necker was a strict disciplinarian; she insisted that her daughter should be brought up in the most rigid principles of the Swiss protestant church; she personally supervised her education and saw to it that the little girl was crammed with all the knowledge and accomplishments which Paris of the late eighteenth century could provide.

Her father was more indulgent; he encouraged her precocity and was amused by her pert sallies; even at the age of ten she was allowed to witness, and to share in, the magnificent receptions that he gave. Her childhood was spent amid the last glories and tribulations of Versailles; amid the Gobelins and grandeurs of her father's lavish saloons; in her young ears there echoed the quiet and incisive modulations of a dying century together with the wilder clamour of the new. At the age of ten, in April 1776, she was taken to London; for two months she lived with her parents in a house in Suffolk Street. She saw the whig statesmen; she watched Garrick act Shakespeare; she witnessed the order and fantasy of English life; she imbibed her father's anglo-mania.

It was in 1784 that she paid her first visit to Switzerland. Her father had only just acquired Coppet and while the rooms were being redecorated he rented the Château de Beaulieu on the outskirts of Lausanne. It was then that she met Gibbon, her mother's old admirer, who was at the time sharing La Grotte with Deyverdun. "Mlle. Necker," he wrote to Lady Sheffield on October 22, 1784, "—one of the greatest heiresses in Europe, is now about eighteen; wild, vain, but good natured—and with a much larger provision of wit than of beauty." It was then also that she met Albertine de Saussure, the fiancée of her cousin Jacques Necker, who became her life-long companion, critic and admirer. Yet even at that age she was bored by Switzerland and Swiss society; she yearned for Paris.

In October 1784, while Benjamin Constant was revelling in his last happy months at Edinburgh, the Necker family moved from Lausanne to Avignon on account of Madame Necker's health. They were already contemplating a husband for their plain but gifted daughter, and were determined that, whatever nationality he might belong to, his religion must be Protestant. At one moment the Neckers are said to have thought of William Pitt, whom they had met at Fontainbleau in September of the previous year, and whose talents and bearing they had much admired. Eventually the choice fell upon young Baron de Staël-Holstein, a man of excellent family and fine appearance who was at the time attaché to the Swedish Embassy in Paris. Long negotiations followed, in which the King of Sweden and the Queen of France took an active, and to our minds exorbitant, part. One of the conditions of the contract was that as recompense for the immense dowry which Germaine would bring with her, young de Staël should be promoted from attaché to Ambassador. In the end the contract was drafted and signed; they were married with great pomp on January 14, 1786.

The Baron and the Baroness de Staël established themselves in the Swedish Embassy in the Rue du Bac. Madame de Necker-Saussure who was in Paris at the time described her cousin as ill-dressed and noisy; she found her snobbishly contemptuous of her Swiss relations. Already she was forming in the Rue du Bac a circle of intellectuals, liberals and constitutionalists. Already it was evident that she desired something more than social success; something more even than literary fame; it was evident that she desired power.

For her husband, until he was almost dead, she never displayed the slightest affection or even consideration. He was a feeble, lascivious, querulous man. She seriously compromised his position, and eventually lost him his Embassy, by abusing her diplomatic status in order to intrigue in French internal affairs. Her whole preoccupation during those years immediately preceding the revolution was with the successes and defeats, the dismissals and recalls, of her father; she sought to construct in her salon of the Rue du Bac a strong group of liberal progressives pledged to the support of Monsieur Necker's plans and politics. In the pursuit of that aim she was indefatigable, lavish, self-assertive, vociferous and inconceivably indiscreet.

In 1788 Madame de Staël published her *Letters on the Works and Character of J. J. Rousseau* which immediately established her as a writer of influence and note. From that moment she saw that she could expand her authority and enhance her fame, by the written as well as the spoken word. It was at that moment also that she met Count Louis de Narbonne for whom, with her habitual recklessness, she developed a passion which she sought neither to mitigate nor to conceal. Her powers of persistence were thereafter devoted to obtaining for Narbonne a post of importance in the government; in spite of the dislike with which she was regarded by Marie Antoinette, in spite of the suspicion which she aroused among the politicians of the left, she was in the end successful. In 1791, a few days after the flight to Varennes, Narbonne was appointed Minister of War.

During the previous year (in August 1790) her son Auguste was born and so soon as she was convalescent she went to Coppet to be with her father in his exile and to "contemplate this majestic example of the mutability of human fortunes." The winter of that year was passed at Geneva and Lausanne. "One is swept away," wrote Rosalie de Constant at that date, "one is completely subjugated by the force of her genius. When she is present, other people just become the audience. . . . Strange it is to find in this remarkable woman, a sort of childishness and good-fellowship which eliminates all taint of pedantry."

In January 1791 she returned to Paris burning once again to be with Narbonne. She knew that he was not faithful to her; there was Madame de Coigny, there was Mlle. Louise Contat of the Comédie Française. She suspected that he did not deeply care for her. "Supposing," she asked him, "that Mlle. Contat and I were both about to drown; which of us would you save first?" "Madame," he replied, "I am convinced that you are an excellent swimmer."

In spite of the protests of her husband and the King of Sweden she continued to use her official position to intervene in French politics. By 1792 however the situation was becoming dangerous. On June 20, from the diplomatic gallery, she saw Louis XVI place upon his head the red bonnet of the revolution; on July 14 she watched Marie Antoinette attending the festival of the Champ de Mars with tears streaming down her cheeks. All former animosities were forgotten. Madame de Staël spent the next month devising a plan to smuggle the royal family to England via Dieppe. On August 10 came the attack upon the Tuileries and the massacre of the Swiss Guards. During the panic that followed she displayed amazing intrepidity. Profiting by her diplomatic immunity (which by then was but slight protection) and by her immense fortune (which was perhaps more efficacious) she created an underground organization for the rescue of aristocrats threatened by the increasing Terror. As her chief agent at this time she employed a German of the name of Justus Erich Bollman, a young man of romantic disposition and great courage.

It was evident that the Jacobins, who had always detested Narbonne, would, after the events of August 10, be out for his blood. He took refuge in the Swedish Embassy where he hid for three nights. Bollman was able to obtain passports for himself and "an English friend" and succeeded in passing Narbonne through the barriers. They reached Dover on the evening of August 20th and from there proceeded to Talleyrand's house in Kensington.

Madame de Staël then got into touch with Manuel, a member of the Paris commune. Through him she managed to obtain the release of Lally Tollendal and Jaucourt. She was at that date expecting her second baby and felt that it was time to leave for Switzerland. On the morning of September 2, the day of the massacre of the prisons, she started off from the Rue du Bac in her great chariot with six horses and postillions. The tocsin was already clanging in the streets and she had not got far when her carriage was intercepted by a horde of demented hags who flung themselves on the horses screaming that she was escaping with the nation's gold. Surrounded by an ever-increasing mob she was conducted to the Hôtel de Ville; dishevelled faces, forearms, red with recent murder, were thrust into her carriage windows; it was almost with relief that she entered the Hôtel de Ville and found herself in the presence of Robespierre. She was detained there for six hours without food or water while the massacres continued; from the window of the room in which she was segregated she could see the assassins drenched in blood streaming across the Place de Grève. When night fell she was re-conducted by Manuel through unlit streets to the Rue du Bac. On the next morning, accompanied only by her maid and in an ordinary post-chaise, she was escorted by Tallien past the barriers. In this manner she escaped from Paris and eventually to Switzerland.

A month later her second son, Albert, was born at Coppet. He bore no resemblance to Monsieur de Staël.

3

As always, she was restless in Switzerland and afraid that Narbonne, who was never dependable in such matters, might in her absence become involved in some entanglement. Shortly after reaching London he had joined the colony of French

MADAME DE STAËL

refugees established at Juniper Hall, the seat of Mr. Jenkinson, near Mickleham in Surrey. The expenses of this establishment were borne by Madame de Staël. The Juniper Hall colony consisted of Madame de Châtre, Madame Victor de Broglie, Mathieu de Montmorency, Narbonne, Jaucourt, Malouet, Lally Tollendal and Narbonne's great friend, General d'Arblay. From time to time Talleyrand would come down for a night or two from London.

The relations between France and England were by then increasingly strained. The provocative actions of the Convention, especially their disregard of Dutch rights over the estuary of the Scheldt, had brought the two nations to the brink of war. The execution of Louis XVI on January 21, 1793 rendered a rupture inevitable. On January 24, Chauvelin, the representative of the Convention in London, was ordered to leave the country. On February 1 the Convention declared war on Great Britain and Holland.

Madame de Staël, having recovered from her confinement, was determined to join Narbonne in England. In vain did her father beg her to abandon so insane a project. In spite of her experiences during the September massacres, in spite of the fact that war was impending, she left Coppet in January, drove through France, reached England in safety, and appeared at Juniper Hall unruffled and garrulous in the first days of February, 1793.

It was there, a few days later, that she was visited by Fanny Burney, who found that she resembled Mrs. Thrale "in the ardour and warmth of her temper and partialities" but with "infinitely more depth." In fact Fanny Burney found the company at Juniper Hall "a marvellous set for excess of agreeability." Dr. Burney, on receiving these enthusiastic letters, was disturbed. He was ready to believe, having read the little book on Rousseau, that Madame de Staël possessed "captivating powers"; but it was his duty to warn his daughter that there had been unpleasant rumours about the French colony at Juniper Hall. It had been whispered even that Madame de Staël had been accused "of partiality to M. de N . . ." Fanny was incensed by such suggestions. "Indeed," she replied to her father, "I think you could not spend a day with them and not see that their commerce is that of pure, but exalted and most elevated, friendship." Miss Burney was a well brought up girl. "Nevertheless," she added, "I would give the world to avoid being a guest under their roof, now that I have heard even the shadow of such a rumour."

Madame de Staël realized that it might be difficult to maintain her colony at Juniper Hall in time of war. On February 26, 1793 she wrote to Gibbon. "Tell me," she asked him, "whether you could find some house not far from your own at Lausanne where I could bring M. de Narbonne and another younger man whose name I have mentioned to you. Would it be possible for us all to live together, supposing we were three or four? What would be the moral and political reaction out there to such a scheme?"

Gibbon appears to have replied that both the moral and political reactions would be severe. Madame de Staël in spite of her father's renewed protests, remained on in England for several weeks. On April 27 she had a two hours' interview in London with Charles James Fox. In May she returned to Coppet via Germany but without Narbonne. During the course of the year she managed to gather her émigrés around her again in Switzerland. "Two gentlemen," we find her writing on December 21, 1793, "have been living with me here under Swedish names—Monsieur de Montmorency and M. de Jaucourt. M. de Narbonne will be arriving shortly under a Spanish name." Meanwhile, from the comparative safety of Coppet, she continued to organize and expand her underground escape organization. She employed several different agents and spent much money; she saved many lives.

In the late autumn of 1793 the Necker family left Coppet for Lausanne in order that Madame Necker, whose health was causing anxiety, might be under the care of Dr. Tissot. Once again they rented the Château de Beaulieu on the outskirts of the town. Madame Necker did not improve under Dr. Tissot's treatment and on May 15, 1794 she died. She had always been obsessed by the dread of being buried alive; she had left instructions that her corpse should be preserved in a stone coffin filled with spirits of wine; the lid of the coffin was to be of glass. The mausoleum at Coppet had not yet been constructed; for five months, until the work was completed, the corpse of Madame Necker remained in a room at Beausoleil.

The Bernese authorities, who regarded all Madame de Staël's émigrés as dangerous revolutionaries, were threatening to expel the whole party from the canton of Vaud. The only hope was to move to Zurich. Madame de Staël was unwilling to leave her bereaved father and he refused to part from what, with some irreverence, she called "that wretched coffin." It was thus that, in September 1794, she decided to make a direct appeal to the Standrecht at Berne and to produce Louis de Narbonne for their inspection. Their Excellencies were not impressed, and Madame de Staël as has been recounted in the previous chapter, made her way back, via Colombier, to Coppet. By that date (it was September 26, 1794) the mausoleum was ready and the coffin of Madame Necker was installed.

The revolutionary ferment had by then spread to the town of Geneva. In 1792, General Montesquiou, commanding the army of the South, had occupied Savoy and was threatening the Genevese Republic. The citizens put themselves into a state of defence, manned the ramparts and called out the home guard. Benjamin's uncle Samuel, and his cousin Victor, donned their uniforms and kept watch upon the barricades. General Montesquiou was at heart anxious not to attack the city; he negotiated a treaty with the Genevese under which their neutrality was to be respected. This treaty was promptly repudiated by the National Assembly, whereupon General Montesquiou, realizing that his life was in danger, escaped to Lausanne, where a few weeks later he unsuccessfully proposed to Rosalie de Constant.

The National Assembly thereafter felt that it would be wiser not to attack Geneva directly but to undermine the place by means of a fifth column. They sent there a French agent, of the name of Soulavie, with instructions to work upon the proletariate of the city, and to induce them to rise against the local patricians. Riots took place in July and August 1794, revolutionary tribunals were set up, and many of the leading citizens were murdered. Madame de Staël's uncle, Necker de Germany, was thrown into prison from which he only extricated himself by sacrificing a part of his fortune. H. B. de Saussure, the distinguished father-in-law of Mme. Necker de Saussure, was deprived of all his possessions. A decree of banishment was issued against Jacques Necker himself. The French émigrés at Lausanne thus found their numbers swollen by Swiss refugees from the terror which reigned at Geneva.

By September 1794 the situation in the town had to some extent been restored and the French agitator Soulavie had been arrested. It was still unsafe to remain for long in the vicinity and so soon as the mausoleum had been closed and the necessary funeral honours tendered, M. Necker returned to Beausoleil; his daughter prepared to follow him to the Château de Mézéry, also near Lausanne, which she had rented for the winter.

MADAME DE STAËL

In the late afternoon of September 28, 1794 (3), Madame de Staël entered her huge yellow travelling carriage with its six horses and the postillions in their green liveries. On leaving Coppet, she drove along the road to Nyon and Lausanne. That morning Benjamin Constant had also been at Geneva, enquiring doubtless as to the fate of his relations and friends. On his way back he stopped at Coppet to ask whether he could be of any assistance in these troublous times; he sent in his card, and was told that Monsieur Necker had returned to Beausoleil that morning and that Madame de Staël had left only a short while ago in the same direction. Riding briskly, he came up with her carriage just outside Nyon. He introduced himself and offered his services. She invited him to join her. Giving his horse to the groom to lead, he entered her carriage.

She had been incensed that morning on reading in a Lausanne periodical (*La Quinzaine,* then edited by L. F. Cassat) an article attacking M. Necker and criticizing the "constitutional mongrels" by whom his daughter was surrounded. Constant contended that no true liberal should ever question the freedom of the press, even when it attacked his family or himself. They stopped at Nyon for the night, taking supper with M. de Vincy. The dialogue which began upon the road to Nyon continued, almost without intermission, for thirteen years.

On the next day, September 29, they continued their journey. At Rolle they dined together with M. Rollaz where they met a bevy of refugees from Geneva. They then drove on to Mézéry where they arrived in time for supper. Constant it seems, then returned to his rooms at the Lion d'Or at Lausanne, but next day he was back at Mézéry.

4

In the afternoon of that day he returned for a short while to the Lion d'Or and wrote to Madame de Charrière informing her that he had at last met Madame de Staël. "It seems to me," he wrote, "that you judge her too severely. I admit that she is very pushing, imprudent and loquacious; but good at heart, confiding, devoting herself to others in complete good faith." Madame de Charrière sent an acid reply saying how much he must have enjoyed showing off in front of all those grand people. In the three weeks that followed Constant spent most of his days at Mézéry. Monsieur de Charrière in the first week of October went to Lausanne on business; on his return to Colombier he must have informed his wife of the sudden friendship which had sprung up between Madame de Staël and Constant. The acidity of Madame de Charrière's comments produced a devastating reply:

> I have had the happiness recently [Constant wrote to her on October 21, 1794] to be able to master my sensation of sterility. Now that I can look forward with some hope to the future, I hate having to flounder in the past. . . . As for Madame de Staël, I have seldom seen such a combination of astounding and attractive qualities; so much brilliance coupled with so much good sense; such expansive, positive kindness; such immense generosity; such gentle and sustained politeness in society; such charm and simplicity; such absence of all restraint within the circle of her intimates.
>
> She is the second woman in my life who could be the whole world to me, who could constitute a whole universe in herself.
>
> You know who was the first.

We can judge of the effect of this upon Madame de Charrière from the letters which she addressed at the time to her confidante Mlle. L'Hardy:

A few days ago [she writes on November 1] I had a quarrel with Constant, and I now see him with horns and a tail. But you will agree that he is a very ugly man. Red hair, little peekly eyes like bits of glass, yellow splotches all over his face. [A week later she wrote again.] Constant has been here since the day before yesterday and left this morning at God knows what hour. I told him that he had every right to love Madame de Staël, as much as, or even more than, me, and that this was not a *wrong* with which I could justly reproach him. But I contended that, apart from all the fuss and bother which might tire me, I had every right to find displeasing something that was not actually a *wrong* towards me: so displeasing in fact, that I preferred to break off all correspondence between us rather than have to suffer the outpourings of this new passion. "Very well," I said to him, "fall in love! Get all excited about it! That's solely your affair, just as it is solely my affair whether I go on writing to you."

I send you the note I received from him. Now these are not conjugal quarrels; not lovers' quarrels; why is it therefore that they are so bitter? I know that in all this I may be making myself ridiculous. I see this clearly. But I must go my own way and say what I think.

These bickerings continued throughout the autumn and winter. "You tell me," she wrote to him on November 27, "that I tried to turn you into a satellite. That is a lie. Sparkle, sparkle as much as you like; sparkle all by yourself." She suggests to him that the time is come when he might sit down and write "a modest little work" on which she would be glad to advise him. He replied that he had no desire at all to write a modest little work. He wanted to embark again upon a most ambitious work; to throw all his renewed energies into his study of comparative religions.

She composed and sent him at this date a pathetic fable:

> Un vieux barbet, cher à son maître,
> Chien caressant et dévoué,
> S'il se voyait quelquefois rabroué,
> Se consolait, tout prêt à reconnaître

Que c'était là le droit du jeu.
Chacun de bile a quelque peu,
Et qui reçoit tous les jours des caresses
Peut bien parfois supporter des rudesses . . .
Mais ne voilà-t-il pas
Qu'un jour son maître fait emplette
D'un petit chien (Bichon, Levrette,
L'un ou l'autre, il importe peu) :
Son allure est vive et brillante
Son poil luisant, son oeil de feu,
Et sa manière en tout charmante;
Car, sans compter que pour l'esprit
Il est de race précieuse,
Dans l'école la plus fameuse
Pour les tours on l'avait instruit.
Le maître a l'excès s'en engoue,
Et sans merci le flatte et loue
En présence du vieux Barbet,
Lequel, d'abord tout stupéfait,
Baisse l'oreille, fait la moue,
Puis de l'humble rôle qu'il joue
Se dégoute enfin tout à fait.

Benjamin meanwhile, finding himself somewhat unequal to the elegant and self-assured circle of his new Egeria, began to take trouble about his clothes. Madame de Charrière noticed the change: "Your hair brushed straight, those yellow trousers of yours, the note you sent me yesterday which smelt of ambergris . . . all this has struck home." "Benjamin," she remarked to him, "you are beginning to take trouble about your personal appearance: you no longer love me."

Yes, she knew it was the end. It was no good making formal reconciliations and shaking hands in solemn compact. It was the end. A letter reached him in Lausanne sealed with the little head of Perseus which six years before had made his heart turn over in joy when he found it on the table of his Brunswick lodgings. It was dated December 12, 1794:

"When I have have a touch of fever," she wrote, "I notice the fact because the candle, or the tallow dip, seem to take on a yellower tinge than usual. For some time past the whole world is no longer lit for me except by this faint yellowish light. I like this subdued tone; I ask for no other. What I have written does not seem somehow to hang together. The connection between my images takes place within my own mind."

The rupture was neither sudden nor complete. They continued to correspond from time to time in a tone of irritable regret. In April 1795 he came over to Colombier again and remained for the day. It was not a successful visit. "I found him very changed," she wrote to Mlle. L'Hardy. "Perhaps it is that today I look at him with different eyes. In place of the old simple gay childishness there was something mysterious about him, something self-important, something busy and restless. I am not in the least interested in his present career— half amorous, half political. I said nothing: I asked no questions. Except when we squabbled as we used to do (but with more acerbity) we were glum in each other's presence— solemn, absurd. . . . All this is pretty sad and bitter. . . . A friendship that fades out is a wretched thing; the greater the former intimacy, the greater the subsequent wretchedness; one probes for the old sympathy and fails to find it. . . . In order to give you some idea of the Constant of today I must tell you that he is dressed with care; the hair that falls down his back is no longer plaited and held together by a comb; his front hair falls down over his forehead and around his ears. I find all that extremely ugly, perhaps because it is so different."

When in March 1796 he paid a visit to the Hubers, who were now established at Bôle, quite close to Colombier, she refused at first to see him. She then consented to receive him for a short hour. They parted quite amicably. "In my detachment from you," she wrote a few days later, "there is something which would make one of the most beautiful attachments one could conceive."

Their friendship, none the less, was broken for ever. In the years that followed she would sometimes write asking him to procure books for her in Paris, asking him to obtain a publisher for her last story, *Sir Walter Finch and his Son William*. By 1802 she was a confirmed invalid, melancholy and ill-tempered; Monsieur de Charrière became afflicted with softening of the brain and would sit for hours by the stove mumbling mathematics. Madame de Charrière died during the night of December 26-27, 1805. The field in which she was buried at Colombier has now been turned into a tennis court.

Monsieur de Charrière died in 1808. Mlle. Louise died in 1810. Mlle. Henriette, who in the last years had nursed her sister-in-law with devoted affection, remained on alone at Colombier until she also died in 1814.

That was the end of the family of Charrière de Penthaz.

CHAPTER VIII

The Directory

[1794–1796]

The Château de Mézéry—Constant is introduced into the society of the émigrés—He succumbs completely to the vitality of Madame de Staël—Nature of their early relations—The poison scene—Their compact—The Thermidorean reaction in France—Madame de Staël and Constant leave for Paris—She opens her salon—The Constitution of the Year III—The "two-thirds"—Constant's change of attitude towards—Directory established November 3, 1795—The 13th Vendémiaire—Interview with Barras—Madame de Staël expelled from France—Constant's pamphlet—Madame de Staël in Switzerland—Rosalie's comments—Constant attacked by Bertin de Veaux—His duel—The question of his nationality—Hérivaux.

1

THE Château de Mézéry stands a mile or so to the northwest of Lausanne among the orchards and the vines. It is a modest, two-storied little house with an attic and dormers. On the ground floor there are three windows to the right of the entrance and three windows to the left; there are brown shutters against buff coloured walls. On the south side, facing the distant lake, is a gravelled terrace with a fountain in the centre and in one corner a small arbour of limes. In the pediment of this trim villa a clock strikes the hours.

The whole Juniper Hall colony had been transported by devious means from Surrey to the Canton of Vaud. There were Madame de Châtre, Mathieu de Montmorency and his mother, the Comtesse de Laval, Lally Tollendal and Jaucourt. A few days later Narbonne joined them from Greng. Madame de Staël, avid for even further society, had for weeks been urging Talleyrand (who had been expelled from England and taken refuge in the United States) to join them at Mézéry. It remains a mystery how Madame de Staël was able to house so large a court in so small a house; there can have been but little space in those small rooms.

Into this patrician company (united as they were by all the shibboleths of the most select côterie of Paris, bound as they were to each other by common tragedies and perils, extremely class-conscious as they had remained in spite of their progressive opinions) was introduced late at night on September 29, 1794 a Swiss gentleman, with the appearance, and in some ways the manners, of a student from some provincial German university. It can scarcely have been for them a welcome intrusion.

Constant was not in the least a snobbish man; he was proud in a quiet way of the Artois origins of his family and of the fourteenth-century seigneurie of de Rebecque. But he did hate being thought Swiss. Few societies that have ever existed have been so self-conscious about their own nationality and hierarchy as was that of the late eighteenth century in France; their sense of solidarity had been intensified by persecution; it led them to emphasize, rather than to modulate, the small tricks of intonation, phraseology and gesture which distinguished them from the provincial and lesser nobility, from the intellectuals and from the financial world. Constant was naturally a shy man, he possessed few drawing-room aptitudes; and although Madame de Charrière had instructed him in some at least of the modes and reticences of the Parisian world, she can never have known, or been able to impart, the highly specialized canons of this esoteric clique. He must have felt ill at ease when so suddenly confronted with the careful worldliness of Madame de Châtre, the grand manner of Madame de Laval, the ascetic distinction of Mathieu de Montmorency, the exquisite but faintly patronising courtesy of Narbonne (1).

In contrast to the chill of all this, was the incandescent exuberance of Madame de Staël herself. However much she may have revelled in, and sometimes shown off about, the historic names of France, hers was never a selective or exclusive friendship. Few people, unless it were Constant himself, have ever possessed such a mania for conversation; it was an excitement for her to have discovered a young man who might become her partner, perhaps even her rival, in dialectical duets. It is never possible to recapture the conversations of the past, or to convey even a fleeting conception of the rapid interchange between these two of ideas, associations, paradoxes, epigrams and images. We must rely upon contemporary evidence and it was not Sismondi only who averred that a dialogue between Madame de Staël and Benjamin Constant had about it an electric quality, compared to which the arguments of other people rumbled like farm-carts along a lane.

The nucleus of their affinity towards each other was this common delight in the quick interchange of verbal flashes. For Constant at least the excitation of this experience at once spread widening circles of intellectual and emotional rapture. The wealth by which she was surrounded, the extreme luxury in which she lived, meant little to him; he was a natural bohemian, who took slight notice of such matters and was content enough to sew on his own buttons and to heat a saucepan on a spirit lamp. It was rather that after all those years of Madame de Charrière's negatives he found in this heroic woman a superb affirmation—the prospect of adventure, the stimulus to self-confidence, the revelation of ambition. She also was Swiss by origin and French by predilection; she also knew that under all the mistakes and cruelties of the Revolution there lay some tremendous truth; she also believed with passionate intensity in the sanctity of the individual, in the evil of all despotic government, even of all social prejudices and conventions; she also was convinced that the time had come when the humane doctrines of English liberalism might find for tortured France a middle way between the old autocracy and the blood-stained dictatorship of the proletariate. The opportunity was impending: might they not, hand in hand together, fusing her will-power with his acuteness, seize that opportunity and achieve, not fame and power merely, but a beneficent usefulness? The years of waste were over; a new epoch, a new century, was about to dawn; in his excitement at this revelation Constant was filled with passionate gratitude and expectancy. Ardently he desired to weave the loose threads of his life and character into the magnificent tapestry which she dangled before his eyes.

The little fibre within him of intemperate adolescence—the fibre indeed of actual childishness—which had survived all his disillusions, induced him at this stage to fabricate one of those flamboyant scenes, which are of such annoyance to his admirers, in that they cast doubt upon his inner seriousness.

The actual date, and even place, of the episode are uncertain. In the *Memorial de J. M. de Norvins* (not a reliable source) the incident is said to have occurred on October 28. It is referred to in a letter from Montesquiou of April 3, 1795. It probably took place at Mézéry some time in November or December 1794, at a moment when Benjamin

THE DIRECTORY

Constant left his rooms at the Lion d'Or and established himself in the house of Madame de Staël.

The story is told in some detail in the memoirs of Count Golovkin. One night, when the inmates had retired to bed, sudden shrieks of agony resounded through the house. They proceeded from the bedroom of Benjamin Constant. Mme. Rilliet-Huber was the first to arrive. She found him writhing in convulsions. He told her that he had taken poison and that all that he asked was to see Madame de Staël before he died. M. de Chateauvieux, (a friend of M. Necker) who had also been aroused, rushed along the passage to fetch Mathieu de Montmorency whom he found reading the Confessions of St. Augustine in a quilted dressing-gown. Montmorency was not sympathetic. "Throw the man out of the window," he snapped. "He upsets the whole thing and will cause a scandal by his suicide."

By that time Madame de Staël, swathed in multicoloured scarves, had hurried to the bedside of the dying man. "It is for you," he gasped, "that I perish." She muttered some words of solace, at which he drew her arm towards him and covered it with passionate kisses. His recovery thereafter was immediate.

The most interesting part of this story is related by Madame Rilliet-Huber, who accompanied Madame de Staël back to her room so soon as it was evident that Constant was out of (and indeed had never been in) danger. According to this account, Madame de Staël, on reaching her own bedroom, poured scent into her washing jug and plunged therein her arm and hand. "That man," she said, "fills me with an insurmountable physical repulsion."

This story is significant, since Constant, who was extremely sensitive to his own ugliness, was driven by her lack of response to an extremity of nervous excitation, to one of those paroxysms of frenzy which he mistook for love and which did certainly create in him a momentary will. His persistence was such that she was obliged to forbid him to sit up with her after the clock had struck midnight. One evening, when they had been alone together, she reminded him that the hour had struck. He denied it, saying that the sound that she had heard from the clock outside must have been the hour of eleven and not that of twelve. "Look at your own watch," she said smiling. The dial on his watch stood at five minutes past midnight. In a sudden passion he took his watch and smashed and ground it against the marble mantelpiece.

"I shall not need," he noted the next morning, "to buy myself another watch."

Madame de Staël appears thereafter completely to have mastered her physical repulsion. With the new year, they entered into a compact together, the text of which has been preserved:

> We promise to dedicate our lives to each other; we declare that we regard ourselves as indissolubly bound together; that our future destiny shall in every sense be a common destiny; that we shall never either of us contract any other connection; and that, the moment we are in the position to do so, we shall render even closer the bonds which now unite us.

To this joint statement Benjamin Constant added a codicil of his own:

> I declare that it is from the very bottom of my heart that I enter into this engagement; that I know nothing on earth so adorable as Madame de Staël; that during the four months I have now passed in her company, I have been the most blissful man on earth; and that I regard it as the greatest good fortune of my life to be able to render her youth happy, to grow old gently by her side, and to reach the final bourne in company with one who understands me and without whom nothing on this earth would be worth while.

THE DIRECTORY

2

Meanwhile in France events had entered upon a new phase. The days of Thermidor (July 27–28, 1794) had seen the fall of Robespierre, his arrest and execution. An anti-Jacobin reaction had set in. The red cap of liberty was derided, the busts of Marat were thrown into the sewers, the clubs were closed. The Revolutionary Tribunal, the Committees, the National Guard, the Commune had either been dissolved or deprived of power. In March 1795 those of the Girondin deputies who survived were invited to return, and on April 23, 1795 a Committee of Eleven was appointed to draft a new Constitution. On that very day, Madame de Staël obtained a passport enabling her to come back to Paris. On that very day also Monsieur de Staël, who had been in disgrace both with the French Government and with his own master, was publicly acclaimed at a sitting of the Convention as Ambassador Extraordinary from his Majesty the King of Sweden. The opportunity had arrived.

She had been able, since the Bernese authorities were still suspicious and adamant, to find a refuge for her émigrés at Neuveville, which was a dependency of the Bishopric of Basle. They had all departed in a long procession on the road to Greng. In the first carriage were Madame de Staël, Constant and Madame Rilliet-Huber. In the second carriage followed Mathieu de Montmorency, Narbonne and Madame de Laval, to whom Narbonne had of late renewed his former attentions. In the third carriage came Jaucourt and his wife. The procession was rounded off by the heavy *fourgons* carrying the luggage of the whole party. At the Château de Greng, Madame de Staël remained for a few days under the hospitable roof of M. de Garville and then said goodbye to her refugees, promising, the moment she got to Paris, to intercede for their return and for the restitution of their properties.

When they had left for Neuveville she drove to Coppet, alone with Benjamin Constant.

Monsieur Necker was distressed by their proposal to return to Paris. He addressed a note to his daughter: "Do not forget, my dearest Minette, all the troubles and worries in which you involved yourself last time. May I beg Monsieur de Constant in this note not to encourage you, but to give you frequent lessons in prudence and patience? Be careful also regarding Monsieur de Staël's extravagance. I am already spending more than my income, and cannot manage to defray the follies of others."

Fortified by this excellent advice, they left Coppet and crossed the French frontier on May 22, 1795.

3

Early in June they reached Paris, hand in hand together, determined to lose no time in conquering this new world. Madame de Staël returned to the Rue du Bac and at once opened the splendid salons of the Swedish Embassy. Constant perhaps with a wry smile, took rooms in the Rue du Colombier.

The society which the Ambassadress now entertained, was disparate, apprehensive and distrustful. The failure of the insurrection of Prairial on May 20 had weakened the extremists; the royalists had been dumbfounded by the death of the Dauphin on June 10. In spite of this, the Republicans of the centre were all too conscious that their position was threatened both from the right and the left. Madame de Staël gathered around her a motley group of Girondins, members of the now moribund Convention, artists, journalists, men of letters, diplomatists, and a few returned émigrés whom, as Constant slyly remarked, "she was pleased, but embarrassed, to receive."

Apart from her general desire to shine, to dominate and to manoeuvre; apart from her determination to push Constant into politics and to have M. Necker recalled from exile; she was actuated by a more immediate motive in seeking to win the favour of those in power. She wished to induce the Government to repay to her father the two million livres which from his personal fortune he had lent to the Treasury in 1778 (2). What she did not realize was the active suspicion with which she was universally regarded. This suspicion was not due solely to her well-known propensity for intrigue; the French agents in Geneva and Lausanne had for long been reporting upon the protection she had given to the émigrés and other "dangerous enemies of the Republic." It had been suggested even that she had been in secret communication with Mr. Wickham, the British Minister at Berne. Monsieur de Staël, who was by no means desirous of falling once again into trouble either with the French authorities or his own sovereign —who may also have wished to be left alone to his own somewhat sordid pleasures—suggested to the Committee of Public Safety that it would be an excellent thing if they issued an order of expulsion against his wife. They contented themselves for the moment with demanding from her a declaration of Republican faith. She gave this in all innocence and all sincerity. She had small conception, either of the force, or of the weakness, by which she was surrounded.

Benjamin Constant at first was delighted by all this high excitement, by all this semblance of personal activity; he was also happy in his affections. Camille de Rousillon, who saw him at this stage, reported on June 30, 1795 that he was "in love as one is no longer in love after the age of eighteen. . . .

As jealous as a tiger, as coquettish as ever. He retains his childish look none the less."

The Committee of Eleven charged with the task of preparing the Constitution (to be known as the Constitution of the Year III) submitted their report on June 23. To some extent their draft was a reactionary document. Universal suffrage was to be abolished, political clubs were to be closed, no armed assemblies were to be permitted, and the members of the Legislature must be over thirty years of age and possess a property qualification. The Corps Législatif was to consist of two chambers, the lower chamber, or *Conseil des 500*, was to be elected by Primary Assemblies, the upper chamber, or *Conseil des Anciens*, was to number 250 and to be chosen from and by the entire Corps Législatif. The executive was to be in the hands of five Directors, selected by the Anciens from a list of fifty names proposed by the Five Hundred.

The members of the old and expiring Convention were terrified by this proposal. They well knew that the feeling in the country was by now strongly anti-revolutionary and that if any system of direct election were permitted, they would not only lose their employments but perhaps also their liberty, loot and lives. They therefore induced Pierre Baudin, a member of the Committee of Eleven, to bring forward an amendment to the draft Constitution on August 18, under which two thirds of the members of the old Convention were automatically, and without any further electoral process, to become members of the new Corps Législatif. The controversy thereby aroused became intense.

Benjamin Constant, who had by then not had time to assess the complicated dangers of the situation, approached this controversy in the true spirit of the Speculative Society. To him it seemed a monstrous act of usurpation that the members of an expiring Parliament should allocate to themselves two thirds of the seats in a new Parliament. He therefore wrote

MADAME DE STAËL

Baron Gerald. Versailles Museum. Photograph by Giraudon, 9 Rue des Beaux-Arts, Paris

three successive letters against the Baudin amendment which were published anonymously in the periodical of his old host Monsieur Suard, *Les Nouvelles Politiques*. These letters were hailed with delight by the royalist faction, and Constant realized at once that he had started off on the wrong foot. The Girondin Louvet, who was a friend of Constant's and unaware that he was the author of the letters, attacked them as "impudent and foolish royalism." Louvet went so far as to invite Constant himself to assist him in refuting the views which had been expounded. Benjamin spent two days and two nights in pulling to pieces his own thesis and in proving that if M. Baudin's amendment were rejected the Republic would be doomed.

He had in fact been sincerely convinced by Louvet that the attitude which he had at first taken was ignorant, dangerous and incorrect; that some continuity was essential as between the Convention and the Corps Législatif if renewed civil war was to be avoided. "This measure," he wrote to his uncle Samuel, referring to the Baudin amendment, "has become absolutely necessary; it will be passed by a large majority in despite of the howls of certain incendiary journalists and the foolish denunciations of unenlightened men." The Baudin amendment, as he foresaw, was passed on August 18. The Convention was dissolved on October 26 and the Directory and the new Corps Législatif installed on November 3, 1795.

4

Constant was aware, that owing to the age limit introduced into the Constitution of the Year III, (a limit which was reduced only for the exceptional case of Tallien) he would not be eligible for Parliament until he reached the age of thirty in October 1797. He therefore hung about somewhat fecklessly, gambling a good deal, making such friends as he could, devoutly attending the court of Madame de Staël.

The impossibility at such a stage of introducing normal representative institutions on the English model was brought home to him by the rising of the 13th Vendémiaire (October 4, 1795). The royalists, profiting by the agitation aroused by the controversy over the Baudin amendment, exploiting the resentment of the Paris mob at the high cost of living, staged an insurrection, which, owing to the weakness of General Menou, was on the very verge of succeeding. The Convention, which was in the last month of its existence, decreed full powers to Paul Barras, one of the leaders of the Thermidorean revolution (3). Barras sent for the young General Bonaparte who had attracted his attention during the siege of Toulon (4), and made him his second in command. Bonaparte, realizing that grape-shot was the solution of all Parisian riots, quickly prevented the insurgents from seizing the artillery park at Les Sablons, and blew them to pieces on the steps of the Église Saint-Roch in the Rue St. Honoré. Barras and Bonaparte between them had saved the Republic.

Constant's own part in these events was not distinguished. Walking home late at night from the Palais Royal, where he had been gambling with François de Pange, he was arrested on suspicion and lodged in the Quatre Nations prison for twenty-four hours. He was eventually rescued by Marie-Joseph Chénier. All that remained to him of this episode was "the sounds, when in prison, which one hears in the street outside; the footsteps of those who are at liberty."

On November 3, 1795 the Directorate was established and the five new Directors (Larevellière-Lépeaux, Rewbell, Barras, Letourneur, and Carnot) installed themselves, clad in fantastic uniforms, in the Palace of the Luxembourg. Madame de Staël realized from the first that the only one of these five who possessed the necessary power, and who was at all amenable to the charm of her conversation, was Paul Barras. She laid siege to him with battering persistency. She waylaid his carriage; she thrust herself into his study; on one occasion she seized both his hands so that he should be unable to reach the bell. In the *Memoirs of Barras,* published posthumously by his executor, M. Rousselin de St. Albin, there occurs a description of one of the first of these interviews which, although faulty in its chronology, does convey a startling impression of the assaults which she delivered:

> I should not venture to say which of the two led the other, which was the man and which the woman, since I have never really been able to make out to which of the two sexes Madame de Staël belonged. She advanced towards me, holding Benjamin Constant by the hand. "Here," she said, "is a young man of astounding intelligence who is on our side; he is devoted to the good cause; he belongs entirely to us." Madame de Staël's protégé was a tall, affected and foolish looking youth, with fiery red hair, and small eyes which one would have supposed to be also red, had they not been hidden by green spectacles. A delicate, ironical, mouth—seeming to make fun of everything—even of its owner—such was Benjamin Constant at the age of twenty (*sic*).
>
> I thanked Madame de Staël, and waited for the young neophyte to say something in his turn. Twisting his body into all sorts of contortions, he stammered out: "Citizen Director, it would make me very happy if you would accept this short treatise which I now have the honour to offer you." This sentence was spoken with a thickness of utterance and an effeminate stutter, in which the letter "s" was pronounced as if it were "z." I have been told that the pronunciation of M. Benjamin Constant has much improved. France and Europe have since become acquainted with his progress and achievements in the Tribune.

Madame de Staël had not profited by the advice of her father to exert patience and to practise discretion. She would sit in the diplomatic gallery of the Corps Législatif and scribble notes and instructions to the deputies, which she would despatch to them by summoning the ushers with a boisterous wave of her arm. Constant's own position was equivocal and he had not the talent of making himself liked. He was regarded as nervous, unstable, and potentially treacherous. "He cannot even," wrote Pauline de Beaumont to Joubert, "manage to like himself."

This, their first irruption into the world of post-revolutionary politics, had proved a fiasco. "One is no more," wrote Madame de Staël, "than a stone thrown into the whirl of a huge wheel." Benjamin's own disappointment went even deeper. "I cannot tell you," he wrote to his uncle Samuel on December 8, 1795, "how I long to leave Paris. The dumb fermentation below the surface, the discouragement of some, the audacious, guilty, hopes of others—all this renders it unbearable to be here."

They had not long to wait. The deputy Legendre rose in the Council of the Five Hundred and denounced Madame de Staël as an alien intriguer. This denunciation was warmly applauded. An order of expulsion was issued against her. She left Paris on December 21, 1795 for Coppet, with Constant in her train.

5

It was not agreeable to return thus worsted from Paris after all the vaunting of their departure ten months before. Nor was the year 1796 any more successful. Madame de Staël occupied herself by writing *De l'influence des passions sur le bonheur des individus et des nations*. Constant gave a final polish to his pamphlet in support of the Directory, to which he gave the title *De la Force du Gouvernement actuel et de la nécessité de s'y rallier*.

THE DIRECTORY

The theme of this pamphlet was that principles are more important than either men or institutions; that the very essence of liberty is the subjection of all arbitrary methods to the rule of law:

> In the absence of principles [wrote Constant] arbitrary methods become the sole alternative. . . . In science, the arbitrary method means the destruction of all science; in morals, the destruction of all morals; in politics, the destruction of all institutions. . . . Always there exists between the nation and the government a reciprocity of duties. If the relation between the government and the people is founded upon the rule of law, then the relation between the people and the government will similarly rest upon the rule of law. But if the relation between the government and the people is an arbitrary relation, then the relation between the people and the government will in its turn be also arbitrary. An arbitrary system is the supreme enemy of Liberty, the corrupting vice of every institution, the germ of death which must be extirpated and destroyed.

Madame de Staël had been notified by the French resident in Geneva, M. Félix Desportes, that if she tried to cross the frontier into France she would immediately be arrested. He introduced into her household a police spy of the name of Monachon. It is possible that her steward Joseph Uginet, whom she called "Eugène," and his wife Olive, who was her personal maid, were also in the service of the French secret police. Sick with longing for the "gutter of the Rue du Bac" she moved restlessly from Coppet to Geneva and from Geneva to Lausanne. "The all-too-famous," wrote Rosalie to her brother, "is here with all her basse-cour." "She loves Benjamin passionately," wrote Rosalie again, "God alone knows where all this is going to lead them!" The fascination which the Ambassadress had at first exercised over Rosalie had now given place to frightened resentment. A lampoon had appeared in Lausanne in which Madame de Staël was referred to as "Mrs. Potiphar"; there were rumours that she intended to divorce M. de Staël and marry Benjamin. Rosalie was hurt moreover by Madame de Staël's outspoken dislike of Switzerland and her disdain of local society. "The moment she enters, the thing ceases to be a party and becomes an arena." What was even harder to bear was that Madame de Staël, bursting in one morning when Rosalie was painting her herbal, had snorted in contempt. "What an extraordinary taste to have!" she said, "It would bore me to extinction." "They are the sort of people," Rosalie decided, "whom it is best to know at a distance."

Meanwhile Constant's pamphlet had been published in May and he left Coppet for Paris to witness and exploit the effect. It had certainly pleased the Directory who ordered long extracts from it to be inserted in the *Moniteur*. Others were less enthusiastic. Bertin de Veaux, on June 5, 1796 wrote an article in the *Feuille du Jour* in which he attacked both the pamphlet and its author. "What a good thing it would be," he wrote, "if Monsieur Carnot were to show this little Swiss gentleman the door, and send him back to hide his shame in his own country, bearing a placard on his back with the words "unwanted rubbish." Constant thereupon challenged Bertin de Veaux to a duel, which ended in a reconciliation. The incident convinced him none the less that he could never hope to play any part in French politics unless he could first establish his right to French citizenship. He therefore wrote to Rosalie asking her to ascertain from the family muniments the exact identity of the ancestor who, for religious reasons, had emigrated from Artois to Geneva. Rosalie discovered that this gentleman, on settling in Geneva, had most inconveniently changed his name to Agostino Costante (5).

There was a further step which must be taken; he must acquire French domicile. He therefore sold what remained of his properties in Switzerland, borrowed money from M. Necker and bought the ruined abbey of Hérivaux near Luzarches. Rosalie and her father, who until then had been living at La Chablière, were thus obliged to leave it; they moved into a small flat near the cathedral at Lausanne. La Chablière was bought by a Viennese banker of the name of de Fries. It is now the property of Madame Wallon-Gaulis.

Charles de Constant, who came to Paris during the first week in June 1796, sent to Rosalie an account of Benjamin at that period. He found him surrounded by politicians, very "worn-out and worried." "He has," wrote Charles, "cropped his hair in order to resemble Brutus. But he looks more like a December sun than a Roman of the Republic." In August Constant returned again to Coppet, where Monsieur de Staël, who had now been finally dismissed from his ambassadorial post, was also spending a lugubrious holiday. Rosalie rather liked Monsieur de Staël. "I find him," she wrote, "far more attractive than any of his wife's lovers. He has a timid, overwhelmed, crushed sort of look; she treats him with haughty disdain."

On October 10, 1796, Constant returned again to Paris in order to secure a good press for Madame de Staël's book on "the influence of the passions." Two months later he appeared suddenly at Lausanne and assured Madame de Staël that she would now be allowed to return to France, although not to Paris itself. They crossed the frontier at Rousses on Christmas day, travelling on an old passport. They were permitted to reside at Hérivaux.

The little town of Luzarches is situated some twenty miles to the north of Paris and a few miles only to the south of Chantilly. About a mile from Luzarches, nestling under a steeply wooded hill, is the old abbey of Hérivaux. It had been acquired as a *bien national* by a certain Colin and it was from him that Constant purchased the property for the sum of 50,-000 francs. The abbey, as it stood, was far too large for his needs; he therefore pulled down the central block and the right wing and turned the left wing into a comfortable private residence. He had no sense of architecture and did not realize that this detached section of what had once been a building three times as large was too high for its own length or breadth. The place had been much neglected by M. Colin, and Constant set about planting fruit trees and plane trees and creating a pièce d'eau in front. He was not successful. A visitor at the time described it as containing "young acacias which give no shade, lawns which are not green, a pond which is half empty of water and fruit trees which bear no fruit."

Today the place has a certain ill-proportioned beauty. The plane trees which Constant planted are today immense. The ruins of the ancient chapel, with its arched doorway and statues, suggest a damaged Newstead; there is the sound of running water in the wood (6).

Madame de Staël was not a woman to enjoy the repose of country life. Benjamin himself, much as he relished the combat of wits or the noise and bustle of the agora, could be perfectly happy alone with his books. What he could not tolerate was a mixture of loneliness and noise, of solitude and interruptions. He was polite, considerate, affectionate and very amusing. But during those damp dark winter afternoons at Hérivaux the enchantment of their first rapture assumed more subdued tones. Madame de Staël always envisaged life in terms of orange, emerald and scarlet; for her, grey was drab.

He had become, and he remained, the strongest affection of her exorbitant life. It is important to remember that underneath all her egoism, vanity and possessiveness; underneath her fuss, her restlessness, her self-display, her desire to manage and exhibit him, her desire to manipulate him as a marvellously constructed maumet in the puppet-show of politics; that underneath all this was a deep, sincere, simple and completely normal devotion. Constant was aware of this. When in later years he sought desperately to free himself from the iron chains with which, in the eyes of the whole world, she had bound him hand and foot, it was always the knowledge of her simple love for him which checked his resolution and led him to so many subterfuges and betrayals. It is assumed—and almost entirely on the evidence which in his own self-depreciation he has himself supplied—that Benjamin Constant behaved heartlessly towards women. He was never heartless to Madame de Staël.

CHAPTER IX

The Tribunate

[1797–1801]

The inconsequence of Constant's actions and character—His first uneasiness regarding the de Staël relationship—Birth of Albertine—Further pamphlets—Talleyrand becomes Minister for Foreign Affairs—He writes to Bonaparte on Constant's behalf—The *coup d'état* of the 18th Fructidor—Barras supreme—Attitude of Constant towards 18th Fructidor—He is made President of the Canton of Luzarches—The return of Bonaparte from Italy—Madame de Staël tries desperately to secure his friendship—Constant stands for Parliament and is unsuccessful—The 18th–19th Brumaire—Constant goes out to Saint Cloud—He solicits some appointment from Bonaparte and Sieyès—The Constitution of the Year VIII—Constant is appointed Tribune—Constant's maiden speech enrages Bonaparte—The effect on Madame de Staël's position—Constant continues to oppose all arbitrary methods—He is dismissed from the Tribunate on January 19, 1801.

1

IT WOULD be possible to simplify the biography of Benjamin Constant by dividing it into four main sections, each directed by a single personality. One would thus have the first nineteen years, from 1767 to 1786, during which his father's erratic dominion became for him an exterior conscience. There would follow the eight years from 1786 to 1794 when Madame de Charrière numbed his energy with her astringent negatives. This would be succeeded by the thirteen years, from 1794 to 1807, during which, as the slave of Madame de Staël, he was first driven into all manner of political experiments and then held captive at Coppet. And in the last section there would come the twenty-three concluding years of his life in which, protected and warmed by the soft eiderdown of Charlotte, he was able to become for France the champion and the interpreter of pure liberal doctrine.

So schematic a method would add clarity to the narrative, but it would not be true. The interest of Constant's actions and character is to be sought, not in their consistency but in their inconsistency, not in their continuity but in their alternations. The current of his life did not flow with equal speed; there were moments when it dawdled in backwaters; there were other moments when it rushed, with intemperate impulse, down the rapids of events. Nor would it be correct to regard him solely as a passive agent, who could be stimulated to activity only by a will-power more forcible than his own. He was an ambitious man; he possessed high intelligence, great capacities, and exceptional physical and moral courage; he was extremely egoistic, and even in his liberalism (which was sincere) there was a strain of anarchic ego-mania. Yet he was for ever hampered by those doubts which assail the intellectual who mixes with the world of action, above all the intellectual who has acquired the habit of self-examination: doubts regarding the sagacity and good-faith of others, doubts regarding the absolute validity of any formula, doubts above all regarding his own prescience and judgment.

Constant was a most incredulous man; it was as an escape from his own scepticism that he sought in others, not guidance, not resolution, but conviction. It was owing also to his disbelief in the capacity of human beings to control their destiny, that he attributed an almost primary importance to the element of chance; and that he was apt, at critical moments in his career, to act, not with forethought or calculation, but on the fall of the cards, the spin of the wheel, the tumble of the dice. *Vogue la galère*—"Let's chance it!" was the motto which came most often to his mind.

A biography of Benjamin Constant cannot for these reasons be symmetrical. There are periods in his career when every day, every hour, is significant and decisive; there are other periods when his life became an inconsequent series of little bits, almost wholly unconnected with each other. The former periods can be examined in detail; the latter must be skipped.

By May 1797 he was already becoming conscious that his relation to Madame de Staël might become a servitude rather than an adventure; that she herself might prove for him a liability rather than an asset. His habit of analysing every passing mood with vigilant precision should warn us not to attach too great an importance to each incidental remark. Yet in a letter to Madame de Nassau of May 1797 there occurs a passage of foreboding; he refers in this letter to "a connection which I maintain, owing to a sense of duty, or perhaps (if you insist) owing to my inherent weakness—a bond which renders me thoroughly unhappy and which has kept me in chains for the last two years." He begs his aunt to look out for a suitable wife for him among the eligible young women of her acquaintance. Only a few weeks later he follows up this letter with one couched in different terms. He can no longer contemplate doing anything which might possibly wound his friend "having received from her such new and remarkable proofs of devotion."

Albertine de Staël, the future Duchesse de Broglie, was born on June 9, 1797.

In the same year Constant published two further pamphlets which served to increase his already high reputation as a political and controversial publicist. The first, was entitled *Des Réactions Politiques* and resumed the old theme of law versus arbitrary Government. The second was entitled *Des Effets de la Terreur* and was provoked by an article by Adrien de Lezay in which it was sought to justify the crimes committed by the Jacobins. Constant argued that if one desired to save the Republic from reaction, one must separate republican policy from the outrages of the extremists. "Nothing," he wrote, "nothing on this earth, can ever justify a crime. . . . If you accord an amnesty to the past, you are corrupting the future." At the same time he was instrumental in founding a constitutional club, aimed at counteracting the propaganda of the royalist *Club de Clichy*. The inaugural dinner of the constitutionalists was given by Constant himself; they held their meetings in the Hôtel de Salm, the lovely little building which is now the chancellery of the Legion of Honour. Constant was chosen as its secretary.

In July 1797 an event occurred which raised all their hopes. Talleyrand had returned to Paris in September 1796. Mainly owing to the efforts of Madame de Staël, he secured in July 1797 the appointment of Minister for Foreign Affairs. If we are to trust the memoirs of Barras, it was Benjamin Constant who was despatched to break the great news to Talleyrand, and to conduct him into the presence of the Directory. Talleyrand that night had gone to the theatre where Constant found him. As they drove together to the Luxembourg, Talleyrand kept on clapping Constant on the knee, exclaiming: "We have captured the stronghold; we must make an immense fortune out of this, an immense fortune." As they drove through the narrow streets he kept on murmuring the words to himself: "*une fortune immense, une immense fortune.*" "And he kept his word;" Constant would comment in later years, "or at least in so far as he was himself concerned."

Madame de Staël supposed at the time that Talleyrand would repay her for the strenuous efforts she had exercised on his behalf by giving to Benjamin the post of Secretary General of the French Foreign Office, which was then being vacated by Giraudet. He did nothing of the sort. Instead he wrote to General Bonaparte in Italy:

> It seems, Citizen General, that you are desirous of having sent to you some distinguished men—either publicists or philosophers—who, being sincere friends of liberty, may be able to further by their republican convictions your task of expediting the formation of the Italian Republics and welding them together.
>
> I know that the name of Benjamin Constant has occurred to your mind. I have thought it fitting to let you know the opinion of those who have the right to form one. Here it is, and I may add that it is mine also.
>
> Benjamin Constant is a man more or less of your own age, fired with a passion for liberty. He possesses intelligence and capacities of the first order. He has distinguished himself by one or two publications, written in a forcible and brilliant style, and replete with acute and profound ideas. He is an unshakable republican and liberal, and his character is moderate but firm. When his remarkable talents (which are at once youthful and mature) created so great a sensation here, there were those sought to set him aside by saying he was of foreign origin. That is untrue. He is a Frenchman, restored to France by the decree which gave back their nationality to those Frenchmen whose ancestors were exiled for their protestant convictions. . . . I should be glad indeed were you to select him; and I have no hesitation in guaranteeing that you will be fully satisfied with such a choice.

Bonaparte took no notice whatsoever of this commendation.

2

The elections of May 20, 1797 had returned a counter-revolutionary majority. The Directory—already discredited by the ill-success of its foreign policy, by the state of public finances, by the known corruption of some of its members—was now faced with a hostile Legislature which it was legally unable to dissolve. The three left-wing Directors—Barras, Rewbell and Larevellière—realized that they were in imminent danger; they appealed to Bonaparte in Italy; he despatched General Augereau to their assistance. At the end of August Augereau arrived in Paris, covered with diamonds and breathing fire and slaughter.

On the night of September 3, 1797 the three threatened Directors constituted themselves a Committee in permanent session and proclaimed that they had discovered and frustrated a royalist plot. Barthélemy, their colleague, was arrested in his bed; Carnot, their other colleague, being warned, walked quietly across the Luxembourg garden and made his way to Switzerland.

At 3 A.M. on the morning of September 4 (the 18 Fructidor) Augereau occupied the Tuileries and in the course of the day secured complete control of the capital. The Legislature were compelled, under the threat of violence, to pass the law of 19 Fructidor, under which the elections were annulled, the deputies then elected disqualified, and the Directors given power to transport to Cayenne whomever they accused of being implicated in the alleged plot against the Republic. The *coup d'état* of Fructidor was a complete and almost bloodless success. Barras had eliminated the two Directors who opposed him, and the two hundred elected, but dissident, members of the Corps Législatif; what remained of that body did not thereafter dare to resist him; his authority was supreme.

Fifty-three persons were at once sentenced to deportation. They were treated with the utmost indignity, being driven down to the port of Rochefort in open iron cages on wheels, exposed to the insults and missiles of the populace. They were then shipped to Cayenne and interned in the pestilential village of Sinamary, where most of them died. This method of extermination was called *la guillotine sèche*.

Constant and Madame de Staël were placed in a predicament by the *coup d'état* of Fructidor. They had spent the night of September 4 supping in the lavish apartments which Barras had assigned to himself in the Luxembourg Palace. It was difficult for them to criticize a friend from whom they expected so much. As good republicans, they must welcome the supression of a dastardly royalist conspiracy; as good liberals they could scarcely approve the violent methods of Augereau, the unconstitutional annulling of the elections, and above all the deportation of priests and deputies without trial. As Talleyrand remarked: "Madame de Staël approved of the 18th Fructidor; but not of the 19th."

Constant—as so often happened to him on such occasions—fell between two stools. On the one hand, at a speech at the Salm Club and later at Luzarches, he lauded Fructidor as a republican triumph and referred to it as "the immortal day." That annoyed the right. On the other hand, he criticized the deportation of the priests and deputies and contended that it should have been sufficient for a strong Government, confident in the support of the people, merely to exclude those associated with the "conspiracy" from all future public office. That brought him into trouble with the left.

His speech at the Salm Club had been reprinted in the *Moniteur*. It aroused the fury of the Jacobin press. M. Signet, the editor of the *Ami des Lois*, attacked him for being a foreigner, a royalist at heart, a Baron, and a Swiss mercenary. Constant, as was his way, challenged Signet to a duel which took place in the Bois de Bologne.

In later years Constant realized that he had been in error in defending Fructidor. In his *Mémoires sur les Cent Jours* he referred to it, not as "that immortal day," but as "that day of illegality, which had the effect of all days of illegality—namely to destroy confidence between the government and the governed."

Barras felt, none the less, that the support which he had received from Constant, merited some reward. The reward was meagre indeed. Constant was appointed President of the Canton of Luzarches. His functions in that capacity were ridiculous rather than exacting. He was obliged to initiate the inhabitants of Luzarches into the mysteries of the Directory's *Culte Décadaire*. He was obliged to preside as some hierophant at rural festivals, such as the "Festival of Agriculture," "The Festival of the Sovereignty of the People" or the "Festival of Married Couples." He had to deliver republican orations under the statue of Liberty draped in wreaths; he had to preach the religion of patriotism, standing in front of the altar of La Patrie; he had to trace, with his own most inexperienced hands, symbolic furrows in the soil of Seine-et-Oise. The inhabitants of Luzarches remained indifferent to the *Culte Décadaire*.

All these manoeuvres, all these degrading friendships and affiliations, all these humiliating charades, were of no avail. In January 1798 Madame de Staël received the order to return to Coppet. Constant, for the moment remained on at Luzarches.

3

Bonaparte, having concluded the Treaty of Campo Formio, returned with his laurels on December 5, 1797. He at once sent an aide-de-camp to Talleyrand, asking for an audience. The latter replied that he would be pleased to receive him at 11 A.M. the next morning. He at the same time slipped a note to

Madame de Staël (1), inviting her to be present in his anteroom.

Madame de Staël had for long conceived for the young republican General an enthusiasm which was ecstatic and uncontrolled. While he was conducting his campaign in Italy, she had addressed to him some four or five most adulatory letters. In one of these letters, unfortunately, she had expressed the view that it was fantastic that a genius such as he "should marry an insignificant little creole, quite incapable of understanding or appreciating his heroic qualities." For herself, she assured him, he was "the best Republican in France: the most liberal of all Frenchmen." Talleyrand felt that the least he could do for the woman whose influence with Barras had obtained him his Ministry, was to invite her to be present, at least in his anteroom, when the hero of the Italian campaign was about to appear.

She got there at 10 A.M. Bonaparte when he entered, seemed ill and weary. He made a few conventional remarks to her about her father, and then turned aside brusquely to speak to Bougainville. He then walked hurriedly into Talleyrand's office.

Four days later, in the courtyard of the Luxembourg, under the symbolic altar of La Patrie, a reception was held in honour of the victory in the Italian campaign. Bonaparte entered the courtyard looking small and humble; the aides-de-camp who surrounded him "were bowed in respect." His policy at the time was not to arouse premature suspicions, but to act the part of a simple soldier on leave. Madame de Staël was enraptured by such Roman behaviour. She applied to him her accustomed battering tactics. In his own Memorial, dictated at St. Helena, he remembered what a nuisance she had made of herself at this time. She accosted him in public; she pushed her way into his house in the Rue Chantereine; she even penetrated into his bedroom. He shouted to her that he was undressed. "What matters that?" she shouted in reply. "Genius is always clothed." It is not surprising therefore that when at Talleyrand's evening reception of a few days later, she asked him who was the greatest woman in history, he should have replied: "The one, Madame, who had the greatest number of children."

Madame de Staël returned to Switzerland in January 1798, conscious that somehow she had not been a success with her hero. On reaching Coppet she found that the French armies were in the course of invading her country; from the corner tower at Coppet she and her father watched the troops pour past.

Constant, having by now reached the statutory age, was preparing for election to the Council of Five Hundred. In the spring of 1798 he presented himself to the electors of Seine-et-Oise; he was not successful. The moment the Canton of Vaud had been annexed to France under the title of the Department of Léman—whereby the obstacle of his nationality was, at least temporarily removed—he strove with the aid of Madame de Staël to be chosen as one of the two deputies for Geneva. Here again he failed. He assured Madame de Nassau that he was sick of politics and would devote the rest of his life to literature.

The obvious incapacity and debasement of the Directory were now being exploited by their enemies of the right and left. The Royalists' hopes of a Bourbon restoration revived. Boulay de la Beurthe published a pamphlet extolling the English restoration of 1660 and arguing that, not reprisals, but a general sense of comfort and security had been the result. Constant replied with a brochure entitled *Des Suites de la Contre-Révolution de 1660 en Angleterre* in which he drew attention to the confiscations of property and the personal persecutions which had then occurred and argued that a restoration of the Bourbons in France would have even more terrible consequences. As a historical study the work is faulty; as a political pamphlet it was one of the most opportune and incisive that he ever wrote.

Then followed the lull of the Egyptian campaign and finally on November 9–10, 1799, the *coup d'état* of the 18th–19th Brumaire and the end of the Directory.

4

On October 9, 1799, Bonaparte, having abandoned his army in Egypt, landed at Fréjus and drove direct to Paris. For some time Talleyrand had been plotting with Sieyès (2) and Lucien Bonaparte the overthrow of the Directory. He had written to Madame de Staël, hinting that great events were about to take place; she left Coppet immediately and Constant came to meet her half-way. At Charenton, the last relay-post before Paris, they were informed that only an hour before Barras had passed through, going southwards, under an escort of dragoons. Pressing forward in their excitement, they reached Paris on the night of November 9.

At seven that morning the Council of Anciens (a majority of whom were privy to the conspiracy of Talleyrand, Bonaparte and Sieyès) had decreed that in view of a "formidable Jacobin plot," and in order to protect the deputies from menace by the city mob, the Corps Législatif would meet the next day, not in the Tuileries, but in the Palace of Saint Cloud. They at the same time announced that General Bonaparte had been placed in supreme command of all the troops in the capital. During the course of the morning the two Directors who were parties to the plot, Sieyès and Ducos, tendered their resignations; a similar resignation was extracted from Barras who in the course of the afternoon was packed off to Grosbois; the remaining two Directors, Gohier and Moulins, who showed signs of obstinacy, were placed under arrest. "The Directory," Bonaparte announced, "has ceased to exist."

On the next morning, November 10, Constant rode out to Saint Cloud to watch events. Madame de Staël waited in Paris in a state of apprehension. If the Council of Five Hundred won the day, then she must expect definitive exile, even arrest; if Bonaparte won the day, then there could be no limit to her expectation. Constant had taken with him three or four of Madame de Staël's grooms in order to be able to send her hourly messages as events developed; he could gain some idea of what was happening by watching through the high glass windows of the Orangery, where the Five Hundred were assembled.

Bonaparte at that juncture completely lost his nerve. His address to the Anciens in the Gallery of Apollo was so hesitant, involved and uncertain that even his supporters (and they were in the majority in the upper Chamber) began to lose confidence. His appearance at the door of the Orangery, flanked by four grenadiers, provoked a riot. The deputies rose in their places uttering wild cries: "Down with Cromwell!" "Down with the Dictator!" "Outlaw him!" Blows were aimed at the young General who was rescued by his officers in a half fainting condition and dragged outside.

Had the Jacobin deputies put to an immediate vote the proposal for the arrest and outlawry of Bonaparte, the whole course of history might have been changed. The situation was saved by Lucien Bonaparte who was acting as Chairman of the Five Hundred. He refused to put to the vote the motion for outlawry, gained time by an impassioned oration, and then, dramatically casting aside his insignia of office, dashed out on to the terrace and harangued the troops. Within a few minutes the feet of grenadiers advancing in formation along the stone corridor towards the Orangery could be heard above the clamour; through the wide open door could be seen the glint of fixed bayonets; in panic the deputies, casting away their scarlet robes, leapt from the windows of the Orangery on to the terrace outside and dispersed into the park. Within a few minutes the Orangery was cleared. Madame de Staël in Paris had opened the hurriedly scribbled messages which Constant sent back to her. When she heard that Bonaparte was about to be arrested and outlawed, she started to pack her things; when she heard that the Five Hundred were escaping from the windows of the Orangery, she wept, (or says she wept) over the death of Liberty.

Constant's own reactions were more deliberate. Thirty years later, being wise after the event, he recorded that "on that day I witnessed the collapse of representative institutions for a period of fourteen years." At the moment he was delighted. He wrote to his uncle Samuel stating that the triumph of Bonaparte was an "event that I had much desired," admitting at the same time that the results would prove incalculable and that the prospects of the future were sombre indeed:

> The chain of circumstance [he wrote] is far more decisive than the purposes of individuals. The motto of all those who are concerned with politics should be *fata viam invenient*. This has been my motto all along. The only way not to be devoured by indecision is to follow one's own conscience and to make that one's only standard.

Immediately, with Madame de Staël's ardent assistance, he started angling for a job.

5

On November 14 he wrote a letter to Sieyès asking for nomination as deputy, either for the Department of Léman, or for that of Seine-et-Oise. "Today," he wrote, "when the destiny of the Republic is linked with your name, it would be a delight for me to serve under one whose past recalls to Europe the first principles of Liberty."

Madame de Staël meanwhile entered into communication with Joseph Bonaparte and sought the assistance of Chabaud-Latour, who had been a member of the Five Hundred and had since been appointed one of the Committee charged with the task of drafting the new Constitution of the Year VIII. In his *Madame de Staël et Napoleon* Paul Gautier reproduces, on the evidence of Aimé Martin, an unpleasant account given by Chabaud-Latour of what followed. Latour managed to obtain for Constant an interview with Bonaparte. The latter made some polite remarks about Constant's pamphlets; Constant then asked if he might be nominated a member of the Tribunate which, under the new Constitution, it was proposed to establish. "And why not?" said Bonaparte, "Yes—that is not impossible, I shall think it over." Constant expressed his gratitude and added: "You must know, Citizen Consul, that I am your man. I am not one of those ideologues who believe that everything can be accomplished by theories. What I admire is practical activity; if you nominate me you can count on my support."

On leaving Bonaparte, as they were descending the staircase, Chabaud-Latour remarked that he was going across the street to call on Sieyès. Constant asked if he might accompany him. On being presented to Sieyès, Constant asked him for nomination to the Tribunate. "You know," he said to him, "how much I abominate the use of force. I am not on the side of the sword; what I look to are principles, justice, ideas. If you give me your support, you can count on my assistance; I am perfectly hostile to Bonaparte."

This story, although it may be apocryphal, is not improbable. There was some truth in what Constant said to each of these two men. The misfortune was that such stories were widely repeated and created distrust.

The Constitution of the Year VIII was inaugurated on December 25, 1799. It provided for four separate Assemblies, the Senate, the Legislative Body, the Council of State and the Tribunate. The sixty Senators were nominated for life by the three Consuls; the members of the Legislative Body and the Tribunate were nominated by the Senate; the Councillors of State were nominated by the First Consul: the element of popular suffrage was reduced to a minimum. The function of the Senate was to safeguard the maintenance of the Constitution; the function of the Legislative Body was to pass by secret vote, and without discussion, the laws presented to it by the Government; the Tribunate, which contained one hundred members, each receiving a salary of 15,000 francs a year, could discuss projects of law; it could accept or reject them, but could not amend them; it could express opinions, but the Government were under no obligation whatever to consider these opinions. A fifth part both of the Legislative Body and the Tribunate was to be renewed each year. As the Constitution worked out in practice, neither the Senate, nor the Legislative Body, nor the Tribunate exercised any effective authority at all. Power was concentrated in the hands of the three consuls—Lebrun, Cambacérès and Bonaparte; the latter was appointed First Consul for ten years with a salary of 500,000 francs a year. He worked entirely through the Council of State over which he presided in person.

Constant received his appointment as Tribune in the last days of December 1799. On January 1, 1800 the Tribunate held its first meeting in the Palais Royal.

Madame de Staël, undeterred by her previous ill-success, remained confident that she would be able to captivate, and thereafter to advise, the First Consul. Shortly after Brumaire she met him at a party given by Berthier in his honour; determined to make a good impression she had written out in advance the brilliant answers which she would make to the questions which he would be obliged to put to her. He merely made some banal remark and turned upon his heel; she was reduced to the unaccustomed rôle of a spectator. She noticed that he would stand, now on one foot, now on the other, "exactly like the Princes of the House of Bourbon."

Yet Bonaparte, realizing that Madame de Staël might be useful, and could become dangerous, was not in those first weeks unwilling to establish good relations. He sent his brother Joseph to see her with the proposal that if she would give unstinted support to his Government, he would accord her permission to remain in Paris and might even consider repaying to her father the two million livres which in 1778 he had lent to the Treasury. "It is not," she answered, "a question of what I want. It is a question of what I think." Bonaparte interpreted this brave but injudicious reply as a declaration of war. His interpretation was confirmed by the attitude which, almost from the start, Benjamin Constant adopted in the Tribunate.

6

On January 3, 1800, three days after the Tribunate had held its first meeting in the Palais Royal, the Tribune Duveyrier made a speech in which he referred to the gardens below them as "the place where an idol, not of fifteen days but of fifteen centuries, was shattered in a single afternoon." On January 4 Bonaparte inserted in the *Moniteur* a sharp warning that the Tribunes must be more careful not to disturb quiet waters.

It was already known by then that the Government intended, on January 5, to bring forward a motion under which discussions in the Tribunate would be subjected to a rigid time-limit. Madame de Staël insisted that Constant, in his maiden speech, should oppose this arbitrary proposal. Having read the *Moniteur* that morning, he had a suspicion that such a speech on his part would be premature and ill-advised. That evening Madame de Staël gave a grand reception which was attended by Lucien Bonaparte and many other Bonapartists. "Your rooms tonight," whispered Constant to Madame de Staël, "are crowded with people who interest and amuse you. If I make that speech tomorrow, they will be empty. I pray you to consider what I say." "One must abide," she answered, "by one's convictions!"

On the next day, January 5, Constant rose to deliver his maiden speech. He protested against the imposition of a time-limit for their deliberations, and spoke of the "exaggerated and restless impatience of the First Consul." "We are," he said, "being hustled through our examination of the proposals put before us, as if we were an enemy army or a squadron of cossacks."

The reaction was immediate. A cold statement was inserted in the *Moniteur* reproving Constant for his thirst for popularity and for his attempts at self-advertisement. The unofficial Press were encouraged to attack Madame de Staël with overt acrimony. "It is not your fault," wrote the *Peuple*, "that you are ugly; but it *is* your fault that you intrigue; take your Benjamin back with you to Switzerland." The right-wing Press were less crude and more incisive than that of the left:

> This woman [they wrote] discourses about metaphysics which she does not understand; about morals, which she does not practice; about the virtues of her sex, which she does not possess. Madame de Staël was represented as saying to her Benjamin:

"France is ours! Shout, yell, make a noise! That is the way to succeed in this country! You, Benjamin, will be appointed Consul; Papa will be made Minister of Finance; my uncle will be Minister of Justice; my husband will be sent away to a very distant Embassy; and I shall be made Inspector General of Everything and President of the Institut."

It became generally known in Paris that Constant by his speech had incurred the grave displeasure of the First Consul. "These intellectuals," said Bonaparte, "are like vermin in my clothes; I shall shake them off." "I am a soldier," Bonaparte remarked when referring to this episode, "I am a child of the Revolution; I am not going to allow people to insult me as if I were a King." Years afterwards, at St. Helena, he could still recall the incident: "At eleven, Benjamin Constant was begging might and main; at midnight, when the favour had been granted, he had already started to become offensive. He put himself into opposition, thinking I would pay a high price for his co-operation; he should have known that I do not buy my enemies; I stamp on them."

Constant had himself foreseen that his maiden speech would not be welcomed. Even Madame de Staël, on receiving at the last moment as many as ten letters from those whom she had invited to her dinner party, regretting that for one reason or another they would be unable to attend, realized that something had gone seriously wrong. She consulted Fouché, who advised her to retire from the capital, at least for a time. Indignantly she removed herself to St. Ouen. In a few weeks, undaunted and still unaware, she was back in Paris. She wrote to Talleyrand, "in the name of our ancient friendship," begging for an invitation to his ball on February 25. "In the name of our ancient friendship," he answered, "I beg you not to come." She attended a reception given by Madame de Montesson. Even to her iron sensibilities the impression was conveyed that a very large number of people turned their backs. Bonaparte sent his brother Joseph to her with a sharp if irrevelant message. The First Consul wished her to know that he was displeased by the fact that Monsieur de Staël was living on the verge of penury while his wife indulged in ostentatious extravagance. On February 19 she took her stand in the Plâce du Carrousel to watch the ceremonial entry of the First Consul into the Tuileries; he did not cast her a glance. "Evidently," she remarked, "I am condemned to celebrity, without being able to make myself known." And it was then that she applied herself to writing her book on *De la Littérature considérée dans ses rapports avec les Institutions Sociales*. It was intended as a justification of the part which intellectuals could and should play in politics.

Constant was distressed by the unfortunate turn which his affairs had taken. He wrote to his uncle Samuel saying that his enemies appeared to have prejudiced the First Consul against him. His uncle replied that he should render himself less sensitive to "capricious favours." Benjamin was stung by this remark. "Believe me," he replied, "no human consideration would induce me to sacrifice what I consider to be right, or worthy, or honourable. You will realize how sensitive I am on this point."

These were no empty words. Constant felt that the Tribunate was falling into the degradation of Cromwell's Parliament and would be unable to "escape the contempt which is the fate of deliberative assemblies when they have not sufficient courage to resist tyranny."

He himself showed that courage. He opposed the law by which political crimes, and crimes against public order, were to be tried by special tribunals and without a jury. He opposed the law under which those who had acquired national property must pay rent to the Government. "Surely," he said in addressing the Tribunate, "surely so vindictive a law will not be passed? No—he who has carried the tricolor to the summit of the Appenines and to the banks of the Nile will not introduce a law of revenge against the families of those who accompanied him in his immortal campaigns."

Bonaparte, when he heard of this in Italy, decided that the vermin must immediately be shaken from his clothes. He instructed Cambacérès to secure that all the opposition Tribunes should be among the first fifth to be retired.

Constant was eliminated, together with twenty other recalcitrants, on January 19, 1801. He did not return to politics for thirteen years.

CHAPTER X

Escape and Recapture

[1801–1804]

Julie Talma—Anna Lindsay—Her origins—Their love affair—Constant finds it difficult to get rid of her—His excuses and fluctuations—Madame de Staël gets into further disgrace with Bonaparte—Necker's *Last Views on Politics and Finance*—Death of Baron de Staël—His widow refuses to marry Constant—She publishes *Delphine*—Bonaparte forbids her to come to Paris—Constant retires to Les Herbages where he is at last able to be alone and work—Madame de Staël descends upon him—She is ordered to remove herself to forty leagues from Paris—She goes off to Germany taking Constant with her—Weimar—Goethe and Schiller—Goethe's low opinion of Madame de Staël and his high opinion of Constant—The death of Necker—The return to Coppet.

1

THE women who dominated, distracted or solaced the life of Benjamin Constant were brilliant, beautiful or tender: he only met one who was wise. In 1798 he had come to know Julie Talma (1), who at that date was still the wife of the actor François-Joseph Talma and had reached the dangerous age of forty-two. She fell in love with Benjamin and faced the situation with her accustomed good sense: there was a short period during which they would walk by moonlight together in the Champs Élysées; but Julie was too straight a woman not to realize that she could find no lasting happiness in the arms of a man eleven years her junior and one who in any case disliked obtaining what he desired. With gentle sagacity she steered their affair into the calm lagoon of a devoted and outspoken friendship. She became the firmest as well as the most penetrating friend that Constant ever had.

In the raffish world of the Directory the Talmas had gathered around them a society which was vivid and mixed. Julie Talma was a revolutionary with a sense of tradition; she appreciated the symmetry of the classical formula while possessing a romantic passion for the disorder of nature. Above all perhaps she was a woman of amused tact. She loved Benjamin, whom she would call "you old flirt," but avoided all exactions; she was highly intelligent but never showed off. She was in every way a marked contrast to Madame de Staël.

It was in October 1800, in the salon of Julie Talma, that Constant first met Anna Lindsay. The love affair which ensued is not in itself of particular interest: it follows the sad but familiar pattern according to which the passion of the man loses its intensity at the moment when the passion of the woman is at last aroused. But it must be examined in some detail since it formed the frame-work, if not the theme, of Constant's single masterpiece, his novel *Adolphe*.

Anna Lindsay was the daughter of James O'Dwyer, an Irish innkeeper at Calais, by his wife Susan O'Rourke. The Duchesse de Fitz-James, who spent a night or two at their inn on her passage from or to Dover, was struck by Anna's vivacity and looks. She offered to educate the child, a proposal to which James O'Dwyer gave his ready consent. It is not known for how many years the girl Anna remained under the Duchess's tutelage or what was the reason for their eventual separation. All that is known is that when Anna was sixteen or seventeen the Duchess suddenly turned her into the street. She became the mistress of M. de Conflans and thereafter of James

Lewis Drummond, subsequently 4th Earl of Perth. By him she had a son who was christened Charles O'Dwyer-Lindsay. For some years they lived together in the Rue Matignon; on succeeding to the title, James Drummond parted from Anna and bought her a flat of her own in the Rue Neuve des Mathurins. In 1789 she became the mistress of Auguste de Lamoignon and during the Terror she showed great courage in housing, and smuggling across to London, several of her protector's relations and friends. She had always possessed a pathetic longing for respectability, and her services during the Terror, coupled with her established and dutiful allegiance to Auguste de Lamoignon (by whom she had two children) earned her admission during the Directory to the fringe of society represented by the Talma salon.

At their very first meeting, Constant was assailed by one of those sudden perturbations of the nerves which formed the prelude to his more reckless passions. He well knew that any such adventure would expose him to difficulties with Madame de Staël and might involve responsibilities which he would be unable to assume. "It gives me," he noted, "an indefinable thrill to stride blindly forward to meet a danger which I dread." He employed all the artifices of seduction. Anna Lindsay was thirty-eight years old at the time; he wooed her as if she were an innocent girl. "You are," he wrote to her, "a virgin to those who know you." He praised in her "that elevation and nobility of soul which heaven gave you and which man has failed to defile." He indicated marriage, a settled home, respectability. "I shall devote my whole life to you," he wrote on December 14, 1800. "The day comes nearer when we shall be united for ever."

A week later, Madame de Staël and Monsieur de Lamoignon both arrived in Paris. Immediately there is a change of tone. "We must wait," he writes, "until we can unite with each other without wounding any of those who trust us not to cause them pain." "You do not need," he wrote on January 4, 1801, "the unhappiness of a third person to convince you that only you can rule my existence." "I never," he wrote on the following day, "allow myself to be swept off my feet."

"In the end," he wrote again, "will come our complete and eternal union. It is with this object—for you alone—that I strive for wealth, fame and power." "Angel of love!" he writes on January 21, "I shall not see you this evening." Anna added a sharp minute on the back of this note in her native language: "The victim was secured and art was no longer necessary." "With what supreme artistry," she wrote to him, "did you force me to love you!"

Constant by that time was becoming seriously alarmed. On February 22 he received from her a letter which showed him that she had taken seriously his suggestion of marriage:

> A cruel destiny has rendered me an outcast launched upon a pitiable career. Desperately I fought to secure some sort of social position—all that I had the right to expect. I might have been accorded more, but never have I encountered anything but selfishness and narrowness of soul. I want to lay down my weapons; to become an ordinary woman; to repeat the words of Milton—"She for God and He"(2). Yes, you will be my whole world for me. Your reputation will cover the defects of mine. Your respect and love will place your Anna high in the world esteem. But will you accord them me eternally?

She promises him that if he will break with Madame de Staël, she for her part will break with de Lamoignon. Constant was shocked by this suggestion; he regarded it as being in the worst taste of *Les Liaisons Dangereuses*. "Your future independence," he wrote, "is conditioned upon your continuing your liaison with de Lamoignon until he makes it up with his wife." Could she not see that his advice was founded upon "profound moral sense?" "Feeling," he wrote, "is not based on contract." "I know," he wrote, "the torture of irreparable situations." What she should aim at was to secure an established position; Lamoignon was contemplating rejoining his wife who had inherited a large fortune; he might be willing to give Anna a handsome indemnity; could she not face the facts and accept a settlement, "which is the only thing that can make one contented once one's youth is gone?" What would the world say of him if he obstructed so sensible a solution? "Surely you do not wish to degrade the man you love?"

The misfortune was that she did sincerely love him. "I find myself unable," she wrote to him on April 14, 1800, "to show my affection for you—even in front of Julie. Real love has about it an element of chastity. When one can display it in public it has already lost its strength."

In the end, in May 1801, Anna Lindsay escaped to Amiens in despair. "I am dying," she wrote to Julie Talma, "I adore and despise him." "Murderers," she wrote, "are executed; men like him are let free to prey upon society."

During the whole of this unhappy episode, Julie Talma was there to help and guide. "In your letters to Anna," she wrote to him, "there is both love and indifference, frankness and duplicity. One half of them must make her despair; the other half revive her hopes. You feeble creature—can't you ever say straight out what you really mean? Is it your pride? Is it your weakness?" (3) "What a charming lover you are!" wrote Julie, "apart from the fact that you are unable to love."

Gradually the storm died down. "I am like a sick man," Anna wrote to him finally, "who has had an illness which he has failed to treat. Do not any longer seek to disturb my soul. Just show yourself a friend." Constant was an adept at deferred solutions; he remained the friend, and on occasions the lover, of Anna Lindsay for several years.

The only person who comes well out of this story is Julie Talma. In a tribute to her which he published many years later Constant praised the subtle sympathy which had enabled her "to console a woman who knew that she was no longer loved, and to advise a man how he could cause the least pain possible."

When Julie died in 1805 Anna Lindsay and Constant watched together beside her deathbed (4). The episode of Mrs. Lindsay produced no lasting tragedy; it produced, or helped to produce *Adolphe*.

2

The relations between Madame de Staël and the First Consul had not improved. On his way to the St. Bernard and Marengo in May 1800, Bonaparte had paused for a few hours at Geneva, where he had been greeted by Necker. The latter had assured him that Madame de Staël, although at times intemperate, was one of his most fervent admirers. On his return to Paris he at first treated her with greater politeness. Lucien Bonaparte has recorded that she confessed to him, "almost in tears," that she was disconcerted by the First Consul's manners. "In your brother's presence," she said, "I become a fool. Such is my longing to please him, and to force him to take notice of me, that I behave like a goose." Lucien repeated this remark to his brother. The First Consul was gratified. "I see—" he answered, "her astonishing genius trembles when faced with my own."

This was the last interlude of amity between them. During the course of 1801 Bonaparte became convinced that the provocative attitude adopted by Benjamin Constant in the Tribunate was due to Madame de Staël's influence. He was annoyed moreover by her book *De La Littérature* which seemed to laud intellectuals at the expense of men of action. When Constant and his friends were removed from the Tribunate, Madame de Staël failed to conceal her displeasure. She accused the First Consul of being an "ideophobe." When someone remarked that Bonaparte had purged the Tribunate she answered with scorn: "Purged?" she answered. "You mean that he has taken off the cream." These remarks were repeated and they did no good.

In April 1802 the Concordat was signed and Bonaparte attended a thanksgiving service at Nôtre Dame in almost imperial state. Madame de Staël who had hoped to see protestantism established as the official religion, absented herself from this ceremony. She had by then abandoned all hope of mastering the First Consul and had decided to defy him. She seems even to have had some wild idea of putting up Bernadotte as a rival. Bonaparte knew of this small stratagem but at the moment he treated it with contempt.

The year 1802 witnessed the complete consolidation of his power. In March he concluded the Peace of Amiens. In August he was appointed First Consul for life with the right to designate his own successor. In September Piedmont was incorporated in France. It was in the latter month that Necker thought fit to publish his *Dernières vues de politique et de finance*. In this portentous work, the old man, while admitting that Bonaparte was *l'homme nécessaire,* expressed the view that he would never be able to found a dynasty and should introduce a liberal constitution centring upon seven Directors. Bonaparte was furious with Necker for having raised the issue of a dynasty at a moment when he had himself not yet prepared the ground. He believed, and with reason, that Necker's *Last Views* had in fact been inspired, and to some extent written, by Madame de Staël. He made known his displeasure. Madame de Staël was overjoyed. "He is afraid of me!" she exclaimed to Lacretelle. "I am delighted. I feel proud and terrified." She had reason to be alarmed. Bonaparte, when this remark was repeated to him, instructed his fellow consul Lebrun to write to Necker and to tell him plainly that Madame de Staël would never again be allowed to reside in Paris.

In the spring of 1802 an important incident occurred in Madame de Staël's domestic life; her husband died. Eric Magnus de Staël had for long been in failing health; as the culmination of a life of excess he fell into the clutches of Mlle. Clairon (5) then well over seventy years of age. He became seriously ill and Madame de Staël, feeling sudden pity for him, decided to take him with her to recuperate at Coppet. In the course of their journey—at the inn at Poligny in the Jura on the night of May 8–9, 1802—Eric Magnus had a stroke and died. He was bundled into a coffin, taken to Coppet, and buried in the village cemetery. Benjamin Constant, who had followed at a discreet distance, felt obliged, after a decent interval, to ask Madame de Staël whether she would be willing to marry him. To his infinite relief she refused to do so; she did not, she explained, wish to exchange a name which she had rendered so famous for one unknown.

In the autumn of 1802 Madame de Staël published her novel *Delphine*. Even today it is an interesting book to read; at the time its success was immediate and universal. In the character of Delphine, Madame de Staël portrays herself as she would like to have been; perhaps even as she thought she was. Delphine was a woman of overwhelming virtue, immense self-sacrifice and irresistible dignity. She was "dominated by her virtues (generosity, kindness, truthfulness) as other human beings are ruled by their passions." The wicked fairy in the story is Madame de Vernon, who on her deathbed confesses to Delphine that "dissimulation has sullied my life." It was not difficult to recognize in Madame de Vernon an exact portrait of Talleyrand. "It seems," remarked the latter, "that Madame de Staël has written a novel in which both she and I are introduced disguised as women." Constant appears in *Delphine* as Monsieur de Lebensei; it is not a convincing portrait. He is represented as a man of deep learning, vivid imagination, and a certain proud shyness of manner which rendered him taciturn in general society; he was Protestant by religion and English in appearance; only to the woman whom he loved could he condescend to display the treasures of his intellect and the depth of his sagacity; under a cold, even sardonic, exterior, he hid a deep well of pity, which he concealed from the world, fearing that it might be sullied. There is only one passage in which this idealized portrait comes alive; it is worth quoting, since it gives a curious and attractive sidelight upon their relations to each other:

> Henri (that was M. de Lebensei's Christian name) has a gay and amusing side which can only display itself in the intimacy of familiar association. It isn't something which he puts on, but something wholly spontaneous and original, the utter ease of which increases its charm. When intimacy has reached a point where it finds pleasure in childish games, in the same joke repeated twenty times over, in small endless details which nobody but you two could possibly understand—then a thousand strands become twisted around one's heart and a single word, a single gesture, the slightest allusion to such sweet memories, suffice to call back to one the beloved object from the uttermost ends of the earth.

The First Consul took strong objection to *Delphine*. Its praise of liberal institutions, its eulogy of the English, it suggestion that personal happiness and ordered society were two incompatibles, its implied criticism of the Roman Catholic as opposed to the Protestant Church, its defence of the institution of divorce—all these unsettling things irritated Bonaparte who wished to impose the habit of order, domestic respectability and obedience. Madame de Staël, impervious as ever, imagined that the success of *Delphine* would oblige the First Consul to summon her back to Paris. In this she was mistaken. He sent her a message that if she tried to cross the frontier into France she would be sent back to Switzerland under an escort of gendarmes. At the same time he sought to induce the Elector of Saxony to prohibit the printing and circulation of *Delphine* in Leipzig.

Constant during that autumn of 1802 was burning to return to his books and to start for the fourth time on his History of comparative religion. He had by now disposed of Hérivaux and bought a smaller house, Les Herbages, a mile and a half from Luzarches between Maffliers and Franconville. It was little more than a cottage, with a paddock, a small wood, and a running stream. Fouché, when consulted, advised him to stay on in Switzerland, at least for a few months more. He therefore remained on at Coppet for the winter of 1802–1803. In the spring he was told that he might return to Les Herbages, although not to Paris. Madame de Staël was hurt and angry at his desertion. He himself was glad to get back to his books and surprised at his own taste for domesticity. "I am conscious of pleasure," he wrote to Rosalie, "when the children of my concierge are glad to see me; the kindness of my servants is most agreeable to me." How happy he would be if he could find a wife!

> Find me [he wrote to Rosalie on May 29, 1803] someone sufficiently rich to render me no longer poor, gay enough to stand out against my moods of depression, calm enough to endure the complete seclusion of this place, elegant enough not to be in any particular ridiculous in society, good enough to love no one but me, passionate enough to love me deliriously, sensible enough not to be delirious when I don't want her to be, and in addition to all this, well educated, gentle and pretty: I would take her, my dear cousin, solely on your responsibility.

Yet how could he possibly marry without inflicting suffering on Madame de Staël? "I am rendered miserable," he wrote to Rosalie, "by the unhappiness which I am supposed to be causing her." Could Rosalie find out whether Madame de Staël was really unhappy at his absence or only pretending? Perhaps she had found another lover? If only he could know for certain that her heart was not broken "then I should recover my calm, the sense of remorse which haunts and torments me would disappear, and I could continue to live in freedom, without that uncanny effect of her voice or letters, without that conviction that she cannot live without me, that I cause her suffering, which combine to destroy my whole scheme of life."

His studious days at Les Herbages did not for long continue undisturbed. In August 1803 Madame de Staël, braving the fury of the First Consul, crossed the frontier and made her way to Maffliers. On October 13, 1803 an officer arrived to inform her that, within twenty-four hours, she must remove herself to within forty leagues of Paris. It was then that she decided to go off to Germany. Even if she had been allowed to stay on at Maffliers, she could not have endured the isolation of that damp spot. "Solitude," she remarked, "is the anteroom of death." For her anything away from Paris was a Siberian exile; yet she was able in her distress to invoke the solace of self-pity and the delights of self-dramatization. She saw herself as "a poor little bird, buffeted by the storm": she also saw herself as Athene Promachos, embattled and resplendent, defending in the eyes of the whole world the citadel of man's unconquerable mind against the wiles and violence of a Corsican despot. She was glad to have the opportunity of trailing across central Europe the pageant of her bleeding heart.

ESCAPE AND RECAPTURE

3

Rosalie at Lausanne was delighted to learn that Benjamin had at last escaped from the concentration camp at Coppet and managed to resume at Les Herbages the studious life which would restore his health, his income and his reputation. He had told her that he rose at four in the morning and went to bed at nine. She was disappointed therefore when she heard that he had resumed his chains and agreed to accompany Madame de Staël upon her flamboyant visit to Germany. "What I respect most on earth," he wrote to her, "is human suffering. I should like when I died to feel that I need not reproach myself for ever having caused it ruthlessly." There was another, more practical, reason which rendered it convenient for Madame de Staël to take Constant with her: she knew not one word of German, whereas he could speak the language even better than he could speak English. After stopping for a few days at Châlons, Metz and Frankfurt, they reached Weimar on December 23, 1803 (6).

The arrival of Madame de Staël created panic in the gentle little town—a town so quiet that the striking of the palace clock could be heard in each of its cobbled streets and out to where the Ilm wound lazily among the meadows and the woods. Goethe, at the time of their arrival, was at Jena; when he returned to Weimar he took to his bed with a severe cold. Schiller, whose knowledge of the French language (even when it was spoken very slowly) was rudimentary, retreated to his attic study and the smell of rotting apples. Madame de Staël was not a woman to be disconcerted by such evasions; each of the two poets was in the end forced to come out.

She was enchanted with the simplicity of Weimar, by the kindness of Karl August and the Duchess Louise, by the intimacy of her tea-table conversations with Goethe and Schiller. Much as she disliked abstract metaphysics, she felt that this German atmosphere was what was needed to cure her of the effects of "the outrage." She had intended to stop for a fortnight only: she remained for more than two months.

She profited by her sojourn to investigate the recesses of Goethe's Apollonian mind. Henry Crabb Robinson—who was of great assistance to her in interpreting the misty philosophies of the great Weimar men—ventured to suggest that she might fail to appreciate in every particular the splendour of Goethe's mind and character. "Her eyes flashed," he records in his Diary, "she stretched out her fine arm—of which she was justly proud—and said in an emphatic tone: 'Sir, I understand everything which deserves to be understood: what I do not understand is nothing.' "

In spite of her habitual self-assurance she did observe, as Boettiger recorded, "that Goethe did not like being asked questions or examined; his whole nature withdraws and retracts when subjected to scrutiny." Madame de Staël—who did not appreciate modesty in any form—upbraided him for being "sulky." At a supper at the Duke's palace, she went so far as to say that Goethe could only be agreeable when he had drunk a bottle of champagne. "She acted rudely enough," wrote Goethe to Schiller, "as if she were on a visit to the Hyperboreans." "All this," he recorded in his *Tag-und Jahreshefte*, "aroused the evil devil within me. I treated every subject that came up in a contradictory, dialectic, problematic vein, and by my obstinate antitheses often drove her to despair." He went so far even as to accuse her of having no conception of what was meant by the word "duty."

When Madame de Staël at last left for Berlin, the whole of Weimar heaved a sigh of relief. "I feel," wrote Schiller to Goethe, "as if I had just recovered from a severe illness."

"We had reason," wrote Goethe, "to be glad that Benjamin Constant was there."

It was on January 22, 1804 when he had been a month at Weimar, that Constant suddenly started to keep the diary which has since been published under the title *Journal Intime*. He found that Henry Crabb Robinson, with all his intelligence and alertness, "combined the English lack of subtlety with the German passion for abstractions." He met Wieland and Herder. He thought the former "cold as a philosopher, frivolous as a poet." He thought the latter "like a soft warm bed, in which one can indulge in pleasant dreams." We are able also to trace the stages by which his initial disappointment with Goethe developed into deep mutual regard. After his first meeting he had summarized his impression of the great man as: "Subtlety, self-esteem, physical irritability amounting to an affliction, remarkable intelligence, fine eyes, face somewhat dilapidated." On January 27 he dined with Goethe and admitted that "I am conscious of embarrassment when conversing with him." He criticized his abuse of analogies, especially those drawn from chemistry and the exact sciences. By February 15 he has revised his first estimate. "He is a man full of intelligence, flashes of wit, depth of thought, new ideas. But I never met anyone less good-natured. In speaking of Werther he said: 'What makes the book dangerous is that I described weakness as if it were strength. But when I write something that suits me I pay no attention to the consequences. If there are a few lunatics who have been harmed by reading the book, then so much the worse for them.' " By February 28 Constant was completely converted: "Supper with Schiller and Goethe; I know no one in the world who can compare with Goethe for gaiety, subtlety, power and range of mind."

What is even more interesting is the impression which Benjamin Constant made on Goethe. In the section of his *Tag-und*

Jahreshefte which he devoted to the year 1804 occurs the following tribute:

> With Benjamin Constant I enjoyed many hours of the most pleasurable and profitable intercourse. Those who are able to appreciate at its true value all that this excellent man accomplished in later years—the zeal with which he so unswervingly followed the line which he had marked out for himself as the line of duty—will be able to form some conception of the noble (although at the time undeveloped) aspirations with which he was at that date inspired. In the intimate talks we had together, he expounded to me his principles and his beliefs; I found that they were philosophically directed towards moral, political and practical ends.
>
> He invited from me a corresponding frankness. If my ways of approaching art and nature were not always very apparent to him, yet the manner in which he strove in all integrity to grasp my point of view—the efforts he made to attune my ideas to his conceptions and as it were to translate them into his own language—all this was of the greatest help to me, in that it brought forcibly to my consciousness, all that was as yet undeveloped, obscure, misty, or impracticable in my method of treatment.

4

In the first week of March 1804 Madame de Staël left for Berlin and Constant for Switzerland. He was able on this lonely journey to take stock of his own position. The domination, he decided, which a woman is able to establish over a man is analogous to the sleep which overcomes travellers lost on the St. Bernard: "They are not satisfied with their situation, but they surrender to the feeling of the moment which at every instant becomes more difficult to shake off. Death overtakes them while they are still planning an immediate escape."

Why [he writes in his Journal for April 1, 1804] should I be assailed today by sad sombre thoughts? Have I lost all power over myself? Is not my destiny in my own hands? Haven't I recaptured my capacity for hard work, even to a greater degree than I had ever hoped? All that I lack to make me happy is strength of will. I must make three decisions. (1) To devote my life to literature. (2) To eschew politics, which I have abandoned after assuming an attitude which was impeccable. (3) To settle in some country where I shall find enlightenment, security and independence. That is all I need. All my energy must be devoted to these three ends. . . . My character, although it displays right feeling and delicacy in action, always goes wrong somehow when it comes to form. It is this which never seems to put me right in the eyes of the world.

On reaching Lausanne he heard that Necker was dangerously ill. Two days later (on April 9, 1804) he was dead. Constant realized at once that there was now no hope whatever of escape; his whole heart went out in compassion to Madame de Staël: he left at once to join her in Germany:

Fate seems to take a delight in condemning me to use up my health (which is good,) and my talents (which are good enough) without any pleasure or success resulting. . . . Oh for a library, sufficient indulgence not to feel starved by its denial, and for once—peace! . . . If I continue to drift, to live from day to day, without taking a definite line to see that my life does not just slip away (as today has slipped away, as last week or last month has slipped away) then I am lost for ever. Shall I have the strength to do this? The memory of twenty lost years—years either wasted or chained to whoever wished to make use of them—all this fills me with a sort of contempt for myself, a sort of discouragement with myself, which will only leave me when I am able to make a firm resolution.

Madame de Staël was in Berlin when the news reached her of her father's serious illness; she started the next morning for Switzerland. It was at Weimar, on April 22, that Constant intercepted her. She was told of Necker's death. "The first moments," he records, "were convulsive."

While in Berlin Madame de Staël had annexed Wilhelm Schlegel (7) the author of the finest translation of Shakespeare that has ever been made. His name had been mentioned to her by Crabb Robinson as a possible tutor for her sons; she arrived in Berlin with a letter to Schlegel from Goethe, who in fact disliked the Schlegel brothers. Wilhelm Schlegel, who had that year instituted divorce proceedings against his wife, was unwilling to leave Berlin where he was conducting a love affair with Sophie Bernhardi. Madame de Staël offered him a salary of 12,000 francs, a pension at the end of a certain number of years service, free accommodation at Coppet, the prospect of her affection, and the suggestion that, in the intervals of tutoring her two sons, he might help her with the book she thought of writing upon German thought and literature. Schlegel was unable to resist these enticements; she exercised upon him, as he admitted, "a supernatural power, against which it would have been vain to struggle." Schlegel at the time was thirty-six years of age, could speak French and English as easily as German, possessed encyclopaedic knowledge, and would clearly be of the greatest value to Madame de Staël in her study of German life, thought and manners. She agreed that he was very ugly, somewhat self-important, and extremely quarrelsome and touchy. Constant took a dislike to Wilhelm Schlegel the moment he first saw him; the antipathy between them did not diminish in the years that followed.

They left Weimar on May 2. Madame de Staël was overcome with grief and the inns at which they stopped on their way from Germany to Coppet would echo with her lamentations. During the day, however, as the carriage lurched southwards, she would consent to indulge in conversation and even in argument. Constant had a quarrel with Schlegel on the subject of Cervantes; they all had a quarrel on the subject of a sense of humour. At Zurich they were met by Madame de

Staël's devoted cousin, Mme. Necker de Saussure, who was able to give her details regarding her father's last illness and death. Her lamentations were renewed. On reaching Coppet she was seized with convulsions; the servants were obliged to lift her out of the carriage and to carry her indoors. Slowly she recovered and settled down to her normal turmoil and to the preparation of her book on Germany. It was not in her nature wholly to resist the temptation of dramatizing her part as Aristides' desolate daughter. Yet of her devotion to her father and of her deep sorrow there can be no doubt at all. She even practised a certain restraint. "The all-too-famous," wrote Rosalie on May 25, "is at Coppet, overwhelmed with authentic affliction. She does not make a display of it, which is the sign of a welcome change in her."

By this affliction, none the less, Constant found himself again rivetted to Coppet. "Madame de Staël," he noted, "shows insufficient consideration for others. It is true that she loves them, with the result that, although she makes many enemies, she also acquires many ardent friends. I show consideration for others, but I do not love them. As a result, I am not much hated, but also not much loved."

He was almost bewildered to find himself back in the old routine. "I have been unable so far," he writes, "to recover the clarity of my mind. I am interrupted at every moment. Oh Solitude! Solitude! more necessary to my talent even than to my happiness! I like everything to do with Coppet, but all those people, all those incessant interruptions, exhaust me and get on my nerves. They drain my natural energy and force me to exclaim with some bitterness—'When will it all end? When will it all end?'"

On their way back from Weimar to Coppet, they had stopped for one night at Göttingen. "Eleven years ago," noted Constant in his diary, "I spent a night like this at Göttingen.

I really was in love then with Madame de Marenholtz; a frenzied passion for her had seized upon me the moment she told me that, in obedience to her father, she had decided to renounce me. Was it pure vanity on my part? I don't think so; but a person who eludes one is clearly something wholly different from a person by whom one is pursued."

CHAPTER XI

Adolphe

[1807]

Coppet and the de Staël system—The Coppet circle of 1804—The tyranny which Madame de Staël exercised over her court—She goes off to Italy—Constant begins again to think of marriage—He meets Charlotte again—Le Vicomte du Tertre—His determination to break with Madame de Staël—He writes *Adolphe*, January 12–27, 1807—The theme of *Adolphe*—The external frame-work of the story is that of his affair with Anna Lindsay—The emotional content reflects his conflict with Madame de Staël—Madame de Staël realizes that he wishes to escape—She redoubles her tyranny—He goes to Lausanne where she follows him—The scene of September 1—He is brought back captive to Coppet—He writes *Wallstein*—Charlotte falls ill at Besançon—Madame de Staël goes to Vienna—On learning that she is about to return to Coppet he decides to marry Charlotte—Their marriage takes place at Dôle, June 5, 1808.

1

NOW that Madame de Staël had become the sole mistress of Coppet, life at the château underwent a change. In Necker's day something of the sumptuous formality of the eighteenth century still hung about the great stone staircase and the tapestried saloons. The footmen wore the powdered wigs, the green state liveries, of the Versailles days; meals were served punctually and with a certain stateliness; old Necker would sit at the head of the table, flinging insults at the deaf butlers, and accepting the compliments which his guests were expected to lavish upon him "with the bland indifference with which saints listen to hymns." When the last ortolan, the last peach, had been consumed, Necker would give his arm to his neighbour and lead a formal procession back into the great drawing-room. For an hour or two he would play whist, with his daughter as partner, and invariably the game ended in mutual recrimination. At the exact hour the sign was given that M. Necker was retiring to rest; the guests dispersed to their bedrooms; the footmen extinguished the candles upon the consoles and in the appliques and the chandeliers.

Madame de Staël changed all this. The luxury of the house remained unaltered; there were still fifteen servants in the kitchen alone; there were still weekly dinner parties of more than thirty people; there were still expensive theatrical performances in what is today the long and lovely library on the ground floor. But like all conceited people Madame de Staël regarded punctuality as the most irksome of all forms of discipline; hating orderliness, she deliberately created disorder. In the morning they would all meet in the dining-room for breakfast at ten o'clock; the main meal was served at five in the afternoon; supper was celebrated at eleven o'clock at night. Yet nobody, and least of all the hostess, was expected to conform to regular hours. "She appeared," records Madame de Boigne, "to be as unoccupied as she was inconsequent. There was no order at all; nobody knew where to go, where to meet, where to wait. There was no room set apart for any special hour of the day. Everybody's door was open; once a conversation started, one set up one's tent in the place it had begun and remained there for hours." Madame de Staël's own bedroom was on the first floor, adjoining the large drawing-room; it has since been turned into a private chapel and her bed and belongings moved down into the corresponding room on the floor below. Constant's room was in the east wing, with a view towards the lake and the hills above Lausanne. Madame de Staël would hurry nosily about the house at all hours of the day and night, penetrating into every bedroom, interrupting all private study or conversation, armed with a little green morocco writing-pad, on which she would inscribe her own thoughts and the compliments of others. Her turbans were of emerald and scarlet, her many scarves were of blue and purple and gold; she would seek by these garish colours to divert attention from her oatmeal complexion and enhance the black brilliance of her eyes. Every morning and every evening the gardeners at Coppet would cut for her a fresh sprig of laurel or mistletoe, of myrtle or osier. She would twirl these green emblems in her fingers or wave them on high, giving thereby a Sibylline grandeur to her gestures and drawing attention to the shapeliness of her hand and arm. On Sunday mornings she would attend the village church. It was the only moment at which her virile voice ceased to bounce along the corridors. It was considered a gross insult if any one of the guests, in any circumstance, suggested that it was time to go to bed.

The society had changed also. The tapping cane, the deep voice, of Talleyrand did not echo upon the stone staircase, the elegance of Narbonne no longer graced the tapestry chairs; Mathieu de Montmorency, it is true, remained for ever faithful; Elzéar de Sabran was often there; but there were new faces now around the table: the clever, sensitive face of Prosper de Barante, the beautiful complacent face of old Bonstetten, the dark uncertain face of Sismondi, the angular, questing, face of Wilhelm Schlegel, the bovine face of his brother Friedrich, the ugly attractive face of Auguste de Staël, the mischievous, merry face of his brother Albert, the angelic childhood face of Albertine, the adorable, ageless, vapid, virginal face of Madame Récamier.

In those empty but strained days of 1804, while Madame de Staël was still in deep mourning for her father, Constant had to rely on the company of Schlegel, of Sismondi (1) and of Bonstetten (2). They would go walks together in the diminutive park, along the path which runs beside the rushing stream. Constant disliked Schlegel, and so did Sismondi. The latter called him "a presumptuous pedant." Bonstetten found the atmosphere of Coppet most exhausting and was irritated by the difficulty he experienced in being able to talk at any length about himself. It distressed him moreover that Madame de Staël should be devoid of all aesthetic sensibility. "All beauty," he wrote, "which does not derive from the intellect or from rhetoric, is non-existent for her." Constant was somewhat shocked (as Thomas Gray had been shocked at Cambridge thirty-five years before) by Bonstetten's friskiness. He decided that he did not like elderly gentlemen who lacked the dignity of approaching age: "perhaps," he added with his unremitting fairness, "it is because I shall end that way myself." Constant rather liked Sismondi, finding him an agreeable, diffident, variable snobbish and uncertain man:

> Went a walk with Sismondi. He reproaches me for never speaking seriously. There is something in what he says. In my present mood I take too little interest in people to want to convince them. I thus fall back upon silence or upon making fun, my jokes amuse me and act as a narcotic. The best quality with which Providence has endowed me is to be amused at myself.

In the last resort there was always his little dog Mou—whom he had bought at Frankfort—Mou and Albertine. What did it matter if Schlegel regarded their romps together as a symptom of infantilism? Albertine, at least, thought Constant the youngest, the most unselfish, the most amusing, the most inventive playfellow there had ever been.

He was utterly aware none the less that, in this Circean captivity he was wasting his youth shamefully. "It is hard," he wrote, "to have neither the amusements for which one sacrifices one's dignity, nor the dignity for which one sacrifices one's amusements." A hanging, crackling, rumbling, thunderstorm—Madame de Staël was always there:

Never have I met a woman who is so incessantly exacting. One's whole life (every minute, every hour, every year) must be at her disposal. When she gets into one of her rages, then it is a tumult of all the earthquakes and typhoons rolled into one. . . . A frightful scene which lasted till 3 A.M. She said that I lacked sensibility; that I did not deserve to be trusted; that my actions did not correspond to my feelings. . . . I don't enjoy being scolded by a woman whose youth is leaving her. I do not enjoy being asked to make love, after ten years of a love affair, when each of us is approaching forty years of age, and when I have told her two hundred times, and ages ago, that I had done with passion. Never have I retracted that statement, except when trying to quieten her torments of rage and fury, which I admit simply terrify me. . . . I must detach my life from hers, while remaining her friend; otherwise I shall not survive much longer.

It is unnecessary to underline any further the strain imposed upon those who loved her by Madame de Staël's infuriate egoism. One final extract from Constant's diary will suffice:

Madame de Staël has gone off to Geneva for the night. Bonstetten, Schlegel, Sismondi and I dined alone together; we behaved like schoolboys when the head master is absent. What an extraordinary woman! It is impossible to explain the dominance she establishes over those who surround her; yet how real it is! If she knew how to rule herself, she could rule the world!

In December 1804 Madame de Staël, accompanied by Schlegel and Sismondi, underwent the Italian journey which produced *Corinne:* it also added several stone to her already buxom figure. She did not return to Coppet until the early summer of 1805. Constant profited by this release to escape to Les Herbages and to plunge back into his study of comparative religion. He had now decided that marriage was the only solution. He once again consulted Madame de Nassau and Rosalie regarding eligible candidates. "I shall marry this winter," he decided, "Obviously I must marry, if only in order to get to bed at a reasonable hour." But the candidates whom his aunt and cousin recommended were not to his taste.

2

In September 1795—at a time when Madame de Staël was pushing and pulling hard to force Constant upon the political world of Paris and a most unwilling Directory—he had received a letter with a Baden postmark:

> Constance, September 9, 1795
>
> Assuming that M. de Constant still remembers a person who will always think of him with interest, and assuming that he does not mind a short journey, Madame de Hardenberg would have much pleasure in meeting him again. She has been some weeks in Switzerland and for the last few days at the above place.
>
> My address is "The Black Eagle."

He returned no reply to this invitation. In 1800, however, he had received a letter from Rosalie telling him that her younger brother Victor had just been at Brunswick where he had met many of Benjamin's former admirers. Constant answered on November 14, 1800 that he was not interested in any of them; but he added the following significant sentence:

> There is one thing I *should* like to know. What has happened to Madame de Marenholtz, or von Hardenberg, who must now be about thirty-one years of age? If Victor met her, don't tell me *where*, but only whether he saw her and whether she said anything about me.

In 1798 Charlotte—having divorced Baron von Marenholtz—had married a French émigré of the name of the Vicomte du Tertre. He was a young man of twenty-four, with a trim tiny figure, chestnut curls, bright blue eyes, meagre intelligence and profound religious convictions. In 1802 he and his wife had come to Paris where they had taken an apartment at No. 274 Rue de l'Université. At a dinner party one evening Charlotte heard a M. de Sanne mention that Benjamin Constant was "in a bad way." She asked him whether it was his health that was causing trouble. No, it was not his health; it was his finances. Charlotte's maternal instincts (which were those of Demeter) were immediately aroused. She asked for Constant's address. He was living quietly in his cottage at Les Herbages, near Maffliers. She wrote to him at once.

One morning in January 1805, as she was entering her carriage, she was handed a letter in which Constant asked to be allowed to visit her. On this, their first meeting since March 26, 1793, they were much embarrassed; she showed him a miniature of her handsome young son von Marenholtz; she complained that Du Tertre was suspicious, jealous, fussy, impoverished, and far too religious; Constant was polite but cold. A few days later he was invited to dinner at the Rue de l'Université:

> A ridiculous dinner with Madame du Tertre. A husband there, who is beginning to show signs of jealousy, and other people who who could only exchange gossip about their county towns. And I— shy in the midst of all this—how absurd for me to feel this sense of inferiority when among such inferior people! That is the worst of shyness—it robs one of all sense of one's own value.

It was shortly after this (as Madame Dorette Berthoud assumes) that their old relations were resumed. She spent some nights with him at Les Herbages. An interlude then occurred.

Charlotte went off to Hardenberg to stay with her brother. Constant once again became entangled in the Coppet machine. She did not hear from him for five long months. From July 1805 until the end of 1806 his life became more feckless, intermittent, interrupted, and dependent than ever. We hear of him at Lausanne, at Geneva, at Dôle, and in the several houses which Madame de Staël rented (at Auxerre and again near Rouen) along the perimeter of her forty leagues from Paris. We hear of him taking part, with extreme ineptitude, in the theatrical performances which she organized. We hear, of course, of scenes of ever increasing intensity. At Auxerre, in the late summer of 1806, there comes an agonized entry in his diary: "In the evening a really terrifying scene. Horrible it was, insane; atrocious things said. Is she mad or am I? How on earth will all this end?" "Always," he writes, "I incline to a rupture with Madame de Staël, but every time I come to this decision I am bound to make a contrary decision the next morning. But her impetuosity and her indiscretion are an abiding torment to me and a perpetual danger. Let it be a rupture therefore, if that can be contrived; it is for me the only chance of a quiet life."

It was now twelve years since that disastrous day when he had first been caught by Madame de Staël on the road to Nyon. What had she done to him during those twelve years? She had damaged his health, she had ruined his weak eyesight, by the long vigils which she imposed; she had injured his reputation by her vaunting display of his subservience. Only the other day he had received from his old father a wounding letter, which had hurt because it was so true. "I should not mind," Juste had written, "if it were you who were keeping her; what distresses me is that it is she who is keeping you." By her incessant intrusions she had deprived him of that peace in which alone he could complete his life's work upon religions; for hours she would oblige him to sit up late while she read aloud her own compositions; never would she listen to, or even allow him time for, his own. Her reckless indiscretion, the vain pique which had led her to provoke the hostility of Bonaparte, had ruined his political career. He was surrounded by men who, although uneducated and far less able than he was, had during those tremendous years made vast fortunes, acquired resounding titles, been accorded stupendous lives. What opportunity had she allowed him? The opportunity of acting the part of Pyrrhus in a most amateur performance in the Salle de Molard at Geneva.

On the first of January, 1807 he entered in his diary a New Year's resolution:

> Yes—assuredly—and more than ever—I must put an end to all this. She is the most selfish, demented, ungrateful, empty and vindictive of women. Why did I not break with her long ago? She is odious to me, unendurable. I shall die if I do not bring the thing to an end. All the volcanoes of the world are less eruptive than she is. She is like an old attorney, her hair entwined with serpents, who in alexandrine verses insists upon the execution of a contract.

It was thus in a mood of indignation and despair that during the month of January 1807, he composed the first draft of *Adolphe* (3). He wrote it at white heat, between January 12 and January 27, within fifteen days.

3

The theme of this short masterpiece is the conflict between duty to oneself and duty to another which confronts a man who has ceased to love a woman by whom he is still adored. Byron, (who had considerable experience of such situations) was induced by Madame de Staël to read the book in the summer of 1816. "It is a work," he wrote to Samuel Rogers, "which leaves an unpleasant impression, but very consistent with the consequences of not being in love, which is, perhaps, as disagreeable as anything, except being so." Yet the theme of *Adolphe* is more subtly intricate than anything that Byron, with his easy-going humour, could conceive.

Constant, during that intense fortnight, was striving to set down on paper the dilemma with which he was then confronted; to analyze the atrocious conflict within him between heartlessness and compassion. Intellectually, he was able to explain, if not to solve, this riddle by an ingenious formula. The emotion of love, he contended, was more transitory in a man than in a woman. For a man, the object of his desire became an "aim"; once he had achieved his object, the woman ceased to be an "aim" and became a "tie." A woman, on the other hand, being more passive, had no "aim" until she had surrendered; her "aim" then became the retention of the lover for whom she had made so great a sacrifice. In irregular connections this time-lag between the two aims led to inevitable dissensions and betrayals; in marriage, the divergence of "aims" was mitigated by the presence of continuing common interests. Marriage therefore was the only reasonable solution of the battle of love.

Constant's misfortune was that he attached such fevered importance to the temporary excitation of being "in love," that he failed (at least until he had been married to soft Charlotte for several years) to appreciate the continuity of mutual respect, gratitude and tenderness which is the foundation of durable love. Those unhappy people who persuade themselves that no emotion can be powerful, or even sincere, unless it be also passionate, miss the balm of ordinary human affection, which is the medicine of distress. Throughout his orphaned life Benjamin Constant had yearned for affection: he was able to bestow it naturally upon animals and children; but in his relations with adult human beings he injected passion even into the docile movements of affection—he injected the passion of pity, by which his very soul was tortured. Thus, although he could find an intellectual formula to explain the disparity of love, he could never find an emotional compromise. Adolphe and Ellénore had reached an emotional deadlock: there was no solution but death.

The theme of his short story can be shortly summarized. Adolphe, partly from desire, partly from vanity, had imposed his passion upon Ellénore; at first she resisted; her surrender when it came was absolute; for him she sacrificed her name, her children, her social position, her fortune and her health. Adolphe, while still striving to love her, could find in his heart only the ashes of satiety and the dead dull weight of duty. He determines to escape; she discovers his intention; and she dies broken-hearted in his arms.

Constant disguised the emotional conflict between himself and Madame de Staël (which is the essential theme of *Adolphe*) by setting his story within the external framework of his affair with Anna Lindsay. Externally, Ellénore is the exact counterpart of Anna and the exact opposite of Madame de Staël. The artistic unity of the story is in fact damaged by this incongruity; a woman as submissive as Ellénore could not in fact have behaved with the violence which is described. Ellénore was of Polish origin, Anna's parents were Irish. For ten years Ellénore had lived with the Comte de P—— (identifiable as Auguste de Lamoignon) whom she had assisted in the days of the Terror and by whom she had had two children. Ellénore, even as Anna, was obsessed by social considerations and by a longing to be rendered respectable. Above all she is described as a woman "of quite ordinary intelligence." This comment, apart from all other disclaimers would enable Madame de Staël to assert and to believe that obviously there could be no resemblance between Ellénore and herself.

It is difficult to suppose, that Madame de Staël, when Constant read his novel aloud to her and Madame Récamier, failed to recognize a certain analogy of emotional content. Byron reports her as being "furious at any supposition" that there existed any resemblance between Adolphe and Constant, between Ellénore and herself. Yet even to her self-enclosed mind some glimmer of supposition must have penetrated. She knew Constant thoroughly; she knew that he was apt to put into writing those daring words which he had not the courage to avow face to face. She must have had some inkling in any case that in this story, Constant was seeking indirectly to convey to her something of the misery of his position, of the sufferings, the humiliations and the denials of opportunity which her despotism imposed.

The device which Constant had adopted in order to disguise the reality of Ellénore and of the emotional situation created by her relations with Adolphe did not for one moment impose upon those who were cognisant of the true circumstances:

> I recognize the author [wrote Sismondi to the Countess d'Albany] on every page. No Confessions that I have ever read provide one with so exact a self-portrait. He makes one understand all his faults, but he does not seek to excuse them or to render himself liked. He has naturally taken every precaution to prevent identification; he has altered all the external circumstances: nationality, social position, appearance, intellect. . . . But in the impetuosity and exactions of her amatory relationships one cannot fail to recognize Her. This apparent intimacy, this passionate domination—in the course of which they would lacerate each other with all the insults which rage and hatred can suggest—all this

is Their story; the story of those two. This resemblance is too forcible not to render futile all external disguises.

In truth, in the pages of *Adolphe* are recorded all the agonizing perplexities by which he was then assailed.

On the one hand there is the sense of wastage and humiliation:

> I am sacrificing my life to her [complains Adolphe] without thereby ensuring her happiness. As for myself, I exist without usefulness, without independence, never being granted a free moment, never being allowed one hour of peace. . . . My life is placed under constraint, my youth is spending itself in inactivity, her despotism dominates my every move. . . . She pursues me everywhere, as if I were her slave, continually recaptured if ever I escape. . . . I recall the hopes of my youth, the confidence with which I once imagined that I could direct my own future, the praise accorded to my early endeavours, a reputation which dawned so brightly and then faded. I repeat to myself the names of my school-friends whom I once treated with haughty disdain and who have left me far behind them on the road of fame, fortune and esteem. On recalling all these things, I experience a rush of rage against her; and, curiously enough, my rage in no way diminishes my terror of causing her anguish.

His nerves could no longer stand the scenes which she imposed upon him:

> My pride was stung by her reproaches; she reviled my character, she represented me as so miserable a weakling, that my anger turned against her rather than against myself. A passion of wild rage seized hold of us; all restraint was discarded, all delicacy cast aside. We hurled at each other every insult which the most implacable hatred could have invented; and there we were—the two beings on earth who alone understood each other, who alone could be just the one to the other, who alone could provide mutual solace and comprehension—there we were, we two wretched humans, in the semblance of two irreconcilable enemies intent on tearing each other limb from limb. . . . Our life became no more

than one long-drawn thunder-storm; our intimacy lost all its charm, our love for each other all its tenderness.

On the other hand, there was the habituation of this long companionship, the terrible sense of loneliness which would darken escape:

> There is something so profound in these prolonged attachments. Without our knowing it, they become so intimate a part of our existence. From a distance, in moments of calm, we resolve to escape; we persuade ourselves that we are looking forward with impatience to the moment of our liberation; but when that moment comes, it fills us with panic; and such is the complexity of our poor human heart, that it becomes an excruciating torture for us to leave the person whose presence causes us no satisfaction. . . . We had been living on the memories of our two hearts.

When Ellénore dies, and Adolphe at last acquires his freedom, he is overwhelmed with solitude and remorse:

> What a load of heaviness now appeared to me that liberty for which I had yearned so long! How deeply I felt the loss of that dependence which had so often irked me! When she was with me, everything I did had a definite purpose, either to cause her pleasure or to spare her pain. I used to resent this, being irritated by the thought that her eyes were watching my every movement, that her happiness was always involved in what I did. There was nobody now to watch my movements; they had become of no interest to anyone at all; there was no one now to claim my time, no voice to call me back. Yes—I was free now! But no longer loved—a stranger to all the world.

We may doubt whether Madame da Staël (who always saw herself as Delphine) derived any profit from the sad story of Adolphe and Ellénore. But Constant's behaviour in the two years that followed only becomes explicable when we realize that he was in fact tortured by the hesitations, the self-reproach, the pity and the remorse by which Adolphe was assailed. For most human beings, remorse comes only after the event; Constant, with his amazing lucidity of intellect, anticipated the remorse which he knew he would experience. He believed to the depths of his soul in the sanctity of human suffering; he foresaw that even if he succeeded in conquering what the world called his weakness, he would emerge from the struggle: "perverted by such a victory, or, if not perverted, then eternally ashamed."

4

By the spring of 1806, Madame de Staël had become convinced (whether from a careful perusal of *Adolphe* or from other indications) that Benjamin was plotting his escape. Her sense of possession thereupon assumed such a degree of ferocity that Benjamin was obliged to resort to the most discreditable stratagems and in the end to find refuge in the cruelty of a secret marriage.

By May of 1806 he had fallen comfortably in love with Charlotte all over again:

I spend much of my time with Madame du Tertre. She has great charm, a lively intelligence, kindliness, and a sweetness of nature which has an immediate effect upon me—making me feel happy. To unite with her would, I feel, mean that at last I had found repose. If M. du Tertre would consent to release her from a bond which means little to him—then my future is assured. Charlotte agrees. To the country [he notes later in his diary] with Charlotte. She is an angel of sweetness and charm and every day I love her more. So gentle, so amiable—how mad I was to reject her twelve years ago! . . . Obviously it is the contrast with Madame de Staël which has brought about this change of feeling; the contrast between her impetuosity, her egoism, her unceasing preoccupation with herself, and the sweetness, the calm, the modest humble ways of Charlotte. Assuredly I am wearied of that man-woman whose iron hands have kept me in chains these ten years, now that I have another woman who enchants and intoxicates me. If I can marry her, I shall hesitate no longer. All depends on the line which will be taken by M. du Tertre.

M. du Tertre, as has been said, was a religious man. He was much affected when informed that his Church could not recognize as binding a marriage contracted with a woman who had not only been divorced by her previous husband but who was also a Protestant. He agreed to annul his marriage with Charlotte, provided everything was arranged in Germany and not in France, and provided suitable financial provision was made for his future maintenance. In June therefore Charlotte left for Hardenberg to make the necessary arrangements, while Constant went to visit his old father at Brévans. While there, he received letters from Madame de Staël—"such as one would not address to a highway robber"—ordering him to return to Coppet immediately. When he showed some lack of promptitude in obeying these instructions, she sent her son Auguste and her steward Uginet to Brévans to fetch him back. She threatened that if he refused to accompany them she would arrive at Brévans and strangle herself before his father's eyes. "Wretch that I am!" confided Constant to his diary, "My weakness has again defeated me. I am going back to Coppet."

The scenes which greeted him on arrival were more lurid than ever:

> She says [wrote Constant to Rosalie] that since I have shown signs of wishing to break away, she is determined not to let me out of her sight. She threatens to commit suicide if I attempt to escape. She has communicated this intention to her children, to her household, to her friends—in fact to the whole world. As a result, they all regard me as a monster for refusing to ease her torments.

On August 1, 1807 Constant went off to Lausanne in order to stay with his aunt Madame de Nassau, who was then living in his own birthplace, the maison Chandieu in the Rue du Grand Chêne. Within two days Madame de Staël descended on Lausanne with her whole court and established herself in the house of M. de Montagny at Ouchy. She had a violent scene with Rosalie, whom she accused of aiding and abetting Benjamin; she shook her by her crippled shoulder; she turned upon her "all the fires of her eyes." She announced that rather than lose Benjamin she would be prepared to marry him.

Meanwhile Constant had broken to Madame de Nassau his intention of marrying Charlotte. His aunt was shocked by the suggestion that he should marry a woman who would have twice been divorced; in the end, feeling sorry for Benjamin in his dilemma, she said that she would be glad to receive Charlotte once she was his wife. Fortified by such support, Constant wrote a letter in which he took a final farewell of Madame de Staël; but on reading his letter over he had a vision of the atrocious anguish it would cause her and he tore it up. In consultation with Madame de Nassau and Rosalie he devised a further stratagem. He would make a second formal offer to marry Madame de Staël, and in the form of an ultimatum. If she agreed, then he would have to assuage Charlotte as best he could; if she refused, then he could with a clear conscience break with her for ever.

Meanwhile Madame de Staël had returned to Coppet. On August 31 she sent her carriage to Lausanne to bring Constant back to his captivity. That night he delivered his ultimatum. His second offer of marriage was anything but a success. She summoned Schlegel, her children and her household to her bedside. "There!" she exclaimed, pointing at Constant, "is the man who wishes to rob you of your name and your fortune." Constant replied that, very well he would promise never to marry her at all. At which she rolled out of bed, twisted her scarves around her neck, and went through all the processes of strangulation. Her children and servants intervened to prevent this suicide.

Next morning, at dawn, on September 1, Constant crept down to the courtyard at Coppet, mounted his horse, and within two and a half hours arrived exhausted and panic-stricken at La Chaumière. He was describing what had happened to Rosalie and Madame de Bavois when loud cries were heard in the hall below. The scene that followed is best conveyed in Rosalie's own account:

> My first movement was to get outside and to turn the key behind me in the lock. I went out on to the landing. I found her lying upside down on the staircase, her neck uncovered, her hair streaming down the steps. She was shouting "Where is he? I must find him!"

Rosalie and her aunt lifted the recumbent woman and led her to an adjoining bedroom. Meanwhile, Benjamin, who had been locked into the drawing-room, banged on the door and clamoured to be let out. Madame de Staël heard his voice, rushed into his arms as he emerged from the drawing-room, and then fell to the ground again screaming bitter reproaches. Rosalie at that lost her temper and shouted at Madame de Staël that she had no right to ruin Benjamin's life. Madame de Staël then let loose upon Rosalie the full stream of her invective. Benjamin made no attempt to defend his cousin. He stood there in livid silence. Rosalie then left the house and took refuge with Madame de Nassau in the maison Chandieu. She refused ever to speak to Madame de Staël again.

In her great yellow carriage with the postillions Madame de Staël drove back to Coppet, with her prisoner inside. It must have been an embarrassing journey:

> She came [Constant recorded that evening in his diary], she fell at my feet, uttering ghastly cries of anguish and desolation.

A heart of iron could not have stood out against it. So I am back at Coppet—and Charlotte who expected me to join her at the end of this month! I have agreed to remain here for six weeks. I am trampling on my whole future happiness.

5

Having recovered her prisoner, having humiliated him in front of his family and her own servants, Madame de Staël realized that a gentler mood was now recommendable. She produced her favourite sedative which, in 1800, she had applied in vain to Narbonne. She urged Constant to adapt Schiller's *Wallenstein* for the French stage.

He was himself delighted by this performance. "It is," he recorded, "the best thing that I have done." The modern reader of *Wallstein* (since that was the title he gave to his adaptation) will be inclined to agree with Napoleon, who said that it proved that Constant had no sense of drama and that he would do well to study the Poetics of Aristotle. Constant, moreover, possessed no ear for poetry; in his hands the French alexandrine (always a difficult metre) becomes a thing of lead. In later years he admitted that he had made a mistake in trying to condense Schiller's trilogy into a French drama, subjected to the unities and the conventions of the classical stage. When he read the play to Madame Récamier and Talma a few months later there was an ominous, an oppressive, silence; he then realized that his autumn months of application had again been wasted.

There are only two things in Constant's *Wallstein* which need detain us. He took Schiller's character of Thécla (who in the original was an ecstatic and rebellious maiden) and turned her into a portrait of Charlotte. And he wrote a preface in which he contrasted in the French and the German conceptions of love. For the French, love is a distracting passion closely connected with animal desire; for the Germans it is a circumambient light, common to man and God, and has about it something religious and mystical.

Charlotte in any case had full need, during the two years that followed, to find comfort in this circumambient and mystical element; it was about all she was accorded. On hearing of his recapture, on learning that he would now be unable to meet her at the end of September, she had faced the situation with her usual devoted submissiveness:

> For the last few days [she wrote] I have been unconscious of what I was saying or doing. I know only that I love you more than life. I never complain about you to anyone. I keep my wound at the bottom of my heart; I keep it hidden there; but if it is to remain there for much longer, then my heart will break.

He assured her that this time he really would be with her in the autumn. By some blessed chance Madame de Staël was off in search of a new lover; she was off to meet Count Maurice O'Donnell in Vienna (4). Charlotte thereupon packed her belongings and drove for eighteen days in the pouring rain to Besançon, where she found, not Benjamin, but seven letters, not all of which were agreeable. Her disappointment was so atrocious that she became seriously ill. Benjamin was at last stung to action. Stating that his old father was on the verge of death, he left Coppet for Besançon and found Charlotte delirious in a bedroom at the Hôtel National. She shuddered at the sound of his voice: "There," she raved, "is the man who is murdering me." So soon as she was convalescent he took her off to Brévans where his father received her with marked courtesy. Madame de Staël by then had really left for Vienna. Benjamin and Charlotte went to Paris; her marriage with du Tertre was finally annulled; they lived peaceably, often together, in Paris and at Les Herbages.

Suddenly, in April 1808, came a letter from Madame de

Staël stating that she was returning from Vienna and summoning him to meet her at Coppet in May. Constant was seized with panic. There was only one thing to be done; he must snatch at the irretrievable.

At the end of May Charlotte and Benjamin went off together to Brévans. Old Juste was delighted that his errant son should at last have found a calm, a comparatively sedate, a sufficiently wealthy companion. He hurried down to Besançon to discuss matters with his friend the Pasteur Ebray. Everything could be arranged quite quietly and without the slightest publicity. On June 5, 1808 at Dôle Constant and Charlotte were married according to the rites of the Protestant Church by Pasteur Jan.

The fact of their marriage was not entered in the parish register.

CHAPTER XII

The God from the Machine

[1808–1811]

The inconsequence of Constant's biography—His inability to finish things off—The mystification which followed his marriage—Charlotte's aunt visits Switzerland—Charlotte accompanies her to Lausanne and Geneva—Their meeting with Madame de Staël who becomes suspicious—Constant and Charlotte go to Brévans and then to Paris—They return in the spring of 1809 to Switzerland—Charlotte informs Madame de Staël that she is married to Constant—The scene which takes place and the conditions which Madame de Staël imposes—She summons Constant to accompany her to Lyons—Charlotte's attempted suicide—Constant takes Charlotte to Paris and then returns to Lyons and thereafter to Coppet—His attempt to lead a dual life—He is summoned to Chaumont—Madame de Staël's court at Chaumont—Miss Randall—Napoleon decrees the confiscation of *De l'Allemagne* and banishes Madame de Staël to Coppet—Constant feels that he cannot abandon her in the midst of such disasters—She meets John Rocca and marries him—Constant is thus released and goes off with Charlotte to Germany.

1

WERE Benjamin Constant a character in fiction, then this story could conform to the accepted rules of composition: there could be clear beginnings and neat ends. But since he was, as he claimed "one of the most real people that have ever lived," then his biography must reflect the uncertain beginnings and the loose ends of actual life. It would be agreeable both for the biographer and the reader if we could at this stage rid ourselves for ever of the wearisome iteration of escapes and recaptures, of revolts and surrenders, of misplaced loyalties and unkind deceptions, which have been described in previous chapters; if we could represent Constant as immediately finding in marriage that combination of protection and independence, of companionship and solitude, which his nature required.

Life does not weave such tidy patterns, nor do men of fluid character permit their biographies to fall into neat compartments. Constant, with his gambler's temperament, was always inclined to allow the hazard of events to determine his action; and to wait until the compulsion of wills stronger than his own had produced the "inevitable" situation. It will thus be necessary to devote one further chapter to the theme of inglorious servitude; since although Constant married Charlotte on June 5, 1808, he did not finally free himself from Madame de Staël until May 10, 1811; this interlude was filled by many discreditable subterfuges and much personal unkindness.

There is a further admission which must be made if the reader is to judge freely, and for himself, the rights and wrongs of this unhappy triangle. A biographer owes a duty to his subject and is justified in making the very most of all favourable fact. He may be tempted therefore to give exaggerated emphasis to the sense of pity, which was assuredly one of the main components of Constant's sensibility, and thereby to extenuate both his cowardice in face of Madame de Staël's violence and his comparative lack of compassion for the suffering which he imposed on Charlotte. At the same time, he may be tempted to concentrate upon Madame de Staël's ferocious egoism at the expense of the magnificent generosity which that splendid woman undoubtedly possessed.

Yet before we condemn Constant too readily, we must force ourselves to visualize the actual physical terror created by Madame de Staël's corybantic passions and to picture the screams and scenes, the spasms and mock suicides, the torturing public dramas, which any emotional conflict with Madame de Staël invariably entailed. It may well be that from an objective point of view, if judging solely by the calm standards of ordinary, reasonable, human conduct, we can find no excuse at all for Constant's weakness; yet we should at least remember that he was bound to approach the issue subjectively, and that the person with whom he had to deal was not calm, objective, reasonable or ordinary. We also, in such atrocious circumstances, might have been overcome, not by pity only, but also by terror.

The tangle of mystification in which they all thereafter became involved composes a veritable cat's cradle of deception. The only other person who knew that the marriage had actually taken place was Juste de Constant, and even he, at a later date, was persuaded to deny the fact. Charlotte had lied to M. du Tertre and had only vaguely indicated to her family that at some distant date she might become "engaged." Constant himself had informed Madame de Nassau and Rosalie that, once he could decently sever his connection with Madame de Staël, he "hoped" to marry Charlotte. And Madame de Staël, even if she may have been told incidentally and humorously of the old Brunswick episode, was not aware that Benjamin and the heroine of the episode had ever met again.

A few days after his marriage, Constant travelled to Coppet with the intention of breaking the dreadful news to Madame de Staël. Charlotte retired to Neuchâtel, where she took a lonely room at the Hôtel des Balances in order to await the result. There was no result. On reaching Coppet, Constant's courage failed him completely. He simply did not dare to tell Madame de Staël the ghastly truth. He hung on miserably, inventing excuses for himself:

> I know very well [he wrote to Madame de Nassau] that if my dual relationship were known, I might be accused of a certain degree of duplicity. But when the truth is certain to cause pain, then it is pride, not duty, which forces one to tell it. . . . True morality consists in avoiding, so far as one can, the infliction of suffering.

In July the falsity of his position was brought home to him by a fortuitous, and somewhat farcical, combination of events.

2

Charlotte's aunt, Frau von Decken, chose that moment to undertake a tour in Switzerland in the company of her son-in-law and daughter, Count and Countess von Wangenheim. Charlotte went to meet them at Berne and accompanied them to Lausanne. They arrived at the latter place on July 20, 1808. Charlotte introduced herself to Madame de Nassau, by whom she was most graciously received.

Madame de Nassau, although she had at the time no knowledge of any marriage, had been told by Benjamin that he much admired Charlotte and that there existed an "understanding" between them. She saw in this attachment a hope of rescuing her nephew from the clutches of Madame de Staël. She therefore wrote to him suggesting that it would be an admirable thing if he also were to join Charlotte at Lausanne. He replied that on the whole he felt that it would be preferable if his aunt were to get to know Charlotte in his absence. Were he to leave Coppet at that moment, Madame de Staël might become suspicious and distressed. His visit might moreover lead to gossip "about two people, neither of whom I wish to compromise!"

All this [he wrote] merely for two or three days, when everything will settle itself quite amicably in the end. No, my dear aunt, I know that on reflection you yourself would not advise me to make this journey.

Frau von Decken, having for some days enjoyed the pleasures of Lausanne society, was anxious to push on to Geneva. The road would lead them past the gates of Coppet, and from Nyon Charlotte scribbled a hurried note to her husband:

Angel mine! If only I could catch a glimpse of you! We are just leaving this place and in two hours we shall be at Geneva. We shall pass close to where you are staying. Couldn't you just stroll about outside for a minute or two? If I could see you, if only from a distance, it would give me a happy moment. Goodbye—I love you. I shall be in the first cabriolet; my cousin will be driving.

There is a small opening in the park wall at Coppet, closed by a small grating, or *claire-voie*, of iron spikes. It may have been from there that Constant gazed out from his internment camp as the cabriolets drove by.

Frau von Decken had engaged rooms for her party at the Hôtel d'Angleterre at Sécheron, on the outskirts of Geneva. This famous hostelry (which figures not only in this story but also in the story of Byron and Shelley) has almost entirely disappeared; all that remains of it today is part of one of the large coach-houses. It was kept by M. Dejean, a curious dwarf-like figure, who would receive his distinguished guests dressed in an apple green coat and white stockings, with a tame heron stalking by his side. Frau von Decken was delighted to find herself in this comfortable hotel, with its wide lawns sweeping down to the lake; she decided that they would all remain there for several days.

Constant was much embarrassed by the proximity to Coppet of his wife and her grand relations. Charlotte had told her aunt that she was more or less engaged to Constant; she had not mentioned one word about the marriage.

> The German ladies [wrote Constant to Madame de Nassau] are to be some twelve days at Sécheron. I shall of course go to see them. I do not know what the aunt will say, but she is sure to examine me with some curiosity. Life consists of getting out of things. Never has there been a situation so strangely contrived as mine. Luckily I begin to foresee the moment when SHE will become more simple; and even the worst that can happen will help to simplify her sooner. . . . I sometimes wonder whether, once I reach calm waters, I shall be surprised at myself for having made such a business about a situation which other men could have solved quite easily. The reason is that all my difficulties occur in my heart.

Charlotte had been three days at Sécheron without receiving a single word from Constant. She uttered a plaintive reproach:

> Can't you realize [she wrote to her husband] that your silence is an agony to me—especially at this moment, when I am so close to where you are, and in such need of comfort? Have pity on me and write, if only a word.

Constant sent her a note by his coachman Audoin fixing a clandestine meeting. She told him that her aunt and the Wangenheims were shocked that her prospective fiancé should be paying court to another woman, while she, a von Hardenberg, was relegated to an inn down the road. Constant was always irritated when Charlotte ventured to remind him of her own awkward position. The clandestine interview was anything but a success.

Meanwhile Frau von Decken, whose social curiosity seems to have been greater than her tact, induced Mme. Odier-Lecointe of Geneva to introduce her to Madame de Staël. "Any day," replied the latter in all innocence, "will suit me for the German ladies." Frau von Decken and the Wangenheims therefore dined at Coppet on July 30. Charlotte absented herself from the party.

> The aunt [wrote Constant to Madame de Nassau] came to dinner with her daughter and son-in-law. She was full of conversation and well received. We discussed my affairs in a desultory, inconsequent sort of way. She showed great interest in me—great friendliness—(which I found agreeable, since it showed what this numerous and distinguished family felt about me). Above all she pleased me by expressing herself in a feeling manner (same as my own) about her niece's character.
>
> But what I need, if I am to be understood, is someone who experiences as I do, and in all their infinite variety, the scruples of the heart. I might have been someone (and there are many such) who can reduce everything to a simple dilemma—who can say, as Charlotte's aunt said—"A door must be either open or shut." Could I take this sort of attitude, then I might create a solution which in appearance would be a peaceable solution; but in fact it would be a poisoned solution.

A few days later the whole German party at the Hôtel d'Angleterre were invited by a Monsieur Dupuch of Geneva to meet Madame de Staël at dinner in his house. This time Charlotte decided to be present. It seems that, in her nervousness at being confronted with her rival, she behaved with foolishness; she showed off lamentably. It must indeed have been a deplorable exhibition, since her aunt went so far as to scold her for her unseemly behaviour. Charlotte at that dissolved into tears. Sobbingly she confessed to her aunt that she had secretly been married to Constant for almost two months. Frau von Decken was a sentimental and maternal woman; Charlotte was forgiven, pitied and caressed.

When therefore, two days later, Madame de Staël paid a formal call on the German ladies at the Hôtel d'Angleterre, she found Frau von Decken in a knowing, and perhaps a combative, mood. Charlotte's aunt emphasized the extreme kindness which had been shown them by Madame de Nassau at Lausanne. Madame de Staël's suspicions were aroused. On her return to Coppet she subjected Constant to an examination in the third degree; he lied furiously. But something of her suspicion must have remained. One of her endless dramatic performances was about to take place in the theatre-room at Coppet. "Do not," wrote Madame de Staël to Madame Odier-Lecointe, "give any tickets to the German ladies. I shall explain why later."

3

In the autumn of 1808, Madame de Staël left Coppet for her winter quarters at Geneva. Constant had made an arrangement with Marianne by which, when warned, she would write him a letter, which he could show to Madame de Staël, expressing urgent anxiety regarding the health of his father. By this stratagem he was able to escape from Geneva and to go to Brévans, where he was joined by Charlotte.

It was not a happy visit. Old Juste pestered him about money, being anxious to make provision for the two children he had had by Marianne. Charlotte set her skirt on fire at the stove, and Constant burnt his hand badly in putting it out. For several weeks he was obliged to wear a glove. In the end they were able to travel to Paris together, where they lived for the winter months, at the Hôtel Vauban, spending short interludes at Les Herbages.

Constant, tortured as he was by the thought of Madame de Staël, had not been able as yet to find the peace of soul for which he yearned:

Everything [he wrote to Rosalie] comes too late in life. When the heart is susceptible to happiness, then happiness just isn't there; when happiness comes, then the heart is no longer tuned to receive it.

To his aunt he expounded a more subtle doctrine. There is no reason, he told her, why intellectuals should not in the end achieve happiness. True it was that for them the period of adolescence is unduly prolonged. But in the end, middle age comes even to them; after all they have experienced they desire repose more ardently than do normal human beings; and at the same time they expect less from life.

During these winter months that he spent with Charlotte she strove to persuade him that so equivocal a situation could not be indefinitely prolonged. She managed to convince him that before the spring arrived, before he was summoned back to Coppet for the summer months, they must confess to Madame de Staël that they were man and wife. Constant suggested that in all the circumstances it would perhaps be better if this unpleasant revelation were made by Charlotte herself, and alone. It would all go so much more easily if he wasn't there.

Early in May 1809, therefore, they travelled down to Switzerland together. Charlotte took a room at the Hôtel d'Angleterre at Sécheron. Constant went off and hid in an inn at Ferney.

In the afternoon of May 9 Charlotte sent a note up to Coppet, signed "Charlotte von Hardenberg," in which she invited Madame de Staël to visit her "in order to receive an important communication." That very night, at ten o'clock Madame de Staël burst unannounced into Charlotte's bedroom. "I obeyed your summons," she said, "because you are a von Hardenberg."

Charlotte was caught at a disadvantage. Fearing that she had a cold coming on she was seated, before going to bed, with her feet plunged in a tub of mustard and hot water.

The interview which followed lasted for six hours, until four in the morning. It was a scene of great ferocity. Madame de Staël confessed afterwards to Madame Récamier (who told Saint-Beuve) that she had lost her temper with Charlotte, not so much owing to the dreadful revelation which she made, as owing to the insipidity of her character and the maddening way in which she repeated the phrase, "But Benjamin is such a kind man." He was not a kind man, she stormed, he was a weak man, gifted with a sense of pity, but at heart an egoist. If in fact he had gone through some form of marriage with Charlotte he had done so only in a fit of momentary aberration, in a mood of sudden weakness. He was far too gifted a man ever to find happiness in association with so flat and soft a mind as that of Charlotte. In the eyes of God, if not of man, he was her husband and not Charlotte's; again and again had he assured her that, whatever temporary connections he might indulge in, his eternal allegiance was pledged to her alone. How could Charlotte suppose that a woman of her feeble character and low intellectual attainments could ever permanently hold the affections of so fastidious and volatile a lover? The whole silly business must be cancelled at once. There was no more to be said. Here were her conditions. First, Charlotte must return to Germany immediately. Secondly, Benjamin must come back to Coppet and remain there for at least three months on end. And thirdly, this absurd marriage ceremony must be kept secret, and if necessary denied.

Before retiring to her aching rest, Charlotte wrote a short and breathless note to Benjamin giving what seems a mild account of that atrocious interview:

> I am even more exhausted than you are, and, what with fatigue and fever, am almost at the end of my tether. She stayed here until four in the morning. I did everything which a human being

could do; everything that one can promise, I promised. Through all her violence and anguish I could see what she wants more than anything is a long respite. Again and again she gave herself away on this point. I refused nothing which is essential to you and her. We simply must talk things over together before you see her. I swore that I had no idea where you were staying, since she threatened to send out a search-party to find you. Make up your mind what you want to do. The details of a six hour conversation are too long to put on paper; yet you must have all these details. In my presence she did not have the slightest symptom of convulsions. I almost forced her by my own attitude to be gentle towards me. Let me know at once when you can come. Come—I entreat you—I doubt whether I could get out to Ferney. All will go well, I hope—only come!

A few days later, Constant was back at Coppet. He assured Madame de Nassau that he would only remain there a fortnight and that thereafter he would rejoin Charlotte:

> I have [he wrote] succeeded in preserving her friendship by promising to conceal for some time longer the fact that I have formed another connection. I thus provide her with the means of preparing public opinion, and of giving the impression that the breach between us was due to her own volition. I swear to you [he wrote again] that there is no human being on this earth whom I esteem, revere, and love as much as Charlotte. Were I offered the riches of Peru, the youth of Hebe, the beauty of the Venus of Medici, I should still prefer my Charlotte.

4

This preference, for the moment at least, was not very marked. He had confessed by then to Madame de Nassau that what he called his "engagement" had in fact been a marriage. She urged him to leave Coppet and to take his wife to Brévans. He made all manner of excuses. In course of time Madame de Staël would accept the situation; in the meanwhile it was in Charlotte's interest that he should remain at Coppet and thereby prevent some atrocious incident. Besides, his father at Brévans was too ill to receive many visitors. Besides, it was more delicate for him not to be present when Charlotte's marriage settlements were being discussed. Besides, if he went to France he might be called up for service with the National Guard. Madame de Nassau was not impressed by these arguments. She accused Benjamin of deceiving even his closest friends; she altered her will, depriving her nephew of the legacy on which he had counted for years.

Meanwhile Charlotte was suffering from a reaction. At first she had been prepared to accept any degree of self-surrender:

> My love, if you can only find peace by sacrificing me utterly, I swear to you that I love you enough to make that sacrifice. What value is a life worn out by all these agitations? I should prefer to be broken on the wheel. Write to me tomorrow and tell me why you are so tortured. Anyhow by tomorrow she may have forgotten the whole thing, that is her way.

This initial mood of abnegation was followed by one of appalling lassitude. She refused to leave Sécheron and go to Germany.

> She is distressed [Constant informed his aunt] by the promises which she made. For the first time since I have known her, she complies but unwillingly with my suggestions. Not because she is opposed to them, but owing to a sort of exhaustion of suffering, which only allows her passive resignation in place of the active resignation which she has so often manifested. This gives me, in the eyes of another person, the appearance of breaking my word of honour from the very start; of violating a solemn treaty. So long as she remains at Sécheron, I feel as if on thorns.

Madame de Staël insisted vehemently on Charlotte's departure. It was difficult, none the less, to persuade Charlotte to leave. "I am so mortally tired," she wrote, "that I cannot drag myself away alone and without anywhere to go to. I have reached the point where I prefer Sécheron just because I happen to be there."

In the end Charlotte agreed to leave (not for Germany, but for Brévans) on the understanding that Constant would join her there in a few days. "I confess," she wrote—"and you must realize it yourself—that her exacting insistence revolts me to a degree which I find it difficult to express. She is deceiving herself if she imagines that she can dispose of my life in the same manner that she has so unfortunately disposed of yours."

As always, Constant, on one excuse or another, postponed his departure from Coppet; he eventually reached Brévans in a mood of trepidation. He had only been there a few days when Madame de Staël's son Auguste, then a youth of nineteen, arrived with a summons to him to proceed to Lyons, where Madame de Staël was taking her court to witness a performance by Talma. When he hesitated to obey this summons, the boy threatened him with a duel. He again capitulated and drove off with Auguste to Lyons.

It was on June 7, 1809 that Madame de Staël and her escort arrived at Lyons. A suite of apartments had been reserved for them at the Hôtel du Parc. Whether with Constant's knowledge or not, Charlotte had followed him to Lyons and taken humble lodgings in the town. It was the anniversary of their marriage and she was feeling desperate. She presented herself at the Hôtel du Parc and asked to see Constant. He was horrified by her arrival and begged her in abject terror to go away at once and not to return. Madame de Staël witnessed this dismissal.

The next morning the following letter was brought round to him at the Hôtel du Parc. He and Madame de Staël read it together:

THE GOD FROM THE MACHINE

You turned me away. That I know did not come from your heart, which is as torn as mine. I pity you more than I do myself. I love you. I believe that I am the only creature on earth that has truly loved you. The woman to whom I owe my death is a hard woman; all that she feels is what she calls her humiliation. The only anguish that I feel is that of parting from you. I pray God to forgive me. Before I die I shall pray for you also—for my son—for that good man du Tertre, who will regret my death. . . . My poor dear friend, I forgive you. At least I should have wished to die in your arms. Even that you could not accord me: she willed it that I should pass my last few hours alone. Without one pang of pity, she saw the state that I was in. She is pitiless; have pity on yourself. Yes! Yes!—you do love me but never again shall I hear your voice telling me so. I should have wished to be granted at least that last consolation. [Charlotte's letter—the handwriting of which becomes increasingly disordered—then breaks into German] Your Lotte, your poor Lotte, kisses you once again. May God bless you and forgive me my life, so that I may find peace after my death. Go on living therefore, and do no harm to anyone —not even to the woman who has destroyed me. I beg you, dear, to take care of all the papers which you will find in the desk. Do not let them bury me until they have made quite certain that I am dead. Great God! Now that I have got everything ready, I am seized with panic. Shall I never see you again? But soon, soon [*bald, bald*].

On reading this letter, Constant and Madame de Staël dashed round to Charlotte's lodgings. They found her writhing in agony upon the sofa but still alive. A doctor was summoned and some of the poison was drained off. Charlotte gradually recovered, although she remained ill for several months. Madame de Staël gave Constant permission to take the woman to Paris where she could be placed under the care of Dr. Koreff. In return he must promise to come back to her immediately and to remain at Coppet for an extra three months. He had only been in Paris two days when he received from Madame de Staël a hard hysterical letter. It is worth quoting, not merely because it is among the very few letters from Madame de Staël to Constant which have been preserved, but also because it indicates that the dilemma which faced him was not quite so simple as has generally been assumed:

> Thank you for having written to me from Roanne. Your letter enabled me to enjoy three hours of sleep. That was something new. For me the last awakening will be the only welcome one. Thank you also for promising to come back here on the 26th. I believe, and desire from the depth of my soul, that those three months you have promised me will mark the gentle end of my miserable existence. . . . At present I know myself to be an unwanted encumbrance, unwanted most of all by myself. I drag out the hours, which pass as wearily as if they were days; everything is dead within me—friends, children, thoughts, sunshine—they are no more to me than shapes of pain.
>
> When I saw you again I seemed to recover my grip on life. Since the last two days I feel that I have something wrong with my lungs. Didn't you tell me once that it was unhappiness which killed Madame Talma in six months? I have just got time. Oh Benjamin! Benjamin! you have twisted my affection for you into a dagger turned against myself. So it was on June 8 (sic) that you married? You know how to pray: pray for me. Never has any poor human being, crippled by life, been in such need of prayer. . . . My soul is left alone to itself; I shall feed myself upon it until I die. I am a sort of Ugolino in the world of the mind; a wall has risen between the world and me. Farewell! Already I have said more than I meant to say. There is no other word to be spoken between us except "the 26th." And to pray God to call me to his presence.

5

Having deposited Charlotte in the scrupulous and tender care of Dr. Koreff, Constant returned obediently to Lyons and thereafter to Coppet. In the eighteen months that followed

THE GOD FROM THE MACHINE

he sought desperately to devise some arrangement by which he could share his life between his mistress and his wife.

He soon discovered that the only argument which appeared to have any effect upon Madame de Staël, was the contention that, since the secret marriage was bound to leak out sooner or later, she would be wise in her own interest to publish it herself and to appear as the divine Delphine, only too happy to arrange the happiness of others. With this in mind he sent to Madame de Nassau the draft of a letter which she should address to him, and which he could show to Madame de Staël, such as would convince her that before long the whole of Lausanne society would be talking of nothing else:

> I was most astonished [Madame de Nassau was to write to him] my dear nephew, by the news your father sends me. He writes to say that you recently married in his house a lady who is in every way suitable, but that you promised to keep your marriage secret until you had had time to inform a certain person whom it might interest. But that suddenly, having brought your wife as far as Geneva, you write and tell him that from consideration of other people's feelings you intend to keep your marriage secret for a much longer period. I beg you, my dear nephew, to consider. . . .

And here was to follow Madame de Nassau's excellent advice about the impossibility of keeping the marriage dark, and the harm which such concealment might do to Madame de Staël's repute.

Madame de Staël was not in the least impressed by this stratagem. If Benjamin was prepared to resort to underhand methods, she would do the same. She spread it abroad that Benjamin, in a moment of weakness, had allowed himself to go through a form of marriage with a German woman, but that this marriage was illegal and therefore invalid. At the same time she sought by every means in her power to get Juste de Constant to deny the marriage, and even went so far as to indicate to him that she would herself in gratitude provide for the future of his son and daughter by Marianne. It seems even that it was she who suggested to the old man that Marianne was right in resenting the amount of property he had in the past transferred to Benjamin and that the moment had now arrived when he should claim it back. At the same time she herself began to demand from Benjamin the repayment of the sums which he had borrowed from M. Necker and herself. It was true that at the time he purchased Hérivaux he received substantial assistance from Madame de Staël's father; but the financial arrangements made between Constant and Madame de Staël at the height of their attachment, the houses which they had jointly rented, the bank account which they had kept in common, represented a problem in accountancy which was in practice insoluble. Even Charlotte, so mild always and so forgiving, was profoundly shocked by this financial manoeuvre:

> I find it incomprehensible [she wrote] that after having assured me that in the eyes of God she was more your wife than I was—after having informed every Dick, Tom and Harry that you were the father of her daughter—she should now hand you the bill, and that (possessing a fortune such as hers) she should insist upon the repayment of the monies she has lent to you.

This sordid wrangle lasted for months. In the end, in March of 1810, he signed an agreement with Madame de Staël under which the sums which he owed her, estimated at 80,000 francs, would be repaid to her at his death, provided that he died without leaving any children. In return for this document he was allowed to go to Paris with the promise that he would return to Coppet for the summer. "I think he will come," she wrote to Sismondi. "I shall suffer from him, but I shall make him suffer also, since I have more than ever the power to do so: this expiation will console me."

THE GOD FROM THE MACHINE

Madame de Staël did not, however, spend that summer of 1810 at Coppet. Pretending that she was on her way to the United States, she rented from M. Jacques Le Ray the Château of Chaumont on the Loire. In this magnificent fortress, (which had received such distinguished visitors as Thomas à Becket, Diane de Poitiers and Nostradamus) she gathered around her a more varied court than usual. There were Mathieu de Montmorency and his brother, Elzéar de Sabran, Monsieur de Barante and his twenty-three-year-old son Prosper, the Baron de Balk, the poet Chamisso (1), Prince Tuffiakin, Madame Récamier, Schlegel, Miss Randall, and Mr. John Izard Middleton of Middleton Place, South Carolina.

Constant, who was living in Paris at the time with Charlotte, was summoned to attend. He promised to be absent only a fortnight. With justified apprehension Charlotte heard his footsteps echoing along the pavement as he walked to the diligence which would take him to Blois. He remained at Chaumont for seven weeks. The relations between the several members of the Chaumont house-party would, in any other society, have led to complications. Apart from her eternal obsession regarding Constant, Madame de Staël at that time imagined herself in love with young de Barante; the latter was in love with Madame Récamier and so was young Auguste de Staël; Madame Récamier, who was in love with nobody except herself, tried out of sheer mischief to upset the sensitive heart of Schlegel; Chamisso got into disgrace for smoking a pipe in the drawing-room; and Mr. Middleton wandered around perplexed. Amid all these emotional tangles one figure alone remained unperturbed. Miss Fanny Randall had in 1809 been imported from England as governess to Albertine. Madame de Staël had a way of annexing for herself the tutors and governesses whom she engaged for the education of her children. Miss Randall was set down to copy out the manscript of *De l'Allemagne*. She was a sturdy, disapproving spinster with a long face and cropped hair. The members of Madame de Staël's court began by regarding her as a comic and pathetic figure; in the end she became for all of them the one person whom they could invariably trust. It is indeed unfortunate that we do not possess the memoirs of Miss Fanny Randall; devoted, angular, ungainly, she stood there as a rock amid all those clashing waves; when Madame de Staël was in her death agony, it was Fanny Randall's hand for which she groped.

During those summer months at Chaumont Madame de Staël was almost happy. Never had her Court been so diversified or stimulating; never had the emotional tangle around her been so intricate; she had recaptured Benjamin before the eyes of the whole world; she was correcting the proofs of *De l'Allemagne*; she was sufficiently persecuted by Napoleon to be a public martyr, but not so persecuted as to be seriously inconvenienced. It was then, one after another, that the blows began to fall.

Napoleon had heard about her forthcoming book; he had heard about the circle she had gathered round herself at Coppet; he determined to strike and to strike hard. He sent the local prefet, M. de Corbigny, to confiscate *De l'Allemagne*; Madame de Staël handed him the proofs she had been correcting, without disclosing that there existed another copy deposited safely with Maurice O'Donnell in Vienna. When this was discovered, M. de Corbigny was dismissed from his post and died a broken man. Madame de Staël two weeks later received orders either to leave at once for the United States or to return to Coppet and remain there. M. de Barante was also dismissed for negligence and for consorting with his master's enemies. An expulsion order was issued against Wilhelm Schlegel.

THE GOD FROM THE MACHINE

Madame de Staël returned to Coppet in despair. Yet during that winter of 1810 to 1811 her friends were startled to observe that her depression suddenly lightened and gave way to feverish effervescence. She seemed to have recovered all her former vivacity; even her youth. Sismondi was utterly perplexed by this transformation. The banishment of which she had so long complained had now become a grim reality; yet never had they seen her so sociable, so self-pleased, so gay. It was some weeks before the mystery was explained.

Constant had left Chaumont in a mood of irritable depression. He took to gambling again and lost 20,000 francs at the Palais Royal in a single night. He was obliged to sell Les Herbages and part of his library (2). There was nothing any longer to retain him in France or Switzerland. Why not escape with Charlotte to Germany; rebuild his life and finish his life's work, in wholly different surroundings? Yet how could he possibly abandon Madame de Staël at the moment when these fresh disasters had come to overwhelm her?

The problem with which he was faced was indeed humanly insoluble. But fate decreed that at that very moment there should enter a young God, beautiful as Apollo, from the machine.

John Rocca was at that date twenty-three years old. He had served in the Spanish War and returned a wounded hero to Geneva. He was a youth of astonishing beauty, romantic disposition and histrionic habits. Madame de Staël at that date was forty-five years of age; she was very stout, her skin was bad, she had a bulbous nose, and her teeth protruded. Yet she managed to evoke in Rocca the passions of his body and soul; she returned that passion with all the ardour of her nature, and with a new-found tenderness. Rocca was not an intellectual; he was not a conversationalist ("Speech,"

she once remarked, "does not happen to be his language");
but he was a man of distinction, as Byron noticed, and of great
devotion and loyalty. He forced Madame de Staël to marry
him and they had a child. Such was a solution of which Constant, in his wildest moments had never dreamed.

In February 1811 Constant and Charlotte came to Lausanne
in order to make some financial settlement with Juste. In
March Madame de Staël and Rocca arrived. On April 15
Constant had supper with Madame de Staël who treated him
with such affectionate intimacy that Rocca challenged him
to fight. They were to meet at nine o'clock the next morning
at the Pont d'Arve. Constant spent the hours before this duel
drawing up his will and writing a letter to Charlotte. "I love
no one," he wrote, "as deeply as I love her. She has been an
angel to me, my last words, if I die, will be a prayer for
her; my last feeling that of gratitude and love."

Auguste de Staël got wind of the impending duel and informed his mother. She told Rocca that never, in any circumstances, would she permit him to kill Benjamin.

On May 10 Constant said goodbye to Madame de Staël
on the staircase of the Curonne d'Or at Lausanne. Five days
later he and Charlotte left for Germany. He did not return
to Switzerland for thirteen years.

CHAPTER XIII

Madame Récamier

[1814–1815]

Constant and Charlotte go to Hardenberg—He spends two and a half years there and at Göttingen—Madame de Staël introduces him to Bernadotte whom she wants to make Regent of France—Constant writes the *Esprit de Conquête*—Analysis of his argument—Its effect—He rejoins Bernadotte at Liège—His letter to James Mackintosh—He goes to Paris—His successive pamphlets—Madame de Staël arrives in Paris—She has lost all interest in him—He falls in love with Madame Récamier—He suffers acutely from this infatuation—She induces him to take up the case of Murat, King of Naples—Madame de Staël raises the question of the money he owes her—Unseemly wrangle over this —The marriage of Albertine.

1

THEY dawdled through Germany, stopping for weeks at a time in places such as Frankfurt, Heidelberg and Wiesbaden. Constant amused himself by gambling at the casinos. He was annoyed because the Germans insisted upon calling him *Herr Baron*. "This exasperates me," he wrote in his diary, "since it would really be too like Harlequin to debaronize myself in order to become French, and then rebaronize myself in Germany." They reached Schloss Hardenberg on August 18, 1811.

Constant was gratified by the welcome he received from Charlotte's august family; he was touched by the domestic affection which prevailed; above all perhaps he relished the proximity of Schloss Hardenberg to Göttingen, with its magnificent library and hordes of learned men. He settled down to intensive work upon his history of religion. He rose at five in the morning and worked until six at night. "I want," he wrote "to intoxicate myself with work and I am still young enough to remain susceptible to this form of intoxication." In the winter he moved into rooms at Göttingen in order to have more immediate access "to the finest library in Europe." He found that the local professors took "no interest in anyone who has not been dead for two thousand years." In February 1812 he paid a short visit to Brunswick; he went to see his first wife Minna von Cramm, and found her immersed in her menagerie (120 birds, 36 cats, 8 dogs, 2 squirrels and a large number of fish). "What memories!" he wrote. "My first wife —Coppet—France! The scattered débris of a finished past. What about my present condition? What about my future?" It was at Brunswick, on February 19, 1812 that he heard of his father's death. "My blood has turned to ice," he wrote. "My head is in a whirl. My heart sad unto death. My poor father!" (1).

The months lengthened into years. Constant, in the library at Göttingen, was writing and rewriting his history of religion. Sometimes his work went smoothly and he would be content; at other moments lassitude would descend upon him accompanied by doubts of the value of his labour. "Worked badly," we find in his diary, "I do not know what has come over me. I write without thinking. My head seems empty. Does this mean that all is over with me in so far as my talent is concerned? Great God! Great God! what will become of me?" At such moments of self-depreciation he would reread his manuscript of *Adolphe* in order to recover the tautness of his own mind. "Read my novel again," he noted in his diary for January 8, 1812. "How one's impressions fade when situations alter! I could not write it again today."

At such moments also the old passion for excitement would descend upon him in recurrent, angry waves. Charlotte assuredly was "the most boring woman that ever encumbered this earth." "I can only really love," he confessed, "when I am absent, or feel gratitude, or feel pity." The thought of Madame de Staël would recur to stab and poison his restlessness. "So long as she lives," he wrote to Prosper de Barante, "I can never feel lonely. My thoughts join with hers; every page that I write is a letter addressed to her." "From time to time," he wrote again, "at somewhat long intervals, I dream of Madame de Staël. These dreams bring me, and for several hours afterward, a surprising renewal of animation: as when our soldiers at Smolensk or on the Beresina came upon a great bonfire lighted."

At Cassel, in January 1813, he met Narbonne who had just endured the horrors of the retreat from Moscow and been appointed Ambassador in Vienna. They discussed their common memories. Constant was shocked to find that Narbonne, who had played so intimate and courageous a part in the great Napoleonic drama, seemed but mildly interested in the fate of empires:

> There is [he wrote] a certain monotony about this French brilliance and this French elegance; yet always it attracts me. I had this feeling when I met M. de Narbonne the other day at Cassel. The essence of the French intellectual manner is to attach no importance to anything (unless it be to those things which one must never mention, such as one's own health or income). They just glide over all other subjects, merely brushing the surface of everything with a faint smile; this gives them a great momentary superiority over those innocents who still believe that there are some things in life of serious importance.

Madame de Staël, accompanied by Schlegel and Rocca, had by then gone off on another of her continental tours intriguing garrulously in St. Petersburg, Stockholm and London. On December 3, 1812 Napoleon from Molodetchno had issued the 29th Bulletin admitting that "an atrocious calamity" had overwhelmed the Grande Armée. There had followed the German War of Liberation, the victories of Wellington in Spain, the formation of the final Coalition, and in October 1813 the triumph of the Allies in the two days' Battle of Leipzig. "Must I always," lamented Constant in his diary, "remain only a spectator?" (2)

2

He had by then spent two and a half years in Germany mainly in the quiet backwater of the library at Göttingen. "What have you been doing," Madame de Staël wrote to him, "with your precious genius?" It was not reproaches only which she addressed to him; she offered a temptation.

Ever since the early days of the Consulate, Madame de Staël had regarded Bernadotte, by then Crown Prince of Sweden (3), as a possible successor to Bonaparte. During her visit to St. Petersburg in 1812 she had almost persuaded the Tsar to agree that the only alternative to a Bourbon restoration was to choose Bernadotte, if not as Napoleon's immediate successor, then at least as Regent for the King of Rome. On reaching Stockholm she had persuaded Bernadotte to accept Wilhelm Schlegel as his Public Relations Officer and Secret Agent. She now suggested that Constant also should put his services at the disposal of her candidate.

On November 3, 1813, scarcely a week after he heard the news of the Battle of Leipzig, Constant left Göttingen for Hanover, where the Crown Prince of Sweden had temporarily established his headquarters. He realized at once that Bernadotte would have little prospect of commending himself to the French people if he arrived in the wake of the Allied armies of invasion. "The soil is shaky," he confided to the *Journal Intime*, "and were I to build my hut upon it I should be building on sand." Bernadotte seems himself to have shared these hesitations. "I found a man," Constant noted later, "who would have given his soul to become King of France, but who did not dare risking the throne of Sweden."

Nor did Constant receive from those who surrounded Bernadotte that welcome to which he felt himself entitled. "How strange it is," he wrote, "that although they realize I am more intelligent than most people, they prefer most people to me!"

On November 13, 1813 he dined alone with Bernadotte. They had known each other in the old days of the Décadi club. Bernadotte suggested to Constant that his real usefulness would not lie in the military, political or diplomatic field; what he ought to do was to write a pamphlet explaining the inherent moral disease which sapped the admitted efficiency of all military dictatorships. Thus encouraged, Constant returned to Göttingen and within a few days wrote his *Esprit de Conquête*. It was published in Hanover in January 1814, and in London during the following March. A copy was sent to Alexander I and to the leaders of the coalition. Constant, to his surprise and delight, discovered that his voice had echoed across the world.

Into this pamphlet—written in the excitement which followed upon his interview with Bernadotte and the prospect of renewed public activity—he flung with lucid eloquence all his boyhood passion for the principles of true liberty.

Europe, he wrote, had become a vast prison, "deprived of all communication with that noble country, England—the generous asylum of free thought, the illustrious refuge for the dignity of the human race." Politics, he argued, are the art of the possible; when dictators attempt the impossible, and thereby outrage the feelings and the moral conscience of their contemporaries, their success can only be ephemeral; they are left with nothing beyond "the crimes they have committed and the sufferings they have caused." War can only be justified if it be in accord with the spirit of the age; in the modern world, military glory was outdated by a thousand years; with the development of modern means of destruction personal prowess in battle had ceased to be effective and had therefore lost its charm. The whole spirit of the age, which was a commercial spirit, was opposed to war; "War is a savage impulse; commerce a civilized calculation"; thus in the modern world the commercial instinct, which is the instinct of peace, had gained ascendancy over "that narrow and hostile emotion which people deck with the name of patriotism." A ruler, above all a usurper, who in the modern world committed his people to an aggressive war was guilty of "a gross and fatal anachronism." Moreover war in the nineteenth century had lost all its old idealism; it had become spoliation; it created a military caste, who were by nature reactionary, contemptuous of the masses, and impatient of the slowness of the democratic method. Militarism must by its very nature remain bellicose; a usurper whose power is founded upon his army can in no circumstances become pacific. He is bound, moreover, to corrupt his own people by telling them lies; he cannot say to them, "Follow me and we shall conquer the world"; they would only reply to him "But we have no desire whatsoever to conquer the world." He is bound therefore to talk to them about "national security," "national honour," or the "need of creating defensive zones." If the people believe these lies, then disaster follows; if they see through these lies, then they themselves lose the habits of veracity. All the vices of the police-state—spies, delation, domiciliary visits, censorship and the disruption of family

MADAME RÉCAMIER IN HER OLD AGE

life—follow inevitably. Moreover these totalitarian systems are not content with conquering other nations, they insist upon imposing upon them their own institutions and ideas. This in its turn leads to a passion for uniformity, which acquires the certitudes and the blindness of "a religious dogma." The system imposed may be in theory better than that which it replaces; but in practice it severs, and therefore outrages, the traditional habits of the conquered nation. Uniformity is in itself an evil: "Variety is an organism; uniformity a mechanism; variety is life; uniformity is death."

The pamphlet ends with a fine rhetorical denunciation of all militarist systems, of all usurpers, and with one resounding appeal to Napoleon: "Man of another world, cease robbing the world of its inheritance!"

It is not surprising that this tremendous denunciation, this lucid statement of first principles, should have produced, at that moment, a profound and wide effect.

3

Had Constant possessed the patience, or even the prudence, to rest upon the laurels he had won by his *Esprit de Conquête;* had he had the sense to remain in Germany until the conclusion of the first Peace of Paris; then he could have returned to France with the reputation of a distinguished victim of Bonapartism, of a man of outstanding political acumen and probity. Had he realized that neither he nor Madame de Staël had any knowledge of internal conditions in France, or of the then state of French public opinion, had he abided even by his early doubts regarding Bernadotte; then he could have slipped easily into the pattern of Restoration politics. His old gambling habits had trained him to attach exaggerated importance to hazard, and to see the finger of destiny in some chance encounter or some momentary opportunity. He was inclined also (as conceited and impatient people are inclined) to prefer the short cuts of politics; to imagine that success can better be achieved by quick admission into the inner councils of a minority, than through the laborious plodding and competition entailed upon a member of a large political group. He thus came to stake everything upon a rapid succession of off-chances; and he thereby forfeited the esteem of his contemporaries and the reputation for sound and consistent judgment which is an essential condition of parliamentary success.

In February 1814, he paid a second visit to Bernadotte, this time at Bückeburg in Schaumburg-Lippe. The Crown Prince decorated him with the order of the Polar Star; he returned to Göttingen much pleased by his reception. The allied armies by that date were approaching Paris. Constant began to fear that he might be too late. "I am tortured," he confessed to his diary, "by this missed opportunity. I am tortured by indecision." Unable to bear it any longer, he left Göttingen and travelled to Liège to attach himself once again to Bernadotte. His arrival was not welcomed. In a fever of agitation he sent to Madame de Staël, who was then in London, a memorandum which he asked her to transmit to the British Government. She replied with spirit:

> I have read your memorandum. God save me from showing it to anyone! I shall do nothing against France. I shall not use against her, now that she is in adversity, either the fame I owe her or the name of my father whom she loved. Her ruined villages lie on that same road on which the women threw themselves upon their knees to see him pass.
>
> Benjamin, you are not a Frenchman! You are not attached to these places by all the memories of childhood. That is the difference between you and me. Would you really like to see the Cossacks in the Rue Racine?

Somewhat chilled by this communication, he hung on miserably at Liège. While there he received a letter from his old Edinburgh friend James Mackintosh. His reply to this letter is worth reproducing, since it illustrates, not merely his adept handling of the English language, but also the qualms of conscience, the doubts and hesitations, by which he was then assailed:

Liège, March 27, 1814.
Your letter found me no longer at Hanover, but at the head quarters of the Prince of Sweden, where I thought it my duty to repair as soon as he entered France. However averse I am in general to any steps which seem to co-operate with foreign forces against French independence, every consideration must yield, in my opinion, to the necessity of overturning the most systemical and baneful tyranny, that ever weighed, with iron weight, on mankind. My last publication, a copy of which I hope you have received, has already explained to you, I suppose, what are my notions on modern patriotism. It cannot, like that of the ancients, be irrevocably confined within the narrow bounds of a particular territory. Liberty, religious feelings, humanity, are the general property of our species; and when the government of a nation attempts to rob the world of all that ought to be dear to every inhabitant of the world —when it tramples on every idea, every hope, every virtue—that nation, as long as it consents to be the tool of that government, is no longer composed of fellow-citizens, but of enemies that must be vanquished, or madmen that must be chained. . . .

Bonaparte draws into his nets those numerous honest men, who wish for the benefit of becoming rogues without publicly changing their colours, and encourages by his protection all the rogues that find it convenient to call themselves honest men. He teaches degradation to the people and tyranny to the men in power; he poisons everything that was pure, levels everything that was high, and makes of this miserable earth a sea of mud and blood, where the huge monster delights to prance and strut, surrounded with the subordinate monsters he has created and instructed. He must fall before we can think of anything else; he must fall, that we may have time to think of anything else. I am sometimes vexed, but never frightened, at the attempts other governments, even while they struggle against him, are making to establish their own despotism. Let us pull down the master, and easy will it be to check those awkward apprentices.

I perceive that I have launched into a long exposition of my political creed; but as I know this creed is not entirely yours, I could not resist the desire of justifying my line of conduct in your opinion, which is to me of so great value.

Alas! All the friends of my youth disappear; and Scotland, if ever I see it again, will present me with nothing but funeral stones.

I have often boasted of our friendship, when your literary and political eminence were my only mode of communicating with you, unknown to yourself, and when I had but very faint hopes of your remembering me. You may, therefore, well believe that the renewal of that friendship has been one of the greatst pleasures I have ever experienced.

Your old and ever,
Devoted and attached friend,
B. Constant.

On March 31 the Allies entered Paris; on April 2 the Senate proclaimed the dethronement of Napoleon; on April 6 Napoleon signed his abdication at Fontainebleau; on April 13 Bernadotte appeared in Paris and established himself in the Hôtel Marbeuf, in the Rue d'Anjou-Saint-Honoré. Realizing that the Allies had decided on the restoration of the Bourbons, fearing that if he gambled for higher stakes he might lose his Swedish crown, Bernadotte returned almost immediately to Stockholm. Constant, who reached the Hôtel Vauban on April 15, was conscious that once again he had put his money on a non-starter. The *Journal des Débats* had mentioned him as "the personal private secretary of the Crown Prince of Sweden." He issued an immediate denial. "It is difficult," he remarked, "to repair one's situation once one has ruined it." But he did his best.

Already, from Liège, he had written a most polite letter to Talleyrand:

> I cannot resist thanking you for having at one stroke disposed of the tyrant and laid the foundations of Liberty. . . . It is agreeable to express one's admiration for a man who is at once the saviour of France and the most charming of Frenchmen.

On April 21 he was granted an interview with Talleyrand at his house in the Rue Saint Florentin. "Not so bad," he noted in his diary. At the same time he paid other adulatory visits to old and influential acquaintances:

> My natural shyness makes me exaggerate the falsity of my own position. . . . What a fantastic imagination I have! Always I am convinced that people want to cold-shoulder me!

He was right, none the less, in concluding that there existed a certain prejudice against him. His Swiss and Protestant origins, the far-flung scandal of his private life, his overt and avowed admiration for English institutions, were not likely to render him acceptable in royalist and clerical circles. His fatuous and impulsive experiment with Bernadotte, the fact that he had returned to France in the wake of the invading armies, would not render him a popular figure or one whom the centre groups would regard as trustworthy. He had never been good at mixing with those (and they were many) whom he regarded as his intellectual inferiors: he was too proud to conciliate, too sensitive to fight:

> The thorns [he had written to Rosalie only a few weeks before] The thorns which encompass one in one's relations with one's fellow men are the same, whether one's sphere of activity be large or small. I cannot abide thorns. I only like addressing my fellow men from a distance, and on the subject of their general interests. There is a morbid spot at the base of my soul which is rendered septic—and most painful—by political and social squabbles. I can only find repose in work, and in the total separation of my own interests from those of others.

He decided therefore that, for the moment at least, he would be wise to eschew active politics and to assign to himself the mission of "teaching France the nature of representative institutions." He thus embarked upon a series of topical pamphlets, the incisiveness of which rendered him before long the acknowledged "king of the pamphleteers."

On April 21, immediately after his arrival in Paris, he wrote for the *Journal des Débats* a long article in which he expounded the doctrine of the neutrality of the Crown—the doctrine upon which any conception of constitutional monarchy must be based. He followed this up on May 24 with a pamphlet entitled *Reflections on Constitutions and the Necessary Guarantees*. In this he contended that the essential elements of any constitutional monarchy were the responsibility of ministers, the neutrality of the crown, a hereditary peerage, an unpaid representative legislature, trial by jury, religious tolerance and freedom of the Press. Any constitution or "Charter" upon which the Bourbon restoration would be based must embody these principles. At the same time the Constitution should be sufficiently flexible to leave room for subsequent expansion. Constant hoped by this pamphlet to convince the royalists that the grant of a constitution would not imply an outrage to the monarchical principle, and to persuade the republicans that it was possible, on the English model, to combine full individual liberty with all the advantages of an hereditary throne.

The Censor objected to this pamphlet, on the ground that if Louis XVIII decided to grant a Charter, then no criticism should be made against it; if he refused to grant a Charter, then nothing must be published in its favour. This led Constant to publish two further pamphlets, the first on *The Freedom of Pamphlets and Newspapers*, the second *Observations on the Speech of the Minister of the Interior*. In these two pamphlets he expounded the view that a people could not be free if men appointed by the Government had the right to limit the expression of free thought. These pamphlets did not please either the right, the centre, or the left; but they did provoke wide discussion; and they did convince men of all parties that Benjamin Constant, at least as a publicist, was not a man who could be ignored.

It was at this moment, on May 2, 1814, that Madame de Staël arrived in Paris and established herself, at first at Clichy, and thereafter in the Hôtel de Lamoignon. She had by then forgotten all about Bernadotte and was "all for the Bourbons." Her known friendship with the Tsar of Russia, her known influence with parliamentary leaders in London, the highly-advertised drama of her long battle with Bonaparte, the purity of her political principles, the great services she had rendered under the Terror—all these combined to give her, during those months of the first Bourbon restoration, a position of unique influence. "There are three Powers," it was said, "in Europe today—Russia, England and Madame de Staël."

Of what immense assistance could she have been to Constant at that moment, if only the old affection, the old confidence, the old creative admiration, could have been maintained! Unfortunately Madame de Staël by then had lost her sense of possession; he was no more to her than a once trusted slave who had succeeded, and in the eyes of the whole world, in making good his escape.

He went to visit her on May 13:

> She is much changed, being thin and pale. I did not allow myself to show any emotion. What would have been the good? Albertine is delightful; as amusing as can be—adorable. It is her whom I regret. I should like to spend the rest of my life in her company.

On May 18 he dined at the Hôtel de Lamoignon and a few days later he read to her the deplorable burlesque poem which he had composed under the title *The Siege of Soissons* (4). It was not a success:

> She has changed from head to foot. She is absent-minded, almost arid, thinking only of herself, hardly listening to what other people say. She seems attached to nothing—even to her daughter only from a sense of duty . . . to me not in the least . . . I read her my poem. It is obvious that she no longer cares for me, since she hardly praised it at all. She only praises what is part of herself—as for instance the man whom she is now keeping.
>
> Seeing her again has lifted a great weight from my life. There can no longer be any doubt about my own future, since there is no vestige in her of any affection for me. Linon (Charlotte) is worth more than she is. Why, oh why, doesn't she come?

Henceforward, he would have to make his own way in a difficult and censorious world.

4

In Constant's *Journal Intime* for August 19, 1814 there occurs an ominous entry:

> Dined with the Suards. My pamphlets are prodigiously praised. I must be on my guard against the vengeance which all this will provoke. But what gets me down, is to have nobody here whom I love. I miss my wife. Really life is becoming too dry.

Twelve days later occurs another entry:

> August 31. Dined at the club. Madame Récamier: my word! Am I going off my head?

Of all Constant's recurrent cerebral passions, his infatuation for Madame Récamier is perhaps the most difficult to explain. He was forty-six years of age at that date and she was thirty-seven. Admittedly, she was one of the most beautiful and ageless women that ever lived. She had a perfect profile, her little head was set as a tulip upon a lovely neck,

MADAME RÉCAMIER

her complexion was unsullied, her grace incomparable, she was able with great skill to hide the ugliness of her feet and hands, she had a faint moustache, and when she raised the curtain of her heavy eyelids the whole world became an April morning and the meadows sparkled with a virgin dew. Admittedly, also, Constant at the moment was in a state of excitation —absent from Charlotte, rebuffed by Madame de Staël, and yearning to find some intimate affection wherewith to solace the self-distrust aroused by the enmity with which he believed himself to be encompassed. What is so strange is that, although he had for years known Madame Récamier intimately, although he had spent months in her company—whether at Coppet, at Chaumont or elsewhere—he had never until that August of 1814 paid any attention to her whatsoever.

He had in fact regarded her hitherto as an empty, bloodless and inhuman flirt. "Madame Récamier," he had written to Prosper de Barante on April 15, 1807, "is ageless. Not a wrinkle, not an idea the more, since I last saw her." "Madame Récamier," he had informed the same correspondent in 1810, "is here—bored with life, light as a ship without ballast . . . either repelling advances regretfully, or resigning herself to them discreetly. She enjoys, neither the repose of virtue, nor the delight of transgression."

Yet there can be no doubt at all that during that summer and winter of 1814 he fell in love with her as desperately as any school-boy.

He had no illusions regarding her abysmal silliness. As he poured out to her the agonies of his distracted heart, her attention would wander, and her lovely eyes would follow the movements of a fly buzzing round the room. "She is a linnet," he complains, "a cloud, without memory, or preferences or discernment. . . . What a childish obsession for a man such as I am! But her claws are fixed, deep in my heart."

He was well aware that by this infatuation he was exposing

himself to ridicule and damaging all prospects of a serious career:

It is absurd, with the political position I now hold in the world, to allow myself to be devoured by a love-affair as if I were a boy of eighteen! . . . My reputation is immense:—how deplorable that this cursed and hopeless passion should render me incapable of deriving any profit from my opportunities!

He was conscious even that this infatuation was a poor reward for all Charlotte's constancy and devotion. Again and again he made firm resolutions; he begged Charlotte to leave Germany and come to Paris; he would himself leave Paris on December 1 and go to Göttingen; he would resume his book on religions; he would tell Charlotte the whole aching truth; he would invest his money in English five per cents; he would obtain the Legion of Honour; he would not return to France until the beginning of March. Yet always the tug of his unsatisfied passion brought him back:

Convulsions of agony! [he noted for September 7] tears—what a curse my temperament is to me! How peaceful it all was at Göttingen! Linon, Linon—oh my God! . . . I have only one thought [he wrote to Madame Récamier] and that is YOU. Politics, society —all gone. I may seem mad to you, but I see your eyes, I repeat your words, I see that school-girl expression of yours which combines so much grace with such deep subtlety—I have every reason to be mad—I should be mad not to be mad—to love is to suffer, but it is also to live; it is so long since I was alive, perhaps I have never lived as intensely as now. I [he writes to her again] who cannot watch you pulling off a glove without all my senses turning upside down within me—and yet who dare not touch your hand if one glance from you reproves me. Be my guide [he begs her]. Take possession of my faculties; profit by my devotion to you to benefit your country and to enhance my fame. Be my guardian angel, my good genius, the God who will restore order to the chaos in my head and heart . . . Give me back that moral sense which you say I lack. . . . I am like a child in your hands. Give me back the virtues which I was born to possess!

Madame Récamier was not at all a safe guide in that world of clashing suspicions and fluctuating loyalties; her political principles were based entirely upon her personal relationships. When at Naples during the winter of 1813–1814 she had been lavishly entertained by Joachim Murat and his consort; she thought it would be an excellent thing if Benjamin Constant, with his facile pen, could be turned on to draft for the Congress of Vienna a memorandum expounding Murat's services and asserting his right to retain the throne of Naples. Constant sat down and wrote a paper, the main purport of which was that, although Murat had no shadow of right to his throne, he might cause a great deal of trouble if he were deprived of it. Murat was so pleased with this somewhat negative defence, that he offered Constant the order of the Two Sicilies, one thousand louis in cash, and a secret mission to Vienna. Constant was attracted by this proposal.

> Apart from my absurd and lamentable passion (which does not diminish and which deprives me of all capacity for work or business) there are other good reasons why I should get away from Paris. My position here is not a good one—lack of money—my wife—the hatred of the aristocratic classes against me—my foreign origin—everything renders a new start necessary. Destiny impels me—let's chance it [*Vogue la galère*]!

He asked the Neapolitan Government to be given an official diplomatic position; they refused. In a fit of pique, and owing also to his complete inability to tear himself away from Madame Récamier, he refused to go to Vienna in a merely clandestine capacity. He returned to Murat's representative in Paris the one thousand louis which he had been given. All that was childish and honourable. Yet the Murat episode did not increase his reputation for political sobriety; and at the same time it aroused against him the hostility, not so much of Louis XVIII himself (who was always amused by human volatility) as of the whole Bourbon clique.

5

Meanwhile Madame de Staël, dominating the precarious and apprehensive world of the first Restoration from her salon in the Hôtel de Lamoignon, had heard with extreme displeasure of this lamentable infatuation. Madame Récamier had been her closest, in fact her only, woman friend; Constant was known throughout the old and even the new world as one of the most gifted and subservient of her many satellites. It was intolerable that these two should combine together in defiance of an authority which, even if she did not desire to exercise it, must still not be ignored.

Her strident virile voice echoed across her crowded drawing-rooms, heaping ridicule upon Constant, holding up to public obliquy this ungainly passion which had suddenly seized upon a man of his mature age. Constant was hurt and disturbed by this campaign of vituperation. On November 8, 1814 we find him writing most ingenuously to Rosalie:

> I am somewhat annoyed with Madame de Staël. I cannot speak to a soul in Paris without her spreading a rumour that I am in love. At my age such a thing would be ridiculous; in my position it would be shocking.

To his diary he expressed himself in less measured terms: "Madame de Staël is a serpent of ferocious vanity; fundamentally she loathes me as much as I detest her. I must protect my money against the claws of that ferocious harpy."

This last sentence refers to the renewed financial altercation which had arisen between them, and which, in the year that followed was to swell to gigantic proportions. It will be remembered that on March 21, 1810 they had signed an agreement together under which Constant had undertaken that after his death his debt of 80,000 francs, with accumulated interest, would be repaid to Madame de Staël or her heirs. In the interval several things had happened. The large amount of capital which Necker, and thereafter Madame de Staël herself, had invested in landed property in Pennsylvania could not by any means be turned into liquid cash. Madame de Staël had placed large sums in Italy which were also frozen. She thus found great difficulty in providing a dowry for her daughter Albertine, who was all but engaged to the young, the gifted, and the high-principled Duc de Broglie. Madame de Staël therefore invited Benjamin Constant to contribute a sum of 40,000 francs (that is one half of the sum which he had borrowed from her father and herself) to swell the dowry of Albertine and thereby enable her to marry. It appears that when she mentioned the matter personally to him early in 1815 he indicated that he would be only too glad to do anything within his power to assist his beloved Albertine. Thereafter, it seems, he changed his mind.

On the return of Napoleon to Paris, Madame de Staël had made her way hastily to Coppet. She wrote to Constant in May 1815 asking him to redeem his promise since this matter of Albertine's dowry was becoming urgent. He replied that he was no longer in the position to dispose of so large a sum. Madame de Staël then wrote to him threatening legal proceedings; it might be that it would be difficult to prove in a law-court that he had ever promised to repay this money; but at least the transactions which would then be publicly disclosed would redound more to his discredit than to hers:

> What sort of man are you [she wrote] to refuse to help my daughter? What sort of a man can you be, in trying to do as much harm to the child as you have already done to the mother? What a man! Imagination shudders in horror at such a prospect! The

whole world will judge your conduct even as I do. The remembrance of your past life will rise before you and make you tremble. However, all is now over between you and me; between you and Albertine; between you and all men of decent feeling. In future I shall only address you through my lawyers and in my duty as my daughter's guardian. Adieu.

It seems that Constant replied to this threat of legal proceedings, by suggesting that, if it came to open court, her own letters to him would not make pleasant reading. This produced a further outburst:

> I did not mean to write to you again on this horrible subject, but the letters that my son brought with him require a final reply. You threaten me with *my letters!* This last stroke is worthy of you! I repeat it—worthy of you! To threaten a woman with her private letters—letters which may compromise her and her children—so as to avoid repaying the money you owe her—that is an action worthy only of the Marquis de Sade. . . . Your malignity robs you even of your intelligence. . . . Take care! You have exploited your talents too far; they will no longer save you from your own character; the latter is too well known by now. . . . It is not a question of legal rights; you know the truth as well as I do. But what you do not know is that all the unhappiness which I owe to you, the horror with which I recollect my youth which was completely ruined by your frightful temper, have given me a strength of will which will enable me to carry through, even if it lasts for twenty years, the law suit which I now intend to bring against you.

This last letter was dated June 12, 1815. Six days later Napoleon was finally overthrown at Waterloo and the second Restoration followed. Louis XVIII repaid to Madame de Staël the two millions which her father had lent to the Treasury; Albertine's dowry was richly ensured; she married the Duc de Broglie and lived happily ever after (6).

But Constant, during the course of this squalid financial wrangle, had been distracted by events of even greater importance.

CHAPTER XIV

The Hundred Days

[1815]

Napoleon returns from Elba—Constant publishes an article in the *Journal des Débats* attacking Napoleon and asserting that he will die rather than abandon the Bourbon cause—On Napoleon's entry into Paris he escapes to Angers and then returns—He assists Napoleon to draft the *Acte Additionnel* to the Imperial Constitution—His justification of this apostasy as contained in his *Memoirs of the Hundred Days*—His mixed motives—His conversation with Napoleon—He is appointed a Councillor of State—His transference of loyalty exposes him to general obloquy—The *Acte Additionnel* and Constant's constitutional theories—The Battle of Waterloo—Interview with Napoleon on his return—the Mission to Hagenau—Constant makes his peace with Louis XVIII—Baroness von Krüdener—He leaves Paris for Belgium and England—His visit to London—Publication of *Adolphe*—His return to Paris.

1

ON MARCH 5, 1815 the news reached Paris that Napoleon, evading the vigilance of Sir Neil Campbell and the English frigates, had landed in the Golfe Juan. Constant's numb zeal for the Bourbons had been fanned into life by his infatuation for Madame Récamier, whose royalism was ecstatic but vague. To win her insipid approval he sent to the *Journal de Paris* a flaming denunciation of the usurper:

> He promises peace: but his very name is a signal for war. He promises victory: yet three times—in Egypt, Spain and Russia—he deserted his armies like a coward.

On March 10th it was learnt that Napoleon was advancing rapidly northwards and almost unopposed; the cities of Grenoble and Lyons had welcomed him with open gates:

> This collapse [Constant noted in his diary] is deplorable. My article which will appear in the *Journal de Paris* tomorrow will expose my life to danger. If one has got to die, one had better die decently. *Vogue la galère*. Everything is uncertain except for the certainty that everything is lost.

By March 17 Napoleon had reached Auxerre. Madame de Staël hurriedly left the Hôtel de Lamoignon, and already her travelling carriage was threading its cumbrous way through the by-roads which led to Switzerland. Constant urged Madame Récamier to escape with him to Germany; with langorous idiocy she replied that this was the moment to prove himself a man.

Constant was a very brave man. His contempt for life rendered fascinating for him the prospect of death. He returned to his room in the Rue Neuve de Berry and within a single excited, impulsive hour he wrote the famous article for the *Journal des Débats*:

> The representatives of the Nation have laid before the throne their devotion and their gratitude. They have assured the King of the admiration felt by the French people for his royal courage; they have expressed the universal desire to see associated with the destinies of the country those men who for the past twenty-five years have fought for the independence, the glory and the liberties of France. It is this sound association which can alone unite all opinions, wipe out the last traces of dissension and give to constitutional monarchy its only possible support: the support of those who in 1789 strove to establish liberty *under* the monarchy, and who in 1815 sought to consolidate liberty *by* the monarchy.
>
> Those who desire only to become the servants of a despot can readily transfer their services from one system to another, confident that under a new despotism they can again assume their func-

tions of obedient tools. But those who love liberty, will prefer to die upon the steps of a throne by which that liberty is safeguarded and assured.

Constant then proceeds (after a deft comparison between Napoleon, Attila and Jenghiz Khan) to define his own attitude and intentions:

> I assert today, and without fear of being misunderstood, that I have always fought for liberty, in its many varied forms. I saw that liberty could be achieved under the monarchy; I saw the King ally himself with his people.
> I am not the man to crawl, a wretched deserter [*misérable transfuge*], from one seat of power to another. I am not the man to veil infamy in sophisms, or to mumble profane words wherewith to purchase a life of which I should feel ashamed.

Here was an outright defiance, a courageous affirmation of liberal principles and personal integrity. "Never," wrote the Duc de Broglie, "Never since the days of Tacitus or Juvenal has tyranny been thus exposed to public obloquy." On March 19 Benjamin Constant had thus proclaimed to the world that he would die for the Bourbons rather than desert to the modern Jenghis Khan; four weeks later he was closeted with Napoleon, drafting with him the *Additional Act* to be appended to the Imperial Constitution, soliciting by every means in his power the appointment and the resplendent uniform of a Councillor of State. So sudden an apostasy requires some explanation.

In his *Memoirs on the Hundred Days*, which he published in 1819, Constant sought, after the event, to justify himself against the criticisms which had been made. His argument is plausible.

His decision, he contended, had not been made upon some momentary impulse, still less had it been influenced by any desire for self-advancement: it was the result of "prolonged reflection." Up to the night of March 19 he had been willing to die for constitutional monarchy; that very day, in fact, he had expressed this willingness in an article published in the *Journal des Débats*. Yet on the morning of March 20 he woke to find that the constitutional monarch had disappeared. Only France remained.

He had regretted the return from Elba and had said so at the time; it had caused him pain. It was "not without distress," "not without misgiving," that he had abjured his opposition to Bonaparte which had become for him a settled habit of mind. Yet who but Napoleon could at that time have driven the foreign invader from the sacred soil of France? And if, after all that had happened, the Bourbons were to return a second time, was there not a danger that they would in revenge have plunged France into all the horrors of a White Terror?

There was no prospect at all, after so triumphant a homecoming, of "despoiling Napoleon of his despotism." The only hope was to persuade him to renounce it, to persuade him that a constitutional system would now be to his advantage. If Napoleon were sincerely converted to liberal principles, then surely he should have received the support of all men of good will. If he were not sincerely converted, then it would be possible to turn against him those very liberal institutions which he had been forced to establish. How could it be suggested that he, Benjamin Constant—who had consistently opposed Napoleon when he was at the summit of his power—could for motives of self-interest have joined him at the moment when he was encompassed by enemies on every side? No—his every action had been dictated by his desire to save France from foreign invasion and from civil war; his only purpose had been to canalize within constitutional barriers the tremendous force and energies which the personality and name of Napoleon could still generate. He had not been working in the interests of Benjamin Constant: he had been working solely in the interests of France.

It is easy to dismiss this defence as a piece of special pleading and to conclude that Constant, in his apostasy, was guided solely by personal motives. Were this the whole truth, then this biography would not have been worth the labour; Constant would be reduced to the level of an ordinary opportunist, who had not the knowledge or the intelligence correctly to forecast the probabilities of the time. It is true that, but for his infatuation for Madame Récamier, he might have hesitated to proclaim with such reckless ardour his devotion to the Bourbons or to risk the vengeance of Napoleon when they had gone. It is true that the overtures thereafter made to him by the Bonapartists flattered his vanity, offered a short cut to eminence and aroused within him the gambler's instinct to play on off-chances for high stakes. But it is also true that his faith in the principles of liberalism, his belief that only through a constitutional monarchy could the wounds of France be healed, was something more than a political or incidental theory; it was perhaps the only conviction to which he consistently adhered, a conviction for which (with damage to himself and benefit to the political education of his contemporaries) he sacrificed what might have become a great parliamentary career. If we regard Constant as an ordinary opportunist, we miss the whole interest of his story; the originality of Constant lies in the fact that he was one of the most extraordinary opportunists that has ever lived. He is not, as Charles du Bos has so trenchantly explained, comparable to other men.

The chain of circumstance in which he at this stage became involved was a regrettable concatenation; his *Memoirs of the Hundred Days* furnish us, as has been said, with an ingenuous explanation; it is necessary to examine the chain as it was forged link by link during those breathless days.

2

The article in which Constant had asserted that he would rather die than join Napoleon appeared in the *Journal des Débats* on the evening of March 19, 1815. At midnight on that same date Louis XVIII shuffled in his felt slippers along the corridors of the Tuileries and down the staircase of the Pavillon de Flore; in wet and blustering darkness he drove away to Ghent. At 9 P.M. the next night, Napoleon, escorted by Polish Hussars with torches flaming, galloped into Paris; he was carried in triumph up the grand staircase of the palace; it was noticed that he seemed exhausted and that the smile on his lips was an uncertain smile.

> My *Débats* article [wrote Constant in his journal] seems to have come out on an unfortunate day. Everybody has collapsed; nobody dreams of putting up a fight.

He knew that he had exposed himself to considerable danger. Yet it was exhilarating to feel that, at such a moment, he had had the courage to defend a cause which Madame Récamier cherished in her little heart:

> In the name of heaven [he had written to her three days previously] force yourself during the next few days to conceal your aversion from me! I need to keep my head. I have risked it for the cause you love. I have defied Bonaparte (and make no mistake he will be here in Paris at any moment) and I have attacked him in every way. I shall remain on, in order to prove to you that I have something within me which is noble and courageous. . . . Other men may be able to make their peace with Bonaparte; I alone, if I fall into his hands, shall perish.

THE HUNDRED DAYS

When Louis XVIII had bolted and Napoleon had clattered into Paris, Constant took it for granted that he could expect no mercy from the man whom he had compared to Attila and accused of military cowardice. He left his rooms in the Rue de Berry and took refuge with the United States Minister, Mr. Crawford. On April 23, accompanied by the American consular official, he passed through the barriers of Paris, hoping to join Prosper de Barante at Nantes. At Ancenis he heard that Nantes also had gone over to the Bonapartists and that the mob had broken the windows of the prefecture. For three days he remained in hiding at Angers. The news then reached him from a friend in Paris that Napoleon was about to proclaim a general amnesty; his own name was not on the short list of exceptions. To remain absent from Madame Récamier—from the intoxication of her seductive prudery—was more than he could bear. Risking everything—his life, his honour, and his reputation—he turned his carriage northwards. At five in the morning of March 27 he arrived at Sèvres, three miles from Paris, and remained there all day in torturing uncertainty. As darkness fell, and the distant lights began to twinkle in the great city, he came to his decision. That night he crept back to Paris. His friends were astounded at his audacity; they were even more startled by what followed.

The next morning, March 28, he visited General Sebastiani (1), who also had openly proclaimed his loyalty to the Bourbons, who also had openly deserted to Napoleon once the latter reached Auxerre. He handed him a letter which could be shown to the authorities; this letter has not been preserved; we can only assume that it expressed contrition for past statements and a lively assurance that he was willing to place his services at the disposal of the Bonapartists. An interview was arranged with Fouché (2), and two days later Constant was charmingly received by Joseph Bonaparte at the Palais Royal.

The latter assured him that his brother, the Emperor, was now fully convinced that in future he must govern by constitutional and not by despotic methods; that he had need of known liberals, such as Constant, to guide his unskilled footsteps along that delicate path:

> Sadness and personal anxiety [is the entry in Constant's diary for March 29] Sebastiani—then safety, hopes. He says my affair is settled. *Vogue la galère.*

Immediately he sat down to write a new pamphlet, which, with his curious affection for cumbrous titles, he called *Political Principles applicable to all Representative Governments and especially to the New Constitution of France.*

On April 13 he received a message to the effect that the Emperor would be pleased to grant him an audience the next morning at the palace of the Tuileries.

In his *Memoirs of the Hundred Days* Constant was at some pains to explain why he accepted this invitation; he was particularly concerned to reply to two of the many criticisms which had been made against him, namely that he was taken in by Napoleon and that he was terrified for his life:

> I did not for one moment believe in the sudden conversion of a man who for so long had exercised so absolute an authority. The habits of despotism are not readily discarded. Nor was I afraid of any persecution; it was made clear to me that the enemies of Bonaparte had for the moment nothing to fear.
>
> It was of my own free will that I accepted the invitation. I wanted to find out for myself what we could still hope for, whether his bitter experiences had in any manner altered his mind. However uncertain may be the prospects of freedom for a people, no man is justified in rejecting such prospects. If I could succeed in inducing him to adopt a single sound principle, to abate one single item of his former arbitrary methods, then the advantage would be one which would accrue to France.

Napoleon, according to this account, spoke to him with engaging frankness:

> I want peace [he said] and I shall only get it by victories. I do not want to give you any false hopes. I allow it to be said that peace negotiations are in progress, but in fact there are no negotiations at all. I need the support of the nation; in return, the nation will ask for liberty; she shall have it. Circumstances have changed. One is not the same man at forty-five that one was at thirty. The repose of a constitutional monarch might suit me quite well; it would even more certainly suit my son.

A more convincing account of the excitements and hesitations, of the many mixed motives, of those eight days is provided by the pages of the *Journal Intime*. Constant had been charged with the task of drawing up an *Additional Act* intended to liberalize the old Imperial Constitution. His day to day record runs as follows:

> *April 14.* Interview with the Emperor: long conversation: he is an astounding man. Tomorrow I am to bring him a draft Constitution. Am I at last going to be a success in life? Ought I to wish for this success? The future is dark. Let God's will be done. Dined with Juliette (Madame Récamier) at the Duchess of Ragusa's.
>
> *April 15.* Second interview. My draft Constitution not much of a success; it is not liberty exactly that he wants. I shall have tomorrow to take a definite line. There is another job he wants me to do which I find distasteful. (Napoleon had asked Constant to draw up a reply to Lord Castlereagh's statement in the House of Commons to the effect that he had owed his return, not to popular support, but only to the army.) I dine with Juliette and go to a reception at the Rovigos'.
>
> *April 17.* Worked hard. I shall bring him the revised draft tomorrow. Rumours that I am to be appointed a Councillor of State. Any chance of that? Evening with Juliette. This futile love affair makes me waste my time.

April 18. Two hours with the Emperor. My revised draft goes better, I am to bring it back tomorrow. My meetings with the Emperor have leaked out in the newspapers. I come in for a good deal of abuse, but I am doing some good, and in any case I want to change my circumstances. Dine with M. Récamier: Juliette isn't there.

April 19. A long interview with the Emperor. He adopts many of my constitutional ideas; we talk about other subjects; he evidently enjoys my conversation. My appointment as Councillor of State is announced. In the evening I read my novel aloud; they all burst into wild laughter. (3) Dine with Juliette. Spend the evening with Fouché. If my appointment is confirmed, then I am in it up to the neck.

April 20. My appointment signed. I have taken the leap. I am right in it now. . . . I must give up gambling and making love; the thing is decided, and I must profit by the decision.

April 21. Meeting with the heads of sections; I thoroughly enjoy official work; I am good at discussing business. . . . With the Emperor till seven. Spend the evening with Juliette—but I must break off this affair and play my own hand.

April 22. Meeting of the Council of State. If they don't alter the Constitution it will be a good one—but! ! ! ! Meeting with the Emperor. The final draft. They have spoilt a good deal of it of course, and there will be criticism; but it doesn't matter—the die is cast—and my own fate along with it.

3

The apostasy of Benjamin Constant brought down upon him, as was to be expected, the fury of the Bourbon party and the objurgations of the royalist press. M. de Sévery wrote a gay and damaging little song, to the tune of *V'là ce que c'est que d'aller aux bois* with the refrain *V'là ce que c'est que d'être constant.* His friends and family were appalled. Madame Récamier was too linnet-brained to realize exactly what had occurred; from Madame de Staël at Coppet (4) he received a scorching note: "I shall say nothing about politics; it is not my way to 'mumble profane words.'"

> He had no conviction whatever [wrote Prosper Barante] he did not believe in the Emperor's assumed liberal sentiments, he did not believe in his own success. Recklessly—at moments gaily—he was playing a game of chance.

Sismondi alone strove to defend him, Sismondi and his devoted cousin Rosalie:

> Please [she wrote to her brother] do not mention Benjamin, unless you have something to tell me. It is not my habit to abandon my friends when they suffer misfortunes or commit mistakes. The lady of Coppet has already done him sufficient harm by spreading stories against him; especially as she will certainly use him to pull her own chestnuts out of the fire.
>
> I have written nothing to Benjamin [she added a week later] except to express my lamentation and distress. I am rendered wretched at his having missed the opportunity of a great career and by the misfortunes which now menace him. His weakness of character transforms into a curse the gifts with which nature has endowed him; his very genius gives prominence to (and even invites) circumstances which he is too weak to resist. As so often happens, he has reduced his faults to a principle of life. In order not to have to fight or struggle, he has come to believe in some sort of fatality, which tempts him to give way to momentary impressions. He has allowed his career to turn into a sort of lottery—and one in which luck is always against him. Now don't abuse him any more to me; I know him so well; abuse is meaningless.

The *Acte Additionnel aux Constitutions de l'Empire* was published in the *Moniteur* on April 24, 1815. The sort of constitution which Constant had wanted to extract from Napoleon had been outlined by him, in May of the previous year, in the form of a plan for an ideal constitution. Since it indicates how far he was affected by what he imagined to be the system then in force in England, it is worth summarizing:

The Monarchy. The royal power is different from the executive power; the monarch represents a neutral institution standing above and between the executive, the legislature and the judiciary. But the Crown must possess certain direct and distinct powers. The monarch must have the right to dissolve Parliament, to appoint and dismiss ministers, to sanction (and thereby to veto) legislation, to appoint the judges, and to decide the issues of peace and war.

The Executive. The Crown is not responsible, but Ministers are. The members of the Cabinet have the right to sit in the Legislature, but not the obligation.

The Legislature. There must be two Chambers. The upper Chamber must consist of hereditary peers on the pattern "set by the admirable English institution of a House of Lords." The lower Chamber must be elected by direct vote, but some property qualification should be imposed before a citizen has the right to vote. Parliaments should be elected for five years and members should not receive any salary. No speech in either Chamber should be read from a prepared manuscript.

Judiciary. Judges are appointed by the monarch. The jury system must be universal. There should be no special tribunals or administrative law.

The Army. The size of the military forces of the State must be determined for each current year by the Legislature.

Personal rights. Every citizen to have the right of trial by jury, inviolability of person and property, and commercial and religious liberty. There should be complete freedom of association and the Press.

It must be admitted that, on paper at least, the *Acte Additionnel* did embody these essential safeguards. It guaranteed religious liberty, the freedom of the Press, inviolability of person, and an elective Parliament. It provided an independent judiciary and laid it down that military service could only be imposed with the consent of the Chambers. These certainly were great gains. Yet Constant could not conceal from himself a certain doubtfulness. When he had suggested that the word "Empire" should be dropped, Napoleon had rasped at him, "You wish to rob me of my past!" When he had suggested that all confiscations of property should be abolished, the Emperor had murmured something about "the need of a strong hand." When he had ventured to suggest that it might be well if the Act were submitted to a Constituent Assembly, Napoleon had said that there was no time. "The Emperor," he wrote as early as April 26, "is not acting as he ought to act." In the evening to the Duke of Otranto: "A vague sort of discouragement seems to pervade all these people. I seem to bring bad luck to whatever party I join."

He was distressed also by the ambiguities of his personal position. He was known to have been the main author of the new Constitution, which was in fact generally referred to in Paris as *La Benjamine*. A pamphlet was circulated, containing a reprint of his article in the *Journal des Débats* of March 19 and bearing the crude title "Traitor!" He had an argument with Montloisier about the feudal system and a duel resulted. Madame Récamier remained gently evasive, softly indifferent. And with Madame de Staël during those weeks there occurred that squalid financial wrangle which has already been described.

Napoleon, who had hoped by his Constitution to rally to his side all liberal and bourgeois opinion, was disappointed by the slight impression it had created. "Well," he snapped to Benjamin Constant, "the Constitution does not seem to have been much of a success." "It is," Constant replied, "because people do not as yet believe in it. Compel them to believe in it by carrying it out." Napoleon thereat signed the decrees summoning the two Chambers. The resultant elections in May returned a liberal majority, which could not be described as Bonapartist. The only hope that remained to Napoleon was to win a resounding victory against the allied armies. At four on the morning of June 12, 1815 he left for his headquarters at Laon:

> He is off [wrote Constant in his journal] and carries all our destinies with him. At bottom nobody really believes he will succeed. A conversation with Caulaincourt. There is general pessimism and a desire to negotiate. I believe that I am the only one of the whole lot who really remains loyal to the Emperor. How odd that this should be so.

On June 18th Constant was awakened by the sound of guns. The battery at the Invalides was firing a salute to announce the victory won by Napoleon at Ligny on the 16th:

> A great victory, so they say. If the news be true, then it is not the end of the story. If it be untrue, then nothing could be worse than to tell lies at such a moment.

On June 20 in the Hôtel Matignon, he was reading *Adolphe* aloud to Queen Hortense. They were interrupted by Savary, Duke of Rovigo, who drew the Queen aside and told her that there had been a disaster on the 18th at Waterloo:

> Read my novel to the Queen of Holland. There is a disquieting silence on the subject of our great victory: there is worse than silence. It seems that there was a disaster on the 18th. God's will be done.

The next day the news was confirmed. "The end approaches," wrote Constant in his diary. "The disaster is complete. Army gone, cannon gone, all means of resistance gone." On that morning of June 21, Napoleon returned to Paris having given orders to his defeated forces to reform at Laon. For a moment he seems to have thought of dissolving the Chambers and of establishing a military dictatorship. On the motion of La Fayette, however, the Chambers had already declared themselves in permanent session and had passed a resolution asserting that whoever sought to dissolve them would be guilty of high treason. Napoleon, shattered by his defeat and his two nights' journey from Belgium, hesitated until it was too late. At seven that evening Constant was summoned to his presence. The Emperor was pacing the garden paths of the Elysée palace. "I found him," Constant records, "serious and calm." Their conversation lasted for three hours.

"It is no longer," Napoleon said, "a question of myself; it is a question of France. Have they considered the inevitable consequence of my abdication? Were I to abdicate today, in two days there would be no army at all. To the army, your parliamentary subtleties mean nothing whatsoever. Do you imagine that a few metaphysical axioms, a declaration of human rights, a few speeches in the Chamber, can stem a rout? One cannot with impunity abolish all authority when the enemy are twenty-five miles from Paris. I am not being deposed by Liberty; it is Waterloo which has deposed me. I am being forced to abdicate in a mood of general panic—a mood from which our enemies will profit."

Napoleon returned to his idea of dissolving the Chambers and driving out the deputies by force. He began to calculate the means at his disposal. As they paced backwards and forwards along the sanded alleys of the Elysée garden, the crowd which had collected in the Avenue Marigny recognized the familiar figure of the Emperor. They climbed up upon the low garden wall and waved at him; the cry of "Vive l'Empereur!" echoed through the twilight trees. "You see—" said Napoleon, "those are not the people upon whom I lavished riches and honours. What do these people owe me? I found them poor and I have left them poor. They are inspired by the instinct of necessity; the voice of the country speaks through them. If I wanted it, if I were to allow it, then within one hour the Chambers would cease to exist. But the life of one man is not worth such a price. I did not come back from Elba in order to drench Paris in blood."

Constant was well aware that Napoleon, if he had wished it, could have let loose upon the deputies the whole fury of the Paris mob. He admired him for refusing to adopt such methods. "A man," he wrote, "who could lay down his throne rather than defend it by massacres deserved well, on that occasion, of the human race."

As darkness descended upon the garden, it became clear to Constant that Napoleon—physically exhausted and utterly demoralized—was prepared for his second abdication. He had spoken of retiring into private life; he would spend such years as remained to him as an ordinary citizen at Malmaison. It was inconceivable to him that the Tsar, the Emperor of Austria, the King of Prussia—who had all fawned upon him in the days of his glory—could treat him as a criminal now that he was a broken man. Constant with a heavy heart went on to Madame Récamier's; realizing his distress, she for once behaved with tact, almost with affection. The next day the Emperor abdicated and the Chambers entrusted Fouché with the task of forming a provisional Government.

4

On June 24 Constant had a final interview with Napoleon. "He spoke of his own position with amazing calm and of the general situation with complete detachment." That afternoon Constant left for French headquarters at Laon. He had been appointed to a Commission entrusted by Fouché with the task of negotiating an armistice with the triumphant enemy. This Commission was composed of La Fayette, Sebastiani, d'Argenson, La Forest and Pontécoulant. Its instructions were to proceed to Blücher's headquarters and to offer an armistice on the basis of the integrity of French territory and a Regency for the King of Rome. Constant was attached to the Commission in the capacity of Secretary General.

Fouché never intended this Commission to be taken seriously; his sole purpose was to remove to a convenient distance from Paris those whom he suspected of Bonapartist or Republican sympathies. The moment they had left, Fouché despatched a second commission to the Duke of Wellington. This second commission was fully accredited, travelled by the direct route without let or hindrance, and was composed of men known to be committed to the return of the Bourbons.

Constant's own Commission was thus doomed to failure from the start. They had a humiliating experience. On reaching Laon they sent a flag of truce to Blücher requesting an armistice. They received a curt reply that permission could not be given them to come to Prussian headquarters. Constant mounted a horse and rode to the outposts of the Prussian army; he was turned back with objurgations. When at last the Commission were allowed to meet the allied representatives at Hagenau, they were coldly received. Lord Stuart, the British representative, was particularly offensive—"perhaps," records Constant, "because he knew more than the others about what was really happening in Paris."

They returned discomforted on July 5, to learn that in their absence Fouché had capitulated and that the Bourbon dynasty was for a second time to be restored. The Chambers had been closed and Prussian sentries were posted at the gates denying all access. The Allied armies entered Paris on July 7. On the next day Louis XVIII returned to the Tuileries.

Constant immediately sat down to write his apology to the King, and to prepare the more considered record which he subsequently published under the title of *Memoirs of the Hun-*

dred Days. The Royalists were determined to wreak their vengeance upon a man who had so flagrantly deserted to the enemy. His name was placed on the list of those to be proscribed. Louis XVIII, who had a taste for literature, himself read Constant's apology. He was much amused. With his own royal hand he deleted Constant's name from the list of those to be exiled. His pardon caused much comment. "You seem," a friend remarked, "to have convinced the King." "That does not surprise me," Constant answered. "I almost convinced myself."

For three months longer, shunned and discredited, he hung on in Paris. His passion for Madame Récamier had now returned to him with all its early ardour:

> This absurd love affair [he notes on July 22] has again given me a dreadful day. I am exhausted, overwhelmed, disgusted with men and Madame Récamier. My heart, my head—in every way I need a rest. Switzerland and my wife; that is what I need and that I pray God to grant me.

At one moment he sought the aid of the famous pietist, Baroness von Krüdener (5). He would attend prayer meetings at her house in the company of Madame Récamier, hoping that they might be rendered "twin souls." The curious jargon of Baroness von Krüdener and her circle begins even to seep into his journal:

> God of Gentleness continue Your work in me! Let Thy will be done and Thy will sanctified.

Before long however he came to the conclusion that Madame Récamier was "ill-adapted to religious ideas." He also began to doubt the efficacy, and even the sincerity, of Frau von Krüdener's séances:

> These people go a little far in their descriptions of paradise; they speak of it as if it were their own bedroom.

He discovered moreover that he only really loved Madame Récamier when he was parted from her. "Her presence always calms me; when one listens to her, one ceases to love her. When away from her one recreates one's own image of her; and the obstacles to seeing her inflame the imagination. . . . But even while I see all this, the least refusal goes to my head; I could kill myself in the agony which results."

Charlotte meanwhile was sending him affectionate letters. "What nobility," he wrote, "what tenderness, what devotion!" On September 19 Fouché was dismissed and Decazes appointed chief of the police. On October 18 the Constitution was suspended. "Things are getting hot," wrote Constant in his journal. He left Paris for Brussels where he was joined the next month by Charlotte. In January 1816 they crossed via Ostend to England. After resting for a few days at Margate, they drove to London.

Before leaving Brussels he wrote to Madame Récamier a letter in which he forgave her for having ruined "my career, my fortune, my reputation and my happiness." It was not an agreeable letter; it ended as follows:

> I shall not come back to Paris for one year from now—not if they offer me the empire of the world. Every person has his own means of doing harm, from the assassin who uses a dagger, to the woman who is so anxious to make quite certain of her charm that she condemns to agony the wretched creatures who allow themselves to be entrapped.

5

They rented a house at No. 32 Upper Berkeley Street and hired a carriage in which Charlotte could drive round leaving cards. Constant was assailed with diffidence. He was conscious of a pervading anti-French atmosphere; he was aware that his own record might tell against him; he disliked the climate and was appalled by the high cost of living; and he was terrified lest Charlotte with her two divorces might not be received in the best society. He had lost touch with all his old English friends; the only people whom he knew were James Mackintosh, Mrs. Bourke, the wife of the Danish Minister, Sir Humphrey and Lady Davy, and Caroline Lamb. His first few weeks therefore were weeks of anger and disillusion:

> I loathe this country [he wrote to Madame Récamier on February 27]. Invitations without cordiality, curiosity without interest, enormous receptions but no conversation, and what I find more painful than boredom is that people of all parties are equally hostile to us and France. All this makes my stay here unendurable. . . . I am glad, none the less, to have come here, since it will rid me of the idea that England could ever become for me an asylum and a recompense. . . . Life here in London is so badly organized. They pay visits in the morning, when one wants to work and have parties at midnight, when one wants to go to bed.

By March he had recovered his self-confidence. He reported delightedly that in thirty-four days they had only dined at home nine times. He paid a visit to the House of Commons and was much impressed. "It was magnificent; my heart beat when I listened to such solid sensible speeches. Of course we have other qualities—eloquence—gesture and so on; but . . ."

By April he was writing, "the sense of security which one has here is reposeful because it is deep and lasting. People began by just being curious about me; they have now become kindly; I enjoy this, since it has all the charm of novelty." Yet he was conscious of a difference. "There is more affinity," he wrote, "between myself and the most extreme French royalist than between myself and the most extreme English liberal."

On April 8 Constant attended the reception to which Lady Jersey, with defiant loyalty, had invited Byron, only a fortnight before he left England in disgrace. Unfortunately Constant makes no mention of this encounter in his *Journal Intime*. The following account occurs in the manuscript diary of J. C. Hobhouse:

> Monday, April 8. Byron and I went to Lady Jersey's tonight. I was introduced by Flahaut to Benjamin Constant and his wife—great compliments—great compliments de part et d'autre—he told me he was going to send me a book. He said that when the news of Waterloo came to Paris, Regnault and other constitutionalists met at his home; they determined to dethrone him—a man came in saying "The Emperor is arrived"—they all dispersed, leaving C. alone as if a stone had been flung into them. . . . Constant said he knew Fouché to be a rogue—he inflamed the war in the Vendée—Constant said that Fouché was the Talleyrand of the mob, and Talleyrand the Fouché of the nobles. He told me my view of the state of things in France previous to the coming of the Emperor was quite correct.

There is no record of whether Constant ever exchanged a word with Byron.

From time to time he would read *Adolphe* aloud to a select company. We find the following record in Miss Berry's Journal for February 14:

> In the evening at the Bourkes where there had been a dinner. Lady Holland, Princess Lieven etc. and where Benjamin Constant read his romance or history; I do not know what to call it as he has not given it a name. It is very well written—a sad and much too true story of the human heart, but almost ridiculously so with the company before whom it was read. It lasted two hours and a half. The end was so touching, that it was scarcely possible to restrain one's tears, and the effort I made to do so made me positively ill. Agnes and I both burst into tears on our return home.

He decided to publish *Adolphe*, ostensibly because he was bored by reading it aloud, actually because he wished to obtain some sterling. There exists in the archives of the House of Murray a letter—as usual undated—from Caroline Lamb:

> Benjamin wishes much to know whether you are inclined to take his novel, and for what. . . . If you affect not Constant's novel, do not say I named it and I will not—it is in my care—send me a positive answer—you may think me partial, which I am not, if I say that it is one of the cleverest things yet written but it will only make one vol.

In the end the book was published, not by Murray, but by Colburn. A simultaneous edition was issued in Paris by Tröttel and Würtz. Charles de Constant was shocked by this publication; it was disgraceful, he said, to sell one's intimate experiences for money. Rosalie, as always, was more tolerant. The book, she said, displayed "profound morality" and made one regret that Benjamin had been denied the blessings of a Christian father and mother. Constant himself regretted afterwards that he had ever consented to let the book be issued:

> I am sorry now that I allowed it. I never see the disadvantages of my actions until after the event. I fear that another person (to whom the book has not the remotest application either in circumstances or character) may take offence.

Having become reconciled to London, he announced that he would like to stay there for two years; the climate however gave Charlotte acute ophthalmia; and the expense was beyond his means. When the season ended, he returned with Charlotte to Belgium. On September 16, 1816 they both left Spa for Paris.

CHAPTER XV

Restoration

[1816–1830]

Constant in the last phase of his life—Miss Edgeworth's portrait—As a deputy—His independent attitude—The politics of the Second Restoration—The failure of the liberal opposition to carry out its own principles—Constant refuses to join any group—His justification of the independent attitude—His pamphlets and journalism—His *Cours de Politique*—Nature of Constant's theory of individual liberty—The common-sense approach—Political troubles—M. Goyet—The Saumur incident—General Berton's conspiracy—His duel with the Comte de Forbin—Loses his seat in the Sarthe but re-elected later for Paris—His declining influence—The nationality question again—His last visit to Switzerland—He has a stroke—As deputy for Alsace—Publication of first volumes of his book on religion—He puts forward his candidature for the French Academy but is not elected—The Revolution of July—He is paid 200,000 francs by Louis Philippe—His increasing paralysis—He dies December 8, 1830—His funeral.

1

THE last fourteen years of Constant's life (from October 1816 to December 1830) were comparatively sedate. In Charlotte he found at last the protective tenderness for which (without knowing it) he had always yearned: the demure enticement of Madame Récamier no longer disturbed him. On July 14, 1817 Madame de Staël died in Paris; he had not been permitted to visit her during her last illness, for fear lest his presence might cause her distress; with the Duc de Broglie, and by the light of candles flickering, he was allowed to keep vigil beside her bier. In July 1818, while on a visit to Madame Davilliers at Meudon, he tried to display his youthful agility by jumping over a garden wall; he damaged his hip-bone so severely that for the rest of his life he was obliged to hobble on crutches. His amatory adventures were thus finished for ever; the one vice which he was never able to master was the vice of gambling; even as an elderly Deputy, even when he was widely regarded as the prophet and champion of liberalism undefiled, he would creep round when the Chamber closed to one of the *tripots* of the Palais Royal. Until the early hours of the morning he would remain in this raffish company, losing dignity and francs.

His personal appearance, now that he was a cripple, became almost venerable; his face rounded; the sharp nose, the mobile sardonic lips, his small peeky eyes, were now set in a circular visage, with invisible eyebrows and faint wisps of sandy hair falling over his collar and tipped with white. A mutilated martyr he appeared; almost benignant, almost benign.

A less pleasing portrait of him, as he struck an English visitor in July 1820, is provided in a letter from Maria Edgeworth to her cousin Miss Ruxton:

> Breakfast with Camille Jordan. It was half-past twelve before the company assembled. At this breakfast we saw three of the most distinguished members of that party who call themselves *Les Doctrinaires*, and say they are more attached to measures than to men. . . . These three Doctrinaires were Casimir Périer, Royer-Collard and Benjamin Constant, who is, I believe, of a more violent party.
>
> I did not like him at all. His countenance, voice, manner and conversation are all disagreeable to me. He is a fair whithky-looking [*sic*] man, very near-sighted with spectacles which seem to pinch his nose. He pokes out his chin to keep the spectacles on, and yet looks over the top of his spectacles, squinching up his eyes so that you cannot see your way into his mind. Then he speaks

through his nose, and with a lisp, strangely contrasting with the vehemence of his emphasis. He does not give me any confidence in the sincerity of his patriotism, nor any idea of his talents, though he seems to have a mighty high idea of them himself. He has been well called *le héro des brochures*. We sat beside each other and I think felt a mutual antipathy.

For ten of these fourteen years Constant sat as a deputy in the Chamber (1). He was a most conscientious Member. He would arrive at the Palais Bourbon punctually and already dressed in his uniform as a deputy in case he might wish suddenly to mount the tribune. He would descend from his carriage encumbered with a variety of objects, which would become entangled with each other, would fall to the ground, would clumsily be recovered. There would be the notes for his speech, the proof of a recent article, a chapter of his work on religions, his little round hat, his spare spectacles, his crutches and the letters which had reached him by that morning's post. He would take his seat at the extreme left of the chamber and remain there all day—gossiping with friends, listening to the debate, scribbling endless notes, sending messages, correcting proofs. From time to time he would struggle out of his seat and hobble up to the tribune to place an interjection or to deliver a speech. He was an effective rather than an elegant speaker; he was apt to muddle his notes and to get them in the wrong order; his effeminate gestures, his lisping accent, the disdain of his manner, did not at first create a favourable impression. But the incisiveness of his wit, the reiterated affirmation of general principles, the lucidity of his argument, compelled attention. His colleague, M. Loève-Veimars, wrote for the *Revue des Deux Mondes* in 1833 his recollections of Constant as a parliamentary orator:

> His pale face, his pale complexion, his long puritan face did not easily become animated. He spoke slowly and in a monotonous

voice, a fact which at first astonished those who had been drawn there by his reputation as an orator. Gradually however his voice would gain in power, would become vital and resonant; his large blue eyes [*sic*] would kindle with a sudden fire; and then the most lucid arguments, a mixture of irony, wit and apposite quotation would blend with the lavishness of his improvisation.

The Chamber, asserts M. Loève-Veimars, could listen to him for hours without the slightest fatigue. It was delightful to watch him deliberately provoking the fury of his adversaries and then replying to their shouts of rage with the most frigid politeness.

> Imperturbable he would remain, while they shouted rude remarks at him (calling him a rebel, a revolutionary, shouting out "Order! Order!")—continuing his speech as if he were in a drawing-room, and from time to time disconcerting his enemies by some joke which obliged them to laugh in sympathy.

He was never, as might be expected, a good party man. At successive periods he was identified with the Constitutionalists, the Doctrinaires and the Liberals. Always he would swerve away from them, either to the left or to the right. He regarded himself as an Independent, and was for ever proclaiming that for him measures were more important than men. He well knew that his conduct during the Hundred Days would disqualify him for office under the Bourbons; he did not believe that another revolution would be good for France and kept aloof from the many plots and cabals in which some of his associates, such as La Fayette and Manuel (2) became involved; he devoted his whole energies to securing that the Bourbons should be forced by parliamentary vigilance to keep to the provisions of the *Charte* which they had granted. His past record proved so heavy a liability that it led him to pursue a lonely and not always a consistent course; above all it tempted him—in that he recognized that he could never now acquire the esteem or confidence of the politicians—to win popularity outside; to court the favour of the uneducated and the very young.

2

It is not the purpose of this biography to enter into the intricate politics of the Second Restoration, except in so far as is necessary to explain Constant's own position.

Louis XVIII was an intelligent and tolerant man, who had no desire to start again upon his travels. Nor had he any illusions regarding the arrogant ineptitude of Monsieur, his brother and heir. "He conspired," he once remarked, "against Louis XVI; he conspires against me; he will end by conspiring against himself." It was around Monsieur that the extreme Royalists or *ultras*, were grouped.

The Chamber elected after the Hundred Days was a reactionary Chamber; it was christened by Louis XVIII *la Chambre des Introuvables*, in that it surpassed the most sanguine expectations of the Royalists themselves. It was dissolved in September 1816 and succeeded by a more equally balanced parliament, in which the opposition, known as the "Doctrinaires" were led by Royer-Collard, Hercule de Serre, Prosper de Barante, Camille Jordan, de Broglie and young Guizot. To the left of the Doctrinaires, although not yet in parliament, were La Fayette, Manuel and Benjamin Constant. In the elections of September 1817, at which one fifth of the Chamber had to be renewed, both La Fayette and Manuel were returned. The elections of October 1818 doubled the number of left deputies, whose strength was further increased by the elections of October 1819, when General Foy was also returned. A moderate Government had been appointed, in which de Serre himself was the leading figure. It was expected that the left wing liberals would support that Government in establishing a constitutional monarchy. It was then, on February 13, 1820, that the Duc de Berry was stabbed by Louvel. The emotion occasioned by this assassination led to the return, in September, 1820, of an enormous Royalist majority; for a month or two the Duc de Richelieu carried on the Government, but in December 1821 Louis XVIII (who was by then ageing and falling more and more under the influence of the Comtesse du Cayla) appointed Villèle as Prime Minister. He remained in power for six years, until December 5, 1827. The de Martignac Ministry which followed, and which lasted from January 4, 1828 to August 9, 1829, represented the last chance of maintaining a constitutional monarchy under the Bourbons; but Charles X as Monsieur had by then become, hated the de Martignac system and the liberal opposition joined with the *ultras* in securing its downfall. "The time has come," said Charles X, "to call a halt." The de Polignac Ministry was placed in power and the stage fully set for the Revolution of July.

In his excellent work, *Le Parti Libéral sous la Restauration*, Paul Thureau-Dangin has shown how the liberals during this period, by their factious opposition and their irresponsible combinations (now with the extreme left and now with the *ultras*) in fact falsified the whole doctrine which they had proclaimed. Their aim had been to combine the principles of 1789 with the continuity provided by the Bourbon dynasty. They wished, they said, to "royalize the nation, and nationalize the monarchy." These were sensible objectives. In practice however, by their irresponsible combinations, they rendered impossible all moderate or efficient government, and allowed their sectional rivalries to discredit the very system which they were, quite sincerely, anxious to support. "It was the Liberals," wrote the Duc de Broglie, "who had learnt nothing and forgotten nothing."

To the left of the official liberals—sometimes supporting them, sometimes acting with volatile and even histrionic independence—were the three outstanding personalities of La Fayette, Manuel and Benjamin Constant. La Fayette brought with him a great historical reputation, immense personal courage, and long experience. His weakness lay in his indecision, his lack of real intelligence and what Jefferson called "his almost canine greed for popularity." Manuel was a more revolutionary type; he detested the Bourbons, had overt Bonapartist sympathies and was inclined to indulge in secret conspiracies. He was expelled from the Chamber in 1823 and died four years afterwards. Constant, with his foreign origin, his volatile past, his contemptuous bearing, his endless hesitations, was not a true representative of the bourgeois radicals of the Restoration period. In opposing successive governments, even when they introduced legislation which was in accord with his own principles, he cast doubt upon the sincerity of his motto "Measures before men"; in courting outside popularity—while lacking the energy, even the courage, to control or lead the forces which he incited—he destroyed such confidence as his talents might have secured him; by the extreme individualism of his political conduct and the reserved disdain of his manner, he failed to attach to himself any influential or loyal adherents; and by his blend of intransigence and vacillation he created the impression that he was not a man upon whom, in any circumstances, it was prudent to rely. For all his brilliance, Constant was not a successful parliamentarian. He suffered the fate of all political independents; the sound party men regarded him as eccentric, cranky, conceited and as such unreliable. They interpreted his independence as an implied reproof to their own party allegiance; and they decided therefore that he could not at bottom be sincere.

Constant himself defended the position of an independent, and incidentally his own record, with fiery eloquence:

> The independents are those who for thirty years have wished for the same thing. They are those who, to every successive government, have repeated the same truths; who have maintained an equal resistance to all arbitrary actions, even when directed against others than themselves. The independents have adopted no symbol, only to sacrifice their principles to that symbol. When they have proclaimed the sovereignty of the people, they have always been careful to remind the people that their sovereignty must be limited by the principles of justice. When France passed from the tempestuous tyranny of popular sovereignty to the more symmetrical despotism of a single man, it was the independents who told that individual that he could maintain his position only by obeying the laws of the State; that these laws, which he regarded as obstacles, were in fact safeguards, to destroy which would sap the foundations of his throne. The independents are those who like constitutional monarchy because it is constitutional, who respect the principle of hereditary succession, since this principle protects the tranquillity of the people against the strife of factions. But at the same time the independents believe that the throne exists for the people, and that to stamp upon the rights of citizens is as destructive of the monarchical principle at it is damaging to the citizens to strive to reverse the legal powers of the crown. The independents represent that generation which, nurtured in the very heart of our recent troubles, often wounded in youth by the arbitrary actions of successive despotisms, have grown up with a detestation of the arbitrary in governance and with a clear insight into falsity of its every pretext. The independents are those who, having no desire to despoil or to banish any person illegally, or to be paid by those who despoil and banish, will have nothing to do with any law which permits people to be arrested, despoiled or banished without trial by jury.
>
> It is from men such as these that we should choose those to whom we entrust our future destinies.

No better statement has ever been made of the very core of Constant's political philosophy.

3

The influence which he possessed (and it was a great and pervading influence) arose, less from his success as a deputy, than from his assiduity as a publicist. Immediately on his return to Paris he had sought to revive the *Mercure*, but it was suppressed by the censorship in January 1818. He then decided to continue it as "a book" to be published at irregular intervals under the title *La Minerve Française*. In the years that followed, the *Minerve* became the official organ of the opposition; after the murder of the Duc de Berry it also was suppressed.

It was however through his pamphlets (and political pamphlets were fashionable in those days) that Constant exercised his greatest influence. He contended, and not without justice, that he had constituted himself "the school-master of Liberty." In his *De la Doctrine Politique qui peut réunir les partis en France*, he replied to Chateaubriand's pamphlet on *La Monarchie selon la Charte* and with glacial objectivity analyzed all the mistakes made by the Royalists since the first Restoration. Between 1816 and 1818 he published his *Cours de Politique Constitutionnelle*, in which he reprinted and extended his previous political articles and pamphlets. In so doing he omitted and even altered such passages as were by then either out of date or inconvenient. This exposed him to a lampoon by Charles Loyson in which the original versions were reproduced and subjected to a critical discussion between Monsieur Benjamin, Monsieur Constant and Monsieur de Rebecque. In spite of this, the *Cours de Politique* is a brilliant, prescient and balanced statement of what had always been for Constant a consistent political faith. "Through his life," wrote Coulmann, "he worshipped liberty as others have worshipped power." "The writings of Constant," commented John Cam Hobhouse, "are a mine of undiscovered truths." It is therefore necessary to summarize Constant's theory of liberty, as expounded in his *Cours de Politique* and in his subsequent *Mélanges*.

He had of course been much influenced by Godwin's *Principles of Justice*, by Bentham's *Principles of Morals and Legislation* and *Fragment on Government*, as well as by Adam Smith's theory of "a natural order" which became the origin of the doctrine of *laisser-faire*. But he disagreed with Godwin that all government was a necessary evil. So long as a ruler remained within his legitimate sphere, which was the protection of the citizen, he should be encouraged to be as strong as possible; it was only when he exceeded that sphere that he became an usurper. Similarly he disagreed with Bentham's use of the word "utility." He contended that a standard of utility was by its very nature less absolute and less precise than a standard of rights and duties. Utility suggests profit; profit is a variable standard, whereas "no error and no caprice can change the concept of duty." "Actions," he wrote, "cannot be more or less just; but they can be more or less useful. Right is a principle, utility only a result: right is a cause, utility only an effect." He admitted the value of Bentham's premises and conclusion, but he disliked the words he used. "It is not his principles which are at fault: it is his terminology which is so vicious."

> For forty years [he wrote] I have fought for the same principle: liberty in all things, in religion, in philosophy, in literature, in industry, in politics. By liberty, I mean the triumph of the individual, as much over a government which seeks to rule by despotic methods as over the masses who seek to render the minority a slave of the majority. Despotism has no rights at all. A majority does possess the right to force the minority to respect public order; but anything which does not affect public order, anything which is purely personal, anything which by its expression does no harm to

anyone else (whether by inciting to a breach of the peace or by suppressing contrary opinions), anything which in so far as industry is concerned limits free competition—all these things pertain to the individual and not to the State. As such, they cannot be subjected to the power of the State.

To this extent Constant (unlike Sismondi who foresaw that economic liberalism must lead inevitably to social injustice) was a complete convert to the doctrine of *laisser-faire*. He was opposed to any interference with the free play of economic forces; for him competition was the very condition of a prosperous industry. At the same time he was well aware that the great crisis which he had himself witnessed was not the last crisis which would mould the shape of human affairs. He foresaw (and at the time his forecasts astonished) that in the immediate future industrial property would become more influential than landed property; that there was bound to be a new distribution of wealth; and that the day would come when education and opportunity would be free for all:

> We have witnessed [he wrote] the collapse of many institutions; many other institutions will collapse in the future. These destructions—or if you will these liberations—are for the future. . . . During this process, many things which have become superfluous will still be regarded as necessary; many things which have become necessary will be decried as subversive, paradoxical or even wicked.
> Let me not anticipate history; let me concentrate upon those doctrines to which my own age has given birth and is now consolidating. It is not for us to occupy ourselves with the problems of a distant future; every century has its own work to do.

It was not merely in its refusal to accept any formula as applicable eternally and universally that Constant's theory of liberty was novel to a generation brought up upon the sentimental absolutes of Rousseau. He denied the assumption of the natural equality of man and described Rousseau's formula of *la volonté générale* as "the evil ally of any kind of tyranny." "An arbitrary act," he wrote, "remains an arbitrary act, even when committed by a whole nation against a single individual." Democracy on the Rousseau model was not liberty; it was merely "the vulgarization of despotism." True democracy is individual liberty based upon a respect for law.

The originality of Constant's teaching lay in his insistence upon the practical rather than the emotional approach. The philosophers and the men of 1789 had made the mistake of applying to modern times what they believed to be the political and social theories of Greece and Rome. They had thereby sadly confused individual liberty with political liberty; the two things were totally different, and often mutually destructive. "Let us be chary," he wrote, "of indulging in such antiquarian reminiscences. What I want is the form of liberty best suited to our modern age. That form is the liberty of the *individual*. To ask people today to sacrifice their individual liberty to political liberty is the surest way to rob them of the former and in the end to deprive them of the latter."

This practical, or as we should say "common-sense," approach, is shown by his treatment of the problems of property and a free press. Property, he contended, was not a natural right, but a social convention; it was a useful convention, since the total abolition of property would render the human race "stationary." Equality imposed by legislation would render impossible the only true equality which was that of "happiness and enlightenment." The freedom of the press, again, was not only ideologically desirable, it was of practical value to the government. Official censorship could never prove effective, since there would always be clandestine publications, which tend to be more damaging and violent than those which appear naturally. By imposing a censorship the government makes itself responsible for everything that is published, and this is bound to place the government in an awkward position at home and even more abroad. Above all a censored press seeks to create a unanimous public opinion, which is not a human possibility. Sound opinion can only be created by a free press such as existed in England. No government can hope to govern unless there exists a sound public opinion.

It may be, as Emile Faguet has contended, that Constant's theory of liberty was the product of his own almost anarchic egoism. It certainly shows little evidence of an acute social conscience. Constant's intelligence was luminous, but it did not emit warmth. He did succeed however, in teaching his contemporaries that there existed a middle line of thought between the ideologues of the Revolution and the hard efficient bureaucracy of the Napoleonic system. He did teach them to realize that it was not power in itself which was evil, but the way in which that power might be misused. And he did do much to convince them that there existed a distinction between self-regarding and other-regarding actions, and that the doctrines of the *Contrat Social* implied a disastrous, and wholly unnecessary, surrender of individual rights.

4

It was not to be expected that so controversial and unloved a figure as Benjamin Constant could plunge into the embittered politics of the second Restoration without exposing himself to much personal animosity and inconvenience. The agent whom he employed in his constituency of the Sarthe was a local journalist of the name of Goyet. He was a passionate radical and regarded with suspicion by the police. He disapproved of Constant's moderation and of his social habits. He would write him letters begging him to dine at home more often and more "conjugally." "Remember," he reminded him, "that it is I who control opinion in the Sarthe." In June 1820, during the period of repression which followed the assassination of the Duc de Berry, the police raided Goyet's rooms and found among his papers certain letters from Constant and La Fayette which were regarded as compromising. Goyet was arrested, but since all that could be proved against him was that he had tried to obtain advance information regarding projected Government legislation, he was released after only a few weeks detention.

Another incident occurred that August, when Constant was making an election tour in his constituency and stopped for the night at Saumur. The cadets of the cavalry school heard of his presence and broke into the inn where he was staying with shouts of "Death to the Liberals!" "Death to Benjamin Constant." He had to be rescued from their clutches by the National Guard. Both he and Charlotte displayed much courage on that occasion.

A more damaging scandal occurred in 1822. In February of that year General Berton was arrested and condemned to death for plotting a military rising at Saumur. Among his accomplices was a local surgeon of the name of Caffé, whom Constant had visited when touring his constituency. Caffé was also condemned to death. Constant wrote to Villèle offering to retire for ever from public life if Caffé could be granted a pardon. He was not granted a pardon and committed suicide rather than face the firing squad. Among General Berton's papers was found a list of the Provisional Government which he intended to put into power if his rising succeeded. The list contained Constant's name. He was therefore summoned to appear before the assizes on November 14 on a charge of "moral complicity." He was sentenced to a fine of 500 francs and to six weeks' imprisonment. Further actions were brought against him for contempt of court for having written two open letters, the one addressed to the Public Prosecutor of Poitiers, and the other to the assistant prefect of Saumur. For these he was sentenced to two and a half months imprisonment and a fine of six hundred francs. Madame Récamier induced Chateaubriand to obtain the annulment of the prison sentences; but the fines were increased.

These incidents certainly added to his reputation as a champion of the oppressed and a martyr to liberty, but they shocked the bourgeois of the Sarthe. In the elections of 1822 Constant lost his seat (3): he did not get back to the Chamber until returned as deputy for Paris in March 1824. In the interval he fought a foolish duel (the twentieth of his recorded duels) with the Comte de Forbin. Being unable to stand without crutches he fought this duel seated in an arm-chair.

With his re-election to the Chamber in 1824 the hostility towards him became intense. When he mounted the tribune the right and centre would try to shout him down. "Go away!" they would shout at him, or sometimes merely "Goodbye." The attacks in the royalist press became even more personal. To the usual abuse lavished on his own past record, there were added attacks upon Charlotte—her German nationality, her double divorce. He was conscious moreover that a younger generation of ardent republicans was springing up around him—men like Thiers, and Guizot and Quinet, for whom he felt but little sympathy. He became aware that something of his old fire of invective was leaving him; perhaps even that his oft repeated aphorisms upon constitutional monarchy were wearing stale; perhaps even that he was becoming a vestige only of the past.

At this stage, an old royalist enemy of Constant's, a Monsieur Dudon, attempted to have his election declared invalid on account of his foreign nationality. Twenty-five years ago Constant had imprudently sought to revive a family legend to the effect that his ancestor Augustin de Constant had been exiled, not merely for his religious opinions, but also because he had wished to establish a republic in France. "Your ancestor," said M. Dudon, "was not therefore expelled for religious motives but for high treason." The dispute was referred to a select committee and Constant hurried off to Lausanne in order to burrow further in the family archives. The law passed by the Constituent Assembly on December 15, 1790, on which Constant based his claim for French nationality, provided fortunately that citizenship could be granted to any person who could prove descent, either on the paternal or the maternal side, from an ancestor expelled for religious reasons. To his delight, Constant was able to trace back his Chandieu lineage to A.D. 942 and to prove that among his maternal ancestors he could count, not only Antoine de Chandieu, personal chaplain to Henri IV, but also Mornay-du-Plessis, the "Pope of the Protestants." The Select Committee were impressed by this documentation and the plea of M. Dudon was disallowed.

This was Constant's last visit to his native country. He took Charlotte up to La Chablière and they sat there under the limes gazing down at the lake. Charlotte was entranced by the beauty of the scenery and urged him to repurchase the property from M. de Fries. For a few months he toyed with this idea: he had never observed the scenery himself.

In October 1824 Constant had a slight stroke. It left him almost unaffected, but was a presage of the end:

> I think [he wrote to Rosalie on December 9] that I shall recover. But the blow struck the root of the tree and echoed through the trunk. I may live ten or twenty years longer, but it will not really be living any more, and I regard myself as struck off the list of those who possess the world and have a future before them. I shall still try to defend the ideas which are dear to me; but I shall

have the feeling of living only from day to day. I shall thank nature, even as a man might bless the Sultan every morning for permitting him to keep his head on his shoulders.

5

Constant did not in fact surrender to decrepitude; in the six years of life that remained to him he experienced the satisfaction of popular acclaim, the excitement of a revolution, and one bitter disappointment: he became the hero of the Alsatian electorate, he witnessed the Revolution of July and he failed to gain admission to the French Academy.

In the elections of 1827 Constant was returned simultaneously for Paris and Alsace. Under pressure from his young admirer, Jean Jacques Coulmann, he accepted the latter constituency.

The Alsatians were delighted to have as their deputy a man of ancient Protestant lineage, who had a German wife, and who could himself speak the German language with extreme fluency. The prefect, Monsieur Esmangart, regarded Constant as a dangerous revolutionary and his supporters as a rabble of *sans coulottes*. Constant did not as a matter of fact desire a revolution or the dethronement of the Bourbons. "I believe," he wrote at the time, "or at least I think I believe—that old governments are more favourable to liberty than new ones." Yet such was his temptation to find in popular demonstrations some compensation for the hostility with which he was regarded by the *ultras*, and even by the liberals, that both his actions and his language gave M. Esmangart good cause for anxiety. The prefect was afraid that the new deputy would stimulate the latent disaffection of the Protestant minority; he subjected Constant to close police supervision; he addressed to the Ministry of the Interior long, angry, anxious reports.

On his visits to his constituency, Constant would stay with young Coulmann at Brumath, paying occasional dramatic and provocative visits to Strasbourg or Colmar. He would drive into these cities in a carriage drawn by eight white horses; the maidens of the villages through which he passed would stand beside the road in their national costumes and present him and Charlotte with enormous bouquets of poppies and cornflowers; the young farmers of the district would escort his processions with a gay and lively cavalcade.

At Strasbourg and at Colmar there would be banquets in his honour. He was presented with an enormous silver vase, on which were engraved the articles of the *Charte* and the semblance of a lion mounting guard. At night time the electors serenaded him from boats upon the river; there were Bengal lights and lanterns; there were cries through the night of "Long live the great deputy!" "Long live the Constitution!"

On one such occasion, when he was attending a banquet at the Hôtel de L'Esprit at Strasbourg, the crowds upon the quay-side and in the decorated boats which thronged the river clamoured for his appearance. He limped out on to the balcony and they held chandeliers before him to illumine his face. He waved his little round hat in the air exclaiming in the German language "Long live the charter!" "Long live civil and religious liberty! Long live the youth of Alsace!" The applause which greeted these remarks was frantic and prolonged. Then a voice rang out suddenly: "Silence! Hats off! The prince of orators is about to address you!" Charlotte tugged hard at his coat to prevent him responding to this invitation. He was able only to mumble a few German words which did not reach the outer crowd upon the quay-side or the enthusiastic young men and women bobbing in their lanterned boats. The cheering was resumed. "Long live," they shouted, "the second Canning!" Exhausted but complacent

Constant was escorted back to Brumath by the students carrying torches and singing songs.

M. Esmangart was much distressed. He sent a police spy to follow Constant to Baden across the river where he went with Charlotte for a cure. He was delighted to be able to report to the Minister of the Interior that the deputy for Alsace was conducting himself in "a shameful and ridiculous manner." He spent his time at this watering-place playing roulette.

His health none the less was causing Charlotte anxiety. It was obvious even to himself that his old vitality had left him. "One feels pretty dry," he remarked to Coulmann, "when one has been devastated by the lava of Madame de Staël for twenty years." Charles de Constant, who saw him at this period, entered the following gloomy observation in his diary for March 1829:

> His health has in fact been much affected. He has been burning the candle at both ends. He always asserts that he does not wish for a long life; old age terrifies him. "I want [he says] to enjoy myself at any cost, regardless of the consequences; I want to win today, whatever may happen tomorrow." It is lucky that the machine is of good material and well constructed: otherwise it would have broken down long ago.

6

He knew full well that he could not now expect any political future; he was aware even that he had lost all influence with the Chamber. "Do not apply to me," he wrote to a petitioner, "my authority in parliament and with the government is nil." His consolation was that the seven volumes of his work on religion had at last been finished and had begun to appear (4). Upon this great labour of research and industry he had been engaged for forty years. He had read thousands of books, accumulated masses of notes, and rewritten his work at least three times. He himself stated that he had found among his papers as many as twenty different versions of his theme; he contended that the material he had collected could accommodate itself to any thesis; "it is a case," he remarked to De Broglie, "of passive obedience." Yet the book when finished was almost valueless; it was not sufficiently scientific to constitute a serious study of comparative religion; it was too long and heavy for the general reader; and in the uncertainty of its argument it discloses the fact that in the course of writing it the author had frequently changed his mind.

His original intention, when under the influence of eighteenth century scepticism, had been to write only about the Polytheism of the ancients, in order to suggest the superiority of pagan over Christian beliefs. Thereafter he became affected by German mysticism and particularly by the Kantian assertion that God cannot be apprehended by reason but only by instinct. He ended by becoming a deist:

> My work [he wrote in 1811] is a remarkable proof of the truth of Bacon's remark that a little learning leads to atheism and much learning to religion. (5)

His main thesis was that religious sentiment is innate in man, in the sense that man is driven naturally to establish some relation between himself and the forces of the invisible world; having established that relation he invests it with a form or dogma; this produces a struggle between religious forms and man's progressive intellect; in the end the mould of dogma is broken and "religion arises younger and more beautiful than ever."

Encouraged by the publication of the first three volumes of his work on religion, Constant presented his candidature for the French Academy. In spite of the fact that he was supported by Chateaubriand, he was not elected. "We do not," they said, "like people who spend the whole night at Frascati's and thereafter go to sleep at our meetings." The successful candidate was a M. Viennet, who has not remained among the immortals. This final failure proved a crushing blow.

Constant was one of the 221 deputies who on March 16, 1830 signed the address in reply to the speech from the throne. It was this address which led to the dissolution of the Chamber, to the ordonnances, and thereby to the Revolution of July. Constant, when the crisis came, was recovering from a slight operation at Montmorency. He received a note from La Fayette, dated July 26, 1830:

> A terrific game is being played here. Our heads are at stake. Bring yours along.

Constant drove at once to Paris and was carried in an ambulance to the Hôtel de Ville. He witnessed the deposition of Charles X and the election of Louis Philippe as the monarch of the bourgeoisie. He was received by a new sovereign, and appointed President of the legislative Committee of the Council of State. He was also handed by Louis Philippe a draft for 200,000 francs wherewith to pay his private debts. "Sire," he remarked, "I accept; but liberty must take precedence over gratitude. If your Government makes mistakes, I shall be the first to join the Opposition." "That," answered Louis Philippe, "is how I understand it myself." This was the last of many unfortunate episodes in the public career of Benjamin Constant.

7

For some years he and Charlotte (6) had been living at No. 29 Rue d'Anjou, a decorous little house, now tenanted by the Association France—U.R.S.S. The general paralysis from which he had for some months been suffering had assumed an acute form; it crept upwards, attacking his bladder and then his tongue. As his sufferings increased, he was moved from the Rue d'Anjou to a private room at the Tivoli Baths (7), where he could obtain medicinal douches. He died there on December 8, 1830.

His funeral on Sunday, December 12 assumed the proportions of a national manifestation. The procession was headed by the Orleans hussars, followed by detachments of the national and municipal Guards, their drums draped in crêpe, their muskets reversed. The four pall-bearers were the Prime Minister, the President of the Chamber of Deputies, the Préfet of the Seine and General La Fayette. The students of the schools of Law and Medicine had obtained permission to carry the coffin on a stretcher; the hearse followed behind. On turning the corner of the Rue St. Honoré one of the handles of the stretcher became loose; they decided to use the hearse, but discovered that the place provided was too short for so long a coffin; a carpenter was summoned and nailed on two extra planks; for an hour and a half the sound of hammering echoed through the Rue St. Honoré. When the coffin had been fixed, the students took out the horses and dragged the hearse towards Père Lachaise. It was half-past three before they reached the Protestant Church, where Charlotte had been waiting and where a short service was held. On leaving the church there were cries of "To the Panthéon! To the Panthéon!" (8) After a momentary confusion, during which some of the escort turned up the Rue St. Jacques, the procession was reformed and proceeded slowly to Père Lachaise.

It was dark when they reached the grave-side. La Fayette delivered his funeral oration by the light of torches flickering in a thin cold rain.

List of Books

1. BOOKS AND PAMPHLETS BY BENJAMIN CONSTANT

1779 *Les Chevaliers*, edited by Rudler 1927.
1796 *De La Force du Gouvernement actuel et de la nécessité de s'y rallier.*
1797 *Des Réactions Politiques.*
Des effets de la Terreur.
1798 *Des suites de la Contre-Révolution de 1660 en Angleterre.*
1809 *Wallstein.*
1814 *De l'esprit de conquête et de l'usurpation* (Hanover, January; London, March).
Le Siège de Soissons, Poligny, 1892.
Réflexions sur les Constitutions.
De la liberté des brochures.
1815 *De la responsabilité des ministres.*
Principes de Politique.
1816 *Adolphe*, (Colburn, London and Tröttel and Würtz, Paris).
De la doctrine politique qui peut réunir les partis en France.
Cours de Politique Constitutionnelle.
1817 *Des Elections prochaines.*
1818 *Entretien d'un électeur avec lui-même.*
1819 *Eloge de Sir Samuel Romilly.*
1820 *Mémoires sur les Cent Jours en forme de lettres.*
1824 *De la religion et cetera.*
1825 *Appel aux nations chrétiennes en faveur des Grecs.*
1827 *Discours.*
1829 *Mélanges de Litérature et de Politique.*

POSTHUMOUS PUBLICATIONS

1832 *Portraits Contemporains.*
1833 *Du Polythéisme Romain et cetera.*

LIST OF BOOKS

2. DIARIES

Le Cahier Rouge, edited by Jean Mistler (Editions du Rocher Monaco 1945).
Journal Intime, edited by Jean Mistler (Editions du Rocher Monaco 1945).

3. LETTERS

Letters to Madame Récamier, Calmann Lévy, 1882.
Letters to Rosalie de Constant, *Nouvelle Revue,* October 1903.
Letters to Prosper de Barante, *Revue des Deux Mondes,* 1906.
Letters to Hochet, *La Révue,* May 1904.
Letters to Fauriel, *see* Glachant below.
Letters to Villers, *Nachlasse des Ch. de Villers,* Hamburg, 1879.
Letters to Coulmann. In Coulmann's reminiscences.
Letters to Madame de Staël, edited by Baroness de Nolde, Putnam, 1907.
Letters to his family, edited by Jean Menos, Savine, Paris, 1888.
Letters to Anna Lindsay, edited by Baroness de Constant, Plon, Paris, 1933.

4. BOOKS ABOUT CONSTANT

Achard, Lucie, *Rosalie de Constant, sa famille et ses amis,* Eggiman, Geneva, 1901, two vols.
Barrès, Maurice, *Un Homme Libre,* Paris, 1905 edition.
Berthoud, Madame Dorette, *La Seconde Madame Benjamin Constant,* Payot, Lausanne, 1943.
Berthoud, Madame Dorette, *Constance et Grandeur de Benjamin Constant,* Payot, Lausanne, 1944.
Blennerhassett, Lady, *Mme. de Staël,* Chapman and Hall, 1887, three vols.
Boigne, Comtesse de, *Mémoirs,* Paris, 1909.
Broglie, Duc de, *Souvenirs,* Calmann Lévy, Paris, 1886, four vols.
Broglie, Prince de, *Madame de Staël et sa Cour au château de Chaumont,* Plon, Paris, 1936.
Coulmann, Jean Jacques, *Réminiscences,* Lévy, Paris, 1862.

LIST OF BOOKS

Du Bos, Charles, *Grandeur et Misère de Benjamin Constant*, edition Corréa, Paris, 1946.

Dury, George, *Memoirs of Barras*, four vols.

Fabre-Luce, Alfred, *Benjamin Constant*, Fayard, Paris, 1939.

Faguet, Emile, *Politiques et Moralistes du XIXe Siècle*, Paris, 1901.

France, Anatole, *La Vie Littéraire*, vol. 1, Calmann Lévy, Paris.

Gautier, Paul, *Mme. de Staël et Napoléon*, Plon Nourrit, Paris, 1902.

Glachant, Philippe, *Benjamin Constant sous l'oeil du guet*, Plon, 1906.

Godet, Philippe, *Madame de Charrière et ses amis*, Geneva, 1906, two vols.

Herriot, Edouard, *Madame Récamier et ses amis*, Payot, Paris, 1926.

Kohler, Pierre, *Madame de Staël et la Suisse*, Payot, Paris, 1916.

Kohler, Pierre, *Madame de Staël au château de Coppet*, Spes, Lausanne, 1943.

Lacretelle, Pierre de, *Madame de Staël et les hommes*, Grasset, Paris, 1939.

Lauris, G. de, *Benjamin Constant et les idées libérales*, Paris, 1914.

Mackintosh, Sir James, *Memoirs of the life of*, Moxon, London, 1836. two vols.

Margerie, Roland de, *Le Comte Louis de Narbonne*, 1944.

Melegari, Dora, *Préface au Journal Intime de Benjamin Constant*, Paris, 1895.

Menos, Jean, *Lettres de Benjamin Constant à sa famille*, Savine, Paris, 1888.

Miot de Melito, Count, *Memoirs*.

Mistler, Jean, *Mme. de Staël et Maurice O'Donnell*, Calmann Lévy, Paris, 1926.

Necker de Saussure, Mme. de, *Notice sur le caractère et les écrits de Madame de Staël*, Tröttel and Würtz, Paris, 1820.

Pange, Comtesse Jean de, *Auguste Wilhelm Schlegel et Madame de Staël*, editions Albert, Paris, 1938.

Pange, Comtesse Jean de, *Monsieur de Staël*, editions des Portiques, 1931.

Pourtalès, Guy de, *De Hamlet à Swann*, editions G. Crès, Paris, 1924.

Rebecque, Baronne Constant de, *Coréspondence de Benjamin Constant et d'Anna Lindsay*, Plon, Paris, 1933.

Rebecque, Baronne Constant de, *Lettres de Julie Talma à Benjamin Constant*, Plon, Paris, 1933.

LIST OF BOOKS

Robinson, Henry Crabb, *Diary Reminiscences and Correspondence.*
Rudler, Professor Gustave, *La Jeunesse de Benjamin Constant,* Paris, 1909.
Sainte-Beuve, *Préface pour Adolphe,* 1867; *Nouveaux Lundis.*
Sainte-Beuve, *Causeries de Lundi, Portraits Contemporains* and *Portraits de Femmes.*
Schemerhorn, Elizabeth, *Benjamin Constant,* Heinemann, 1924.
Scott, Geoffrey, *The Portrait of Zélide,* Constable and Company, 1925.
Sismondi, *Lettres Inédites,* Lévy, Paris, 1863.
Staël, Madame de, *De l'influence des passions sur le bonheur.*
Staël, Madame de, *Dix années d'exil.*
Staël, Madame de, *De l'Allemagne.*
Staël, Madame de, *Delphine.*
Staël, Madame de, *Corinne.*
Thureau-Dangin, Paul, *Le Parti Libéral sous la Restauration,* Plon Nourrit, Paris, 1888.

Notes

CHAPTER ONE

1. In the *Dictionnaire des Familles Française,* published at Evreux in 1912 the Constants are listed as an old territorial family. In the second half of the sixteenth century they owned the Seigneurie of Rebecque, from which they derived their title. Their motto was *In arduis constans.*

CHAPTER TWO

1. *Mackintosh, Sir James* (1765–1832). He was exactly two years older than Constant. Educated at King's College and Edinburgh University. Intended to study medicine but became more attracted by law. Obtained his diploma in 1787 and was called to the Bar 1795. Wrote *Vindiciae Gallicae* in reply to Burke's *Reflections on the French Revolution.* He was a brilliant conversationalist and Coleridge, who disliked him, called him "the king of the men of talent." Became recorder of Bombay, was knighted, returned to England, elected to Parliament, became a member of the Holland House circle and eventually a privy councillor. He saw much of Constant at the time of the Restoration and subsequently in London.

2. *The Speculative Society* was not, and is not today, a purely University Club, although its premises were, and are, within the old University building. A portrait of Constant hangs today in the lobby of the Speculative Society—a fact which must, if he knows it, cause him much pleasure.

3. *Laing, Malcolm* (1762–1818). Called to the Bar but was not successful owing to his poor delivery and harsh accent. Became a historian and in 1802 published his *History of Scotland.* He exposed Ossian. Represented the Orkneys and Shetlands in Parliament from 1807 to 1812. He thereafter retired to his estate in the Orkneys where he died.

NOTES

4. *Suard, Jean Baptists Antoine* (1733–1817). Born at Besançon. Member of the French Academy in 1774. Appointed Censor of plays. He was a moderate monarchist, and during the Revolution he took refuge at Coppet and then at Anspach. He returned after Brumaire and was appointed Permanent Secretary of the French Academy. He published several books of literary criticism. His wife was the sister of the publisher Panckoucke. She was a woman of great beauty and intelligence and her salon rivalled that of Mme. Geoffrin.

5. *Madame Johannot.* Jean Mistler has been able to unearth some facts about the Johannot family. She was born Marie Charlotte Aguiton at Geneva. In 1776 she married Jean Johannot as his second wife. They lived in Paris in the Rue de la Victoire. He possessed a property at Vaucresson. He was elected to the Convention in 1792 and voted conditionally for the execution of Louis XVI. He was regarded as a man of scrupulous integrity in public life. At the Restoration he returned to Switzerland where he died.

CHAPTER FOUR

1. The route followed by Benjamin Constant on his journey to Edinburgh and back was as follows: *Outward journey.* Dover (June 25 and 26)—London-Chesterford (July 22)—Newmarket-Brandon-Stoke-Lynn-Wisbeach-Thrapston-Wadenhoe-Stamford-Thrapston again-Kettering-Leicester-Derby-Buxton-Chorley-Kendal-Edinburgh (August 12). *Return journey.* Edinburgh-Moffat-Carlisle-Keswick-Patterdale (August 29–30)—Ambleside-Kendal-Lancaster (Sept. 1)—Garstang-Bolton-Disley (Sept. 3)—Market Harborough (Sept. 5)—Wadenhoe (Sept. 7)—Kimbolton (Sept. 11)—London-Dover.

2. The dog recovered from its nervous breakdown and was safely delivered to Kentish. Some years afterwards he showed the animal to Charles de Constant as a living pledge of his affection for Benjamin.

3. *Brunswick, Charles William Ferdinand, Duke of* (1735–1806). Nephew of Frederick the Great. Distinguished himself in the Seven Years' War. He rejected the offer to become Commander-in-Chief of the French armies and refused to be a candidate for the throne of France. He was much admired by Mirabeau and Gouverneur Morris

NOTES

as the type of enlightened and constitutional ruler. In 1787 he commanded the Prussian Army which invaded Holland and restored the Stadholder. He commanded the Allied armies and invaded France. His Manifesto of July 27, 1792 threatening the people of Paris with reprisals caused lasting indignation. He married (1764) Princess Augusta, sister of George III.

4. *Cagliostro, Alessandro* (1743–1795). Alchemist and impostor. His real name was Guiseppe Balsamo. He toured the capitals of Europe selling love-philters, elixirs and other profitable concoctions. In 1785 he was implicated in the affair of the Diamond Necklace, and was imprisoned in the Bastille. On his release he went to London where he was interned for a while in the Fleet Prison. He then retired to Rome and was sentenced to life imprisonment in the fortress of St. Leo, where he died.

CHAPTER FIVE

1. The text of this renunciation was seen and reproduced by Sainte-Beuve (*Portraits Litéraires*, III, p. 242, note 2). It has since disappeared. It was a curious document and ran as follows: "By all that is deemed honourable and sacred, by the value I attach to the respect of my fellows, by the gratitude I owe to my father, by the advantages of birth, fortune and education which I have enjoyed, (which distinguish a gentleman from a rogue, a gambler and a blackguard) by the rights I have to the friendship of Isabella [Madame de Charrière], by the share I have in it—I hereby pledge myself never to take part in any game of chance, nor in any game (unless to oblige a lady), from this present date until January 1, 1793.

If I break this promise I shall confess myself a scoundrel, a liar and a cad, and will tamely submit so to be called by everybody who meets me.

Brunswick this nineteenth of March 1788. H. B. de Constant."

2. The "Graue Hof" was burnt to the ground during an insurrection in 1830. The new palace was built between 1831 and 1836 according to the plans of the architect Ottmer. It also was destroyed by fire during a ball in 1865.

3. *Caroline of Brunswick* (1768–1821). Engaged to Prince of Wales 1794. Married him April 8, 1795. Princess Charlotte born

NOTES

January 7, 1796. Separates from her husband April 1796. 1806 "The delicate investigation" exonerates her from ill conduct. 1811 Prince of Wales becomes Regent. August 1813 she leaves England and goes abroad. Her infatuation for her courier Bartolomeo Bergami. November 1817 Princess Charlotte dies. January 1820 George III dies and Prince Regent succeeds. She lands at Dover June 5, 1820. Divorce Bill introduced July 5, 1820 and dropped November 10. King crowned July 19, 1821; she is refused admittance to the Abbey. She dies August 7, 1821.

Charles de Constant met the Princess of Wales at Geneva in October 1814. She mistook him for Benjamin. "It is a long time," she said, "since we have met, Monsieur Constant." Charles described her at that date as "a little woman of forty-six, of vast and shameless obesity." The fair hair and fresh complexion had given place to an enormous black wig and two circles of brick red paint on her cheeks.

4. *Mauvillon, Jacob* (1743–1794). His father, who came from Tarascon, was professor of French at Leipzig University. Jacob Mauvillon was born and educated at Leipzig and did much to introduce into Germany the English theory of economics. He was a liberal, and had been an intimate friend of Mirabeau. After his death Benjamin Constant thought of writing his biography.

5. In July 1789 there seemed a chance of the whole case being revised. Benjamin therefore went to the Hague and spent some months there working up his father's case from the beginning. "I am trying," he wrote, "to do something to make up for all that I did or failed to do in my reckless youth." These efforts were unavailing. On July 16, 1791 all still pending cases were decided against Juste de Constant. He was dismissed from the army and heavy damages were awarded against him. In the end the Colonel triumphed. By a decree of February 19, 1796 all sentences passed against him were quashed. He was given the rank of Major-General and a pension of 2,400 florins a year. But by then he had spent his entire fortune and ruined all hopes of a military career. For sixteen years he lived on at Brévans in a rage.

NOTES

CHAPTER SIX

1. *Thérèse Forster and Louis Ferdinand Huber.* She was Thérèse Heyne, born at Göttingen in 1764. At the age of 20 she married George Forster, the writer and explorer, who had accompanied Captain Cook on his voyages. He was then a professor at Vilna. From there he was transferred to Mainz where he became librarian. It was there that she met Louis Huber.

The latter, born in 1764, was an intimate friend of Schiller with whom he had lived at Leipzig in 1785. He quarrelled with Schiller and became secretary to the Saxon Legation at Mainz. He then eloped with Thérèse and they established themselves at Neuchâtel. Forster died in 1794 and Huber then married Thérèse.

2. Charlotte called Benjamin by his first name "Henri" and seldom used the one by which he was usually known.

3. *La Fayette, Marquis de* (1757–1834). Appointed Major-General in American army at age of nineteen. Wounded at Battle of Brandywine 1777. 1779 returned to France to ask French assistance. 1789 elected to States General. Colonel-General of National Guard. Introduced the tricolour. Retired into private life on proclamation of constitution (September 18, 1791). December 1791 he is put in command of one of the three French armies, but he is suspected by the Assembly and denounced as a traitor August 19, 1792. He fled to Liège whence he was taken prisoner and lodged first in Prussian and afterwards in Austrian prisons. Not till 1797 by the Treaty of Campo Formio was Napoleon able to secure his release. He was opposed to the Empire and only again played a part during the restoration when he became deputy for the Sarthe and a colleague with Constant in the Liberal opposition. Revisited America in 1825. In the 1830 Revolution he took command of the National Guard again. Died in Paris May 20, 1834.

Madame de Staël's plea for intervention was made during his imprisonment in a Prussian fortress where it was said he was being treated with indignity.

4. *Count Louis de Narbonne* (1755–1813). He was reputed to have been the son of Louis XV. He was the first and the most distinguished of Madame de Staël's lovers. They first met in 1789. In

NOTES

1791, largely through her influence, he was appointed Minister of War. He was widely suspected of having offered the throne of France to the Duke of Brunswick. In 1792 his life was threatened and Madame de Staël succeeded in saving him and transporting him to England. He returned to France in 1800. He was a great friend of Talleyrand who was however jealous of his influence with Napoleon to whom he became First Aide-de-Camp. He accompanied Napoleon on the Russian campaign where, in spite of his 50 years, he conducted himself with great courage and endurance. He was then posted Ambassador to Vienna. On Austria's joining the Coalition he was disgraced and made Governor of the fortress of Torgau where he died of typhus in 1813.

During the visit to Greng it became clear to Madame de Staël that Narbonne had lost his affection for her. She was thus fully prepared for his successor.

CHAPTER SEVEN

1. *Suzanne Curchod.* Born 1737, the daughter of Louis-Antoine Curchod, pastor of the village church at Crassier. Being beautiful and highly educated, she captured the affections of Gibbon to whom she was engaged for five years. In 1760 Pastor Curchod died, and Suzanne was obliged to support her mother by giving lessons. In 1763 her mother died and shortly afterwards she had the good fortune to meet Madame Verménoux and thereafter Jacques Necker. She was a hard, cold, calculating, reserved, conventional and snobbish woman. She worshipped her husband and was jealous of his affection for Germaine. But she did see to it that her daughter received a very thorough education.

2. *Château de Coppet.* This ancient castle, with the baronial rights attached to it, stands above the village of Coppet off the road from Geneva to Nyon. It had at one time belonged to the Dukes of Savoy and was the home of Otho de Grandson whom Chaucer called "the prince of French poets." In the seventeenth century it was a castellated fortress with a keep at the north angle and round towers at the three other corners; the moat was fed by a stream which still runs through the park. In the eighteenth century the moat was filled in, the courtyard opened out and only one of the four towers preserved.

NOTES

Necker purchased the property from his partner Thélusson on May 3, 1784 for the sum of 500,000 livres. He took possession, to the sound of cannon firing a salute, on September 1, 1784.

3. The actual date of the first meeting between Constant and Madame de Staël is a subject of controversy. Constant himself, many years later, noted in his diary: "September 19, 1794. Madame de Staël." This has led some authorities to assume that he first met her at the Château de Greng near Lake Morat. It is clear however that although Madame de Staël was at Greng on that date, Constant was at Lausanne. We know that Madame de Staël was at Berne on September 13, at Colombier on September 24, and at Coppet on September 26. We also know that she reached Mézéry late at night on September 29. In Constant's letter to Madame de Charrière of September 30 he says that he had supper with her and Monsieur de Vincy at Nyon, that he lunched with her next day, dined that night with M. Rollaz at Rolle, and supped with her that evening presumably at Mézéry. He also lunched at Mézéry next day the 30th, after which he wrote his letter to Madame de Charrière.

Assuming therefore that Mme. de Staël stayed the nights of the 26th and 27th at Coppet to be with her father during the interment of Mme. Necker, it would mean that they first met on the road to Nyon on September 28 and continued the next day together to Rolle and Mézéry. These dates are admittedly conjectural, but it is at least probable that the dates given in his letter of September 30 to Mme. de Charrière are more accurate than the date entered in his diary many years later.

CHAPTER EIGHT

1. Madame Récamier in her old age told Sainte-Beuve that Madame de Staël at this period was deeply unhappy because Narbonne had resumed his old affair with the Comtesse de Laval. Constant met Narbonne again at Cassel in 1813 when the latter had returned from the Russian campaign and was Ambassador in Vienna.

2. In 1778 Necker deposited with the Treasury a sum of 2,400,000 livres in return for which he received a personal receipt from Louis XVI promising to repay the sum whenever he might ask for it. He accepted 5% interest for this loan, which was far below the then cur-

NOTES

rent rate. When he retired in September 1790 he left two millions of this sum on deposit with the Treasury until the accounts had been audited, withdrawing only the 400,000. The Directory offered to repay the debt in paper money or in national property. Necker refused. Napoleon always refused to pay it because of his rage against Madame de Staël. It was eventually repaid by Louis XVIII.

3. *Barras, Paul Francoise Jean Nicolas, Vicomte de* (1775–1829). Descended from a noble family in Provence. 1789 deputy for Var in Convention. Regarded as a Jacobin. Met Bonaparte during siege of Toulon. Took leading part in 9th Thermidor and subsequently in suppression of Vendémiaire insurrection. Arranged Bonaparte's marriage with Josephine and secured him the command of the armies in Italy. Assisted Bonaparte in the *coup d'état* of 18th Brumaire, but his life was so profligate and his practices so corrupt that Bonaparte thereafter forced him to retire from public life.

4. The main dates in Bonaparte's life up to 1795 are as follows. Born Ajaccio, August 15, 1769. Sent to Military Academy at Brienne 1779. Ecole Militaire in Paris 1784–1785. Enters the artillery. Lieutenant 1791. Captain 1792. Siege of Toulon 1793. Promoted General of Brigade 1794 at age of twenty-five. Serves in Italian campaign under Kellerman. He was on sick leave in Paris in 1795 when Barras summoned him to suppress the Vendémiaire insurrection. As a reward appointed to command armies in Italy.

5. This nationality problem proved a worry to Constant all his life. Under the law of 1790, descendants of Huguenot families expelled from France were allowed to reclaim French nationality. Under the law of 1795, however (a law aimed at the émigrés) those who had remained absent from France for a period of seven years were excluded from French citizenship. Benjamin petitioned the Corps Législatif to the effect that a law of 1795 could not deprive the descendants of Huguenots from benefits conferred upon them by a law of 1790. His petition was filed. When Geneva was annexed to France he became, for the moment at least, a French citizen by right. But after the Restoration he was again exposed, as will be seen, to serious difficulties on the score of his nationality.

Charles de Constant, who was in London at the time conducting a case against the British Admiralty for wrongful confiscation of merchandise, was enraged by Benjamin's action. "Benjamin," he

NOTES

wrote, "with his petition to prove himself a Frenchman, will end by having me locked up as such in England."

6. Constant sold Hérivaux in 1802, and purchased in its place a smaller house "Les Herbages" near the village of St. Martin du Tertre, not far from Luzarches.

CHAPTER NINE

1. The comings and goings of Madame de Staël, her successive expulsions and returns have been tabulated and can be explained. During the whole of the Directory period the decree of expulsion of 1794 remained, in theory at least, in force. But with Talleyrand at the Foreign Ministry she was constantly able to obtain permission to revisit Paris for short periods. The cat-and-mouse policy which they adopted towards her may have been galling and inconvenient, but it was not permanent exile. There were gradations in the permissions allowed her. Sometimes she was allowed to come to Paris for a stated period; sometimes she was allowed to reside in France indefinitely provided she kept within 40 leagues of the capital; sometimes she was forbidden to cross the frontier in any case. The same sort of cat-and-mouse policy was continued by Napoleon. All these comings and goings have been carefully checked by Paul Gautier in his *Madame de Staël et Napoléon*.

2. *Sieyès, Emmanuel-Joseph* (1748–1836). Entered the Church. Elected to the States General. A member of the Convention; withdrew in disgust from politics. He voted for death of Louis XVI. He was offered post of Director but refused it as he disapproved of the Constitution of the Year III. He was given diplomatic missions which he executed ably. Finally he agreed in 1799 to become a Director in the place of Rewbell and began at once to intrigue against his colleagues. It was he who drafted "the perfect constitution" after Brumaire. Having used him Bonaparte politely laid him aside. Sieyès lived in retirement during the Empire, but left France at the time of the Restoration. He returned after the July Revolution (1830) and died in Paris in 1836. He is chiefly remembered for his reply to the question "What part did you play in the Revolution?" "J'ai vécu," answered Sieyès, "I survived."

NOTES

CHAPTER TEN

1. *Julie Talma* (1756–1805). She was the illegitimate child of a bourgeois of Pézenas. At the age of seven she was almost burnt to death in a fire at the Opera House; she was rescued by a stranger who adopted her and saw to her education; she was enrolled in the Corps de Ballet. She became the mistress of the Comte de Ségur. In 1791 she married the actor Talma and ten days later produced twin sons, who were christened Castor and Pollux. In 1801 she divorced Talma. Castor and Pollux died of consumption, an illness to which she herself succumbed on May 8, 1805.

2. Mrs. Lindsay was recalling, somewhat inaccurately, Milton's insufferable line: "He for God only, she for God in him." (*Paradise Lost* IV, 299.)

3. There is an echo of this reproach in *Adolphe* (p. 97). "During my absence I wrote to Ellénore regularly. I was divided between the fear that my letters might cause her pain and the wish not to express an emotion that I did not feel. I wanted her to see through me, but not in such a way as to cause her misery; I congratulated myself when I was able to substitute words like 'affection' 'friendship' 'devotion' for the word 'Love'; when suddenly I pictured poor Ellénore to myself—sad and lonely—for whom letters must be the only consolation; and thus at the end of two cold formal pages, I quickly added a few burning tender phrases, which of course misled her all over again."

4. Those who dislike Benjamin Constant because of his habit of defining with great lucidity the more unpleasant truths regarding human nature, have seized upon a passage in his *Journal Intime* to prove that he was completely heartless. "I spent the day and night by the bedside of Madame Talma who is nearing her end. I take the opportunity to study death [*J'y étudie la mort*]." Is this so very disgraceful? Nobody can doubt the depth of his affection and respect for Julie Talma. After all the Journal Intime *was* his private diary and not written for publication. And what *writer* could deny that, even in moments of real affliction and distress, he is always accompanied by an imp taking notes?

5. *Clairon, Mlle. Claire-Joseph Leris* (1723–1803). In her youth

NOTES

she was one of the leading actresses at the Comédie Française. She crops up again and again in this story. When Madame de Charrière was a young woman she had admired Mlle. Clairon in the part of Phèdre; Madame de Staël as a girl took lessons from her in elocution; and when Benjamin was a boy at Erlangen she was reigning mistress to the Duke of Anspach-Bayreuth. In her old age she wrote her memoirs.

6. Constant on January 22, 1804 resumed his diary (now known as the *Journal Intime*) with the words "I have just arrived in Weimar." This has led some writers to assume that Madame de Staël, who reached Weimar on December 23, had preceded him. Yet on February 29 Constant remarks that he had by then spent "three" months at Weimar. He wrote his diaries and his letters at such terrific speed that he was apt to make mistakes about dates as well as mistakes of spelling and grammar. It seems more reasonable to suppose that they both arrived together on December 23, 1803 and that when Constant wrote "three" months he ought to have written "two."

7. *Schlegel, August Wilhelm, von* (1767–1845). Born at Hanover. 1796 married Karoline Böhmer. Professor at Jena University. Translated Shakespeare. With his brother Friedrich, he started the romantic school of criticism. Divorced his wife 1804. 1813 acted as secretary to Bernadotte. In later years he devoted himself to the study of Sanskrit.

CHAPTER ELEVEN

1. *Sismondi, Jean Charles Leonard, de* (1773–1842). He was a Genevese of the real name of Simonde which he changed to Sismondi for snobbish reasons. The author of the *History of the Italian Republics*. He accompanied Madame de Staël on her journey to Italy. He there met the Countess of Albany, widow of the Young Pretender and mistress of Alfieri, with whom he maintained an interesting correspondence which has been published. At the time of the Hundred Days he was one of the few to defend Constant's attitude. He died in Geneva.

2. *Bonstetten, Charles Victor de* (1745–1823). Born in Berne. Studied at Geneva and Leyden. In 1769 he visited Cambridge and

NOTES

completely upset Thomas Gray by his beauty, vivacity and talents. On his return to Switzerland he entered the service of the Berne oligarchy and held several administrative posts. He wrote books about Switzerland and a study of the influence of climate on national character.

3. In the *Journal Intime* (p. 244) there occur three entries for January 1807, which enable us approximately (since Constant did not always give the day of the month) to fix the date of the composition of *Adolphe*. (1) "I intend to begin a novel which will be my own story." (2) "I finished my novel in fifteen days." (3) "I read my novel aloud to Mme. de Boufflers."

The entry in which the first of these three references occurs mentions also that he had been to see Talma in *Gaston et Bayard*. The date of that performance was January 11. We can assume therefore that *Adolphe* in its first form was written in Paris between January 12 and January 27, 1807. It is true that in a letter from Madame de Staël to Bonstetten dated November 15, 1806 occurs the remark "Benjamin has started to write a novel. It is the most original and the most moving thing that I have read." But, as Professor Mistler points out, the dating of her letters to Bonstetten are not reliable or conclusive. I prefer to stick to the dates indicated in the *Journal Intime*.

4. *Maurice O'Donnell* was an Austrian Count of Irish antecedents. He was only twenty-four years of age, extremely handsome, but not given to literature or conversation. Madame de Staël applied her battering ram to him without the slightest effect.

Madame de Staël, who exacted absolute fidelity from her lovers, was herself less consistent in her attachments. During this period she had affairs with Don Pedro de Souza, the son of a Portuguese diplomatist, and with a Doctor Robertson, in attendance on Lord John Campbell.

CHAPTER TWELVE

1. *Chamisso, Adelbert von* (1781–1838). German poet and botanist. His best known work was his novel *Peter Schlemil, or The Man Who Sold his Shadow*. In 1815 he went on a scientific mission round the world in the company of Otto von Kotzebue. He thereafter be-

NOTES

came Director of the Botanical Gardens in Berlin. He was a coarse rough creature whom Madame de Staël sought to tame.

2. During Constant's absence Charlotte had attended the ill-fated ball of Prince Schwarzenburg at which many people lost their lives in a fire which consumed the specially constructed ballroom. She was knocked over during the panic, but rescued by a Colonel of the Guards. She remarked that evidently she was not destined to die by fire: that was an unlucky prediction.

CHAPTER THIRTEEN

1. Juste died from an urinary operation on February 2, 1812. In the last months of his life he had turned against Benjamin and even accused him of all manner of financial felonies. "Is my father a beast?" Benjamin had noted in despair. In the end he behaved well to his father's second family. By a deed which he signed on June 7, 1812 he undertook to pay 500 francs a year to Charles and 1,000 a year to Marie Louise.

2. The main dates for this period are as follows: 1812, June: Napoleon invades Russia. September: Battle of Borodino. Burning of Moscow. October: Retreat from Moscow begins. December: Napoleon abandons his army and returns to Paris. 1813, February: German War of Liberation begins. May: Battle of Bautzen. June: Wellington defeats the French at Vittoria. October: Battle of Leipzig. 1814, March: Allies enter Paris. April: Abdication of Napoleon. May: First Peace of Paris. 1815, March: Napoleon returns from Elba. June 18: Battle of Waterloo. Second abdication of Napoleon. July: Return of Louis XVIII, October: Napoleon interned at St. Helena.

3. *Bernadotte, Jean Baptiste, Prince of Ponte Corvo and subsequently Charles XIV of Sweden* (1763–1844). Born at Pau. Entered French army and made a Marshal in 1804. Fought at Ulm, Austerlitz and Wagram. In 1810, on the death of the Crown Prince of Sweden, he was elected as his successor to the throne and adopted as such by Charles XIII under the title of the Crown Prince Charles John. In return for the promise of Norway he joined the Coalition in 1812 and rendered useful service in the Battle of Leipzig. In 1818, on the death of Charles XIII he succeeded to the throne of Sweden and Norway. He died at Stockholm on March 8, 1844.

NOTES

4. *Le Siège de Soissons* is an allegorical satire in nine cantos. The main characters are Argaléon, Narbal, Apsimare and Florestan corresponding to Napoleon, Fouché, Talleyrand and Alexander I. The manuscript of this deplorable poem was left by Constant to his half-brother by whom it was bequeathed to the Agricultural Society of Poligny. It was there discovered by Victor Waille who published it in 1892.

It it monotonous, confused and wholly unreadable. The sole interest it possesses is that it proves that Constant had no ear at all, not merely for the French *alexandrin*, but for the French language itself. No French school-boy would venture to write a line such as:

"Sur des sophas dorés vous eussiez vu s'étendre."

5. *Madame Récamier* (1777–1849). She was born at Lyons, the daughter of Maître Bernard, a local lawyer. In 1793 she married the banker Récamier, who was supposed by some to be her father. She first met Madame de Staël during the Directory. When Madame de Staël was exiled she took her side thereby incurring the displeasure of Bonaparte. In 1807 she spent five months at Coppet, where Prince August of Prussia fell passionately in love with her. In 1813 she went to Naples where she made great friends with the Murats. In 1818 she formed a lasting friendship with Chateaubriand. She had rooms in the Abbaye-aux-Bois where she continued to entertain all the eminent figures in the political and literary world. At the end of her life she became completely blind. She died of cholera on May 11, 1849.

6. Albertine's marriage was ideally happy. She was beloved and admired by all who knew her. Her premature death in 1833 caused general affliction and evoked many tributes, above all the magnificent memorial ode, or *Cantique*, of Lamartine. Her husband became Prime Minister of France in 1835 and Member of the French Academy. Her children and great-grandchildren were most remarkable. Her son Albert, Duc de Broglie (1821–1901) was Prime Minister in 1873 and again in 1877: he was also a Member of the French Academy. Of his two grandsons, the present Duc de Broglie is a Member of the French Academy, while his brother, the Prince de Broglie, is a Nobel prize winner. Albertine's daughter, Louise de Broglie, married the Comte d'Haussonville, who became a Member

NOTES

of the French Academy as did their son, the Comte Othenin d'Haussonville.

Few families in any country could boast such a succession of distinctions.

CHAPTER FOURTEEN

1. *Sebastiani, Horace François Bastien, Count* (1772–1851). A Corsican by birth. Assisted Napoleon at Brumaire. Promoted a general at Austerlitz. Sent as French Ambassador to Constantinople where he played an important part. Served in Spain and in the Russian campaign. Accepted Louis XVIII in 1814 but thereafter rejoined Napoleon. Escaped to England after Waterloo, but thereafter became a member of the Chamber of Deputies and Minister of Marine and Foreign Affairs. Under Louis Philippe he was appointed Ambassador in Naples and (1835–1840) Ambassador in London.

2. *Fouché, Joseph, Duke of Otranto* (1759–1820). Intended for the church but in 1792 became deputy in the National Convention. Voted for the execution of Louis XVI. Became a fanatical Jacobin and with Collot d'Herbois was responsible for the Terror in Lyons. He then turned against Robespierre and was closely concerned with the Thermidorean Revolution. Under the Directory he was suspected of having betrayed to Barras the conspiracy of Babeuf. After serving as Ambassador at Milan and the Hague he was on July 20, 1799 appointed Minister of Police. He assisted Bonaparte at Brumaire. In 1802 Bonaparte tried to get rid of him but was obliged to bring him back. He was again dismissed in 1810 and thereafter made Governor of the Illyrian provinces. On the return of Napoleon from Elba he was again made Minister of Police. Although Louis XVIII at the second Restoration was willing to re-employ him, the royalist party regarded him as a regicide. He retired to Trieste where he died on December 25, 1820.

3. This cryptic reference is explained by a passage in the Duc de Broglie's Memoirs. Constant had read his novel aloud to fifteen or sixteen people in Madame Récamier's drawing room. He was obviously tired and when he reached the passage describing the death of Ellénore he broke down completely. The whole audience also burst into tears; their sobs became convulsive and then sud-

NOTES

denly changed into "bursts of nervous laughter," in which Constant joined.

4. *Madame de Staël* during the Hundred Days displayed all her characteristic faults and virtues. Under the first Restoration she had used her influence in favour of the Bonapartists. "She enjoys," said Talleyrand, "rescuing people whom she has drowned the night before." When Napoleon reached Paris and was joined by Constant she expressed all the appropriate motions of horror. But when Constant became a Councillor of State she tried to get him to interest Napoleon on her behalf. She even wrote to Castlereagh assuring him that Napoleon had turned over a new leaf. But once war became inevitable she changed her mind and became firmly anti-Bonapartist.

5. *Baroness von Krüdener* (1764–1824). Barbe Juste von Wietgenhof, born at Riga. After a gay youth she fell under the influence of the impostor Fontaine and became a pietist. She sought to convert the Tsar of Russia and was believed to be the originator of the Holy Alliance. She travelled about Europe telling the peasants "to flee from the wrath to come." She died when on a visit to the Crimea.

CHAPTER FIFTEEN

1. Constant first stood for Paris in 1817; he was not elected. In March 1819 he was returned for the Sarthe and retained that seat until the elections of November 1822. He then remained out of Parliament until March 1824, when he was elected for Paris. In 1827 he was re-elected for Paris and simultaneously for Alsace. He chose the latter constituency which he continued to represent until the Revolution of July.

2. *Manuel, Jacques Antoine* (1775–1827). Deputy for the Vendée in 1818. He was an avowed anti-Bourbonist and in protesting against the Spanish war he stated that Louis XVI had owed his death to a similar foreign invasion. This led to an uproar in the Chamber and a Committee found him guilty of a breach of privilege and ordered his expulsion (March 23, 1823). He retired to the house of his friend the banker Laffitte at Maisons Laffitte, where he died in 1827. His funeral was turned into a demonstration against the Government.

3. The Sarthe did not remain ungrateful to Benjamin Constant. On July 14, 1913 a monument was erected to his memory at Le

NOTES

Mans, at the intersection of the Rue de l'Etoile and the Rue des Ursulins. It contains a replica of the bust of Constant by Bra. It was unveiled by M. Joseph Caillaux.

4. The publication of Constant's long work on religions took the following forms. (1) *De la Religion, considérée dans sa source ses formes et ses Développements.* Vol. I. Paris 1824. Vols. II and III Paris 1825 and 1827. Vols. IV and V. Paris 1831. (2) *Du Polythéisme romain considéré dans ses rapports avec la philosophie grecque et la religion Chrétienne.* Published posthumously Paris 1833, two volumes.

5. Constant was recalling the passage in Bacon's essay on Atheism: "A little philosophy inclineth man's mind to atheism, but depth in philosophy bringeth men's minds about to religion."

6. Charlotte lived on for fifteen years as a widow in the Rue d'Anjou. She would give little receptions at which she would take her stand under the bust of Constant by Bra. She wrote mystical poems in her later years which she would inscribe in a fat album. In July 1845 she went to sleep while reading in bed, with the result that her night-cap became entangled with the lamp. She rushed out on to the staircase, shrieking for help. She died of her injuries after three days of agony.

7. The Tivoli Baths were not, as some biographers have assumed, either situated in the vicinity of Rome or a gambling establishment. They were what would now be called a nursing home. They were situated at 88 Rue St. Lazare, and Galignani's *New Paris Guide* (1830 edition) has the following reference: "In this fine establishment are baths of fictitious mineral waters of every kind, with commodious lodgings for invalids and a fine garden."

8. The Panthéon was not at that date a cemetery for national heroes. The clericals still regarded it as the Church of St. Geneviève and were bitterly opposed to any lay use of the building.

Index

Achard, Madame, 105
Achard, Mlle., 17
Achard, Ninette, 105
Adolphe, 7–8, 80, 175, 179, 201–7, 268, 275, 312, 314
Albany, Countess of, 204, 313
Anspach, Dowager Margravine of, 26–27
Anspach-Bayreuth, Margraf of, 25–26, 313
Audoin (Benjamin's coachman), 219
Augereau, General, 159–60

Balk, Baron de, 231
Barante, Prosper de, 26, 195, 231–32, 237, 249, 261, 281
Barante, Prosper de (son of Prosper), 231
Barras, Paul, 146–47, 157, 159–62, 164, 310, 317
Barrès, Maurice, 80–81
Barthélemy, 159
Baudin, Pierre, 144–45
Baumier, M., 34–35
Bavois, Mme. Charrière de (aunt of Benjamin), 10, 12, 16, 103–4
Beaumont, Pauline de, 148
Bellegarde, Marquis de, 49–50
Benay, Lieutenant de, 56–58
Bentham, Jeremy, 286

Bernadotte, 180, 238–39, 241–45, 313, 315
Bernhardi, Sophie, 190
Berry, Duc de, 282, 290
Berry, Miss, 275
Berthier, General, 169
Berthoud, Mme. Dorette, 199
Berton, General, 290
Beurthe, Boulay de la, 163
Blücher, 271
Boettiger, 186
Boigne, Madame de, 194
Bollman, Justus Erich, 123
Bonaparte, Joseph, 167, 169, 261
Bonaparte, Lucien, 164–65, 170, 179
Bonaparte, Napoleon, 119, 146, 158–59, 161, 164–73, 179–83, 211, 232, 238, 241–44, 254–71, 308, 310–11, 315–17
Bonstetten, Charles Victor de, 195–96, 313–14
Borel, M., 104
Bos, Charles du, 259
Boswell, James, 13, 49
Bougainville, 162
Bourbonne, Madame de, 47, 58
Bourke, Mrs., 274
Bretonne, Rétif de la, 68
Bridel, M. (tutor of Benjamin), 25
Bridges, the Reverend, 61–62

INDEX

Broglie, Duc de, 253–54, 257, 278, 281–82, 296, 316–17
Broglie, Duchess de (*see* Staël, Albertine de)
Broglie, Mme. Victor de, 125
Brunswick, Duke of, 66, 75, 81–82, 88, 90, 105, 113, 304–5
Brunswick, Duchess of, 82, 84, 86, 96, 109, 305
Brunswick, Dowager Duchess of, 82
Brunswick, Prince Augustus of, 83
Brunswick, Princess Caroline of, 83, 100, 305–6
Brunswick, Crown Prince Charles of, 83
Brunswick, Prince Frederick William of, 83
Brunswick, Prince George of, 82
Burke, Edmund, 95–96
Burney, Dr., 125
Burney, Fanny, 125–26
Byron, Lord, 201, 204, 218, 234, 275

Caffé, M., 290
Cagliostro, Alessandro, 73, 305
Cahier Rouge, 20–21, 26–27, 30, 33, 36, 42–43, 47, 53, 55, 61–62, 64, 68
Cambacérès, 168, 173
Campbell, Sir Neil, 255
Carnot, Marie François, 146, 150, 159
Caroline (an actress), 98
Cassat, L. F., 129
Castlereagh, Viscount, 263, 318
Cayla, Comtesse du, 282
Chabaud-Latour, 167
Chaillet, François, 71
Chaillet, le Pasteur, 72

Chamisso, Adelbert von, 231, 314–15
Chandieu, Antoine de (Sadael), 2, 292
Chandieu, Henriette (*see* Constant, Henriette de)
Chandieu de l'Isle, Benjamin de, 4
Charles X ("Monsieur"), 282, 297
Charrière, M. de, 50–52, 56, 72–73, 75, 79, 87, 92–93, 103, 130–31, 134
Charrière, Madame de (Isabella van Tuyll), 13, 17, 56, 58–59, 62–68, 84–87, 91–95, 97, 102–5, 107–9, 111–15, 130–34, 136–37, 154, 305, 309; character of, 53, 68, 71, 76–77, 85, 92, 110, 137, 154; life of, 48–53, 70–78, 134, 313; writings of, 51–52, 112–14
Charrière, Mlle. Henriette, 71, 73–75, 85, 134
Charrière, Mlle. Louise, 71, 75, 79, 85, 134
Chateaubriand, François René de, 17, 285, 297, 316
Chateauvieux, M. de, 139
Châtre, Madame de, 125, 136–37
Chaumont, Château de, 231–32
Chauvelin, 125
Chénier, Marie-Joseph, 146
Clairon, Mlle., 26, 181, 312–13
Clichy, Club de, 157
Coigny, Madame de, 122
Colburn, 276
Colin, M., 151–52
Colombier, 50, 52, 65–73, 75–76, 78–79, 85–86, 92, 95, 100,

INDEX

104–5, 107, 109, 112–15, 133–34
Condorcet, Marquis de, 47
Conflans, M. de, 175
Constant, Augustin, 2, 292
Constant, (Henri) Benjamin: *character of*, 53, 60, 94, 108, 155; childishness, 17, 36, 60, 133, 138, 143–44, 251; as conversationalist, 47, 53, 63–64, 74, 110, 137; courage, 68, 155, 257, 290; Cousin Rosalie's influence on, 14, 17; craving for affection, 203; deceitfulness, 18, 221, 225, 229; dislike of scenery, 4; domesticity of, 183; dual personality, 1–2, 14, 43; effect of mother's death on, 5; father's influence on, 5–8; heartlessness towards women, 153, 176–78, 215, 312; intelligence, 1, 12; love of animals, 59–62, 64, 83, 104, 196; melancholia, 105; nervous excitability, 22–24, 58, 139–40; pride, 136, 245; precociousness, 22, 24, 34; secretiveness, 20; self-analysis, 76, 155–56; shyness, 136, 199, 245; social gifts, 46–47, 136; spiritual loneliness, 79; uneven development of, 5

health of, 5, 79, 105, 200, 295; bad eyesight, 21, 62–63, 68, 147, 200, 278; crippled by fall, 278; operated upon, 297; paralysis of, 299; suffers stroke, 292

opinions of: on British House of Commons, 274; on constitutional monarchy, 246; on degradation of parliaments, 172; on doctrine of *laisser-faire,* 286–87; on England, 239, 246, 274; on Fouché, 275; on freedom of the press, 129, 246, 288–89; on independents in politics, 284; on liberalism and liberty, 32, 155, 158, 239–41, 257, 278, 285–89; on love, 40, 202–3, 211–12; on marriage, 202; on militarism, 240; on Napoleon, 255, 257–58, 270; on property rights, 287–88; on religion, 295, 319; on rule of law, 149, 172; on Talleyrand, 275; on totalitarian systems, 240–41, 244

personal appearance of, 5, 12, 62, 84, 131–33, 136, 139, 147, 151, 278–80

private life of: adolescence, 12; and Anna Lindsay, 175–79; attempted suicide of, 139; baptism of, 5; birth of, 2, 5; buys French property, 151; in Brussels, 35; and Caroline, 98; and Charlotte von Hardenberg, 98–100, 106–7, 199, 215, 273–76, 289–98; childhood letters of, 12, 22–23; death and funeral of, 298, 319; divorce of, 100; dueling, 67–68, 160, 234, 267, 291; early education of, 19–25; early upbringing of, 6, 8, 10–12; in England, 32, 59–61, 273–76; financial difficulties of, 199, 230, 233, 252–54, 267; first marriage of, 91, 97–98; and French citizenship, 150, 291–92; gambling, 26, 30–31, 34, 42, 47, 53–54, 81, 146, 233, 241, 278, 305; in Germany with Charlotte, 235–38;

INDEX

and Goethe, 187–88; and Julie Talma, 174–75; last visit to Switzerland, 292; and Mme. Charrière, 52–53, 56, 58–59, 62–69, 74–78, 84–87, 91–95, 97, 102–5, 107–12, 115, 130–34; and Mme. Johannot, 35–36; and Mme. Récamier, 248–54; 256, 259, 261, 263, 267, 270, 272–74, 277; and Mme. de Staël, 115, 129, 136–41, 147–53, 155–57, 163–73, 181, 183–85, 188–90, 197, 200–11, 213, 215–22, 224–34, 237–38, 242, 247, 252–54, 265, 267, 295, 309; at Oxford, 25; proposes to Mme. de Staël, 181, 209; and Schlegel, 190, 196; second marriage of, 213; sexual development of, 26–27; and the Suards, 32, 34; and Mrs. Trevor, 40–45; at University of Edinburgh, 28–31, 61; at University of Erlangen, 25, 313
public life of: apostasy, 257, 264; appointed to uncredited commission for armistice, 270; appointed Tribune, 168; and Bernadotte, 238–39, 241–45; and Bonaparte, 167, 170–73, 201, 255–71; constitutional club founded by, 157; defeated in election for council, 163, 318; defense of Fructidor by, 160; denied membership in French Academy, 296–97; elected Deputy, 278–79, 291, 318; and French Revolution, 95–96, 107; as hero of Alsatian electorate, 293–94; imprisonments and fines, 146, 290–91; an Independent in politics, 280, 283–84; and Louis XVIII, 271–72; made president of Canton of Luzarches, 161; maiden speech as Tribune, 170–71; mobbed by cadets, 290; monument to, 318; and new Constitution, 265–67; patriotism of, 257–59; as a public speaker, 279–80; in service of Duke of Brunswick, 81–109; in support of Directory, 148–49

writings of, 7–8, 22, 39, 67, 105, 107, 131, 148–49, 201, 211, 239, 265–66; comparative history of religions, 39, 74, 108, 131, 183, 200–1, 236, 295–96, 319; diaries, 20–21, 24, 26–27, 36, 42–43, 47, 53, 55–56, 61–62, 64–65, 99, 187, 200–1, 210–11, 236, 238, 252, 263–64; "king of the pamphleteers," 246, 279; listed, 299–300; pagan mythology, 30, 39; poetry, 45, 63–64, 211, 242, 248; political, 144–45, 148–49, 156–57, 163–64, 169, 239, 246–47, 255–57, 262, 285–86; translations, 29–30

Constant, Captain, 2
Constant, Charles de (cousin of Benjamin), 7, 14, 17, 44–46, 151, 276, 295, 306, 310
Constant, Charles de (half brother of Benjamin), 11, 315
Constant, David (great-grandfather of Benjamin), 3
Constant, la Général de (grandmother of Benjamin), 8, 12
Constant, Henriette de Chandieu (mother of Benjamin), 4–5

INDEX

Constant, Lisette de (cousin of Benjamin), 14
Constant, Louise de (half sister of Benjamin), 11, 315
Constant, Rosalie de (cousin of Benjamin), 6–7, 9, 11, 14–17, 36, 67, 75, 91–92, 122, 128, 149–51, 183–85, 191, 198, 208–10, 216, 221, 245, 252, 265, 276, 292
Constant, Victor de (cousin of Benjamin), 128, 198
Constant d'Hermenches, Baron (uncle of Benjamin), 3, 13, 49
Constant de Rebecque, Baron Juste de (father of Benjamin), 3, 23, 25–28, 32, 34, 36–37, 44–46, 48, 53, 56–57, 65–67, 154, 200, 208, 213, 215, 221, 229, 234, 315; abduction of Marianne by, 10; Benjamin's description of, 7–8; birth of, 5; character of, 6–8, 19, 46; death of, 6, 236, 315; financial ruin of, 4, 6, 90–91, 102; ideas on education, 38; marriage of, 5; military desertion of, 89–90, 306; properties of, 4; second marriage of, 11–12
Constant de Rebecque, Samuel de (uncle of Benjamin), 4, 13–16, 51, 67, 104, 128, 145, 166, 172
Constant family, 303; origin of, 2–3; wealth of, 3
Constitution of the Year III, 145, 311
Constitution of the Year VIII, 167–68
Contat, Mlle. Louise, 122–23

Cooper, Mrs., 72
Coppet, Château de, 114–15, 119–20, 125–27, 155, 193–97, 200, 208–10, 212–13, 216–22, 224–26, 228, 230–233, 253, 308–9
Corbigny, M. de, 232
Costante, Agostino, 150
Coulmann, Jean Jacques, 285, 293–95
Cramm, Wilhelmina von (first wife of Benjamin), 91–92, 95, 97–100, 102, 106, 108–9, 236
Crawford, James, 261
Crouzat (Benjamin's valet), 81
Curchod, Suzanne (*see* Necker, Mme. Jacques)

Dalziel, Professor, 28
d'Arblay, General, 125
d'Argenson, 270–71
Davilliers, Madame, 278
Davy, Sir Humphrey, 274
Davy, Lady, 274
Décazes, 273
Decken, Frau von, 217–21
Dejean, M., 219
Desportes, M. Félix, 149
d'Estournelles, Baroness (*see* Constant, Louise de)
Deyverdun, 104, 120
Directory, the, 145, 164, 176, 311, 317
Doctrinaires, les, 282
Drummond, James Lewis (4th Earl of Perth), 176
Ducos, 164
Dudon, M., 291–92
Duncan, Andrew, 28
Duplessis, M. (tutor of Benjamin), 21–22

INDEX

Duplessis d'Ependes, Chevalier, 67–68
Dupuch, M., 220
Duveyrier, M., 169

Ebray, le Pasteur, 213
Edgeworth, Maria, 278
Edinburgh, University of, 27–33, 60
Emmet, Thomas Addis, 29
Erlangen, University of, 25–27, 313
Esprit de Conquête, 239–41
Esmangart, M., 293, 295

Faguet, Emile, 80, 289
Féronce von Rosenkrantz, Jean Baptiste, 85, 94, 106
Fitz-James, Duchesse de, 175
Flahaut, Comte de, 275
Forbin, Comte de, 291
Forster, Thérèse, 104, 307
Fouché, 171, 183, 261, 264, 267, 270–71, 273, 275, 317
Fox, Charles James, 126
Foy, General, 281
Fraser, Alexander, 28
French Revolution, 3, 29, 95–96, 107, 118, 123, 138, 141
Fries, M. de, 151, 292

Garville, M. de, 115, 141
Gautier, Jeanne-Marie, 117
Gautier, Paul, 167, 311
Gibbon, Edward, 39, 41, 104, 120, 126
Gillies, Adam, 29
Gillies, John, 39–41
Gobert, M. (tutor of Benjamin), 21
Godet, Philippe, 48

Godwin, 286
Goethe, 185–87
Gohier, 165
Golovkin, Count, 139
Göttingen, University of, 105, 236–39, 242, 250
Goyet, M., 289–90
Grange, M. de la (tutor of Benjamin), 20
Grant, James, 29
Gray, Thomas, 196, 314
Guizot, 281, 291

Hardenberg, Georgina Charlotte, Countess of (second wife of Benjamin), 108, 111, 155, 192, 198, 202, 207–8, 212, 215–31, 233–34, 250, 291–92, 294–95, 297–98, 307, 315, 319; courage of, 290; death of, 315, 319; divorces Baron von Marenholtz, 199; divorces de Tertre, 212; in England, 273–76; ill-health of, 276; letters from Benjamin, 106–7; love affair with Benjamin, 98–100; and Mme. de Staël, 222–23; marriage to Benjamin, 215; marriage to de Tertre, 199; meets Benjamin, 98; second meeting with Benjamin, 199
Hardenberg, Graf Hans Ernst von, 98–99
Hardenberg, Schloss, 235–36
Harris, Sir James, 88
Herder, 187
Herivaux, 151–52, 183, 230, 311
Hobhouse, John Cam, 275, 286
Holland, Lady, 275
Hope, Charles, 29
Hortense, Queen of Holland, 268

INDEX

Hôtel d'Angleterre, 218, 220, 222
Huber, Louis Ferdinand, 104–5, 133, 307
Hundred Days, the, 255–72, 280–81, 313, 318

Jan, le Pasteur, 213
Jaucourt, Marquis de, 124–26, 136, 141
Jenkinson, Mr., 125
Jersey, Lady, 275
Johannot, Madame, 35–36, 41, 304
Jordan, Camille, 278, 281
Journal Intime, 68, 187, 239, 248, 263, 275, 312–14
Juniper Hall colony, 125, 135

Kentish, Richard, 29, 60, 64
Koreff, Dr., 227–28
Krudener, Baroness von, 272, 318

La Chablière, 4, 10, 15, 21, 64, 90, 94, 102, 151, 292
Lacretelle, 181
La Fayette, 47, 113, 269–70, 280–81, 283, 290, 297, 307
La Forest, 271
Laing, Malcolm, 29, 303
Lally Tollendal, Comte de, 124–25, 136
Lamb, Caroline, 274, 276
Lamoignon, Auguste de, 176–78, 203
Langallerie, Chevalier de (cousin of Benjamin), 13
Langallerie, Marquise Gentil de (aunt of Benjamin), 12–13
Larevellière-Lépeaux, 146, 159
Lascelles, Edmund, 44, 59–60

Laval, Comtesse de, 137, 141, 309
Lavasseur, Thérèse, 113
Lebrun, 168, 181
Le Ray, M. Jacques, 231
Les Chevaliers, 22
Leschaux, Dr., 68
Les Herbages, 183–85, 198–99, 212, 221, 233, 311
Letourneur, 146
Lezay, Adrien de, 157
L'Hardy, Mlle., 112, 130–31, 133
Lieven, Princess, 275
Lindsay, Anna, 175–79, 202, 312
Loève-Veimars, M., 279–80
Louis XV, 15
Louis XVI, 123, 125, 311, 317–18
Louis XVIII, 246, 251, 254, 260, 271–72, 281–82, 315, 317
Louis Philippe, 297, 317
Louvel, 282
Louvet, 145
Loys, Madame de, 17
Loyson, Charles, 285

Mackay, John, 60
Mackintosh, Sir James, 28–29, 243, 274, 303
Magnin, Jeanne Suzanne (Marianne), 10–12, 20, 66, 91, 221, 230
Malouet, 125
Malmesbury, Earl of, 88
Manuel, Jacques, 124–25, 280–81, 283, 318
Marat, 95, 141
Marenholtz, Baron Wilhelm von, 98, 199
Marenholtz, Baroness von (*see* Hardenberg, Charlotte von)
Marie Antoinette, 15, 122–23
Martignac, Comte de, 282

INDEX

Martin, Aimé, 167
Mauvillon, Jacob, 84, 94–95, 105, 108–9, 306
Mauvillon, Madame, 107
May, Mr. (tutor of Benjamin), 25
Memoirs of the Hundred Days, 160, 257, 259, 262, 271–72
Menou, General, 146
Mézéry, Château de, 128, 135–36, 138, 309
Middleton, John Izard, 231
Minerve, 285
Mirabeau, 83, 96, 119, 304, 306
Mistler, Jean, 304, 314
Monachan, Henriette, 72
Monochon, police spy, 149
Montesquiou, General de, 127–28, 138
Montesson, Madame de, 171
Montloisier, M., 267
Montmorency, Mathieu de, 125–26, 136–37, 139, 141, 195, 231
Morand, Jeanne (Nanine), 11
Mornay-Duplessis, 292
Morris, Gouverneur, 119, 304
Moula, Mlle. (Muson), 71, 74
Moulins, 165
Münchausen, Baron von, 81, 96
Murat, Joachim, King of Naples, 251, 316
Murray, House of, 276

Narbonne, Count Louis de, 114–15, 122–27, 136–37, 141, 195, 211, 237, 307–9
Nassau, Comtesse de (aunt of Benjamin), 7, 17–18, 24, 103, 108, 156, 163, 208–10, 216–17, 219, 221–22, 224–25

Necker, Anna Louise Germaine (*see* Staël, Madame de)
Necker, Jacques, 117–22, 127–29, 139, 142–43, 151, 180–81, 189, 193–94, 308–10
Necker, Mme. Jacques, 117–20, 127, 308–9
Necker, Karl Friedrich, 116–17
Necker, Louis (de Germany), 117, 128
Necker de Saussure, Madame, 120–21, 128, 191

Odier-Lecointe, Madame, 219, 221
O'Donnell, Count Maurice, 212, 232, 314
O'Dwyer, James, 175
O'Dwyer-Lindsay, Charles, 176
Orange, Prince of, 100
Orange, Princess of, 88, 106
O'Rourke, Susan, 175
Otranto, Duke of (*see* Fouché)

Pange, François de, 146
Pérey, le Pasteur, 10
Périer, Casimir, 278
Peyrou, M. de, 71
Pillichody, Captain, 67
Pitt, William, 121
Polignac, Marquis de, 282
Pontécoulant, 271
Portrait of Zélide, The, 48
Pourrat, Madame, 54–56
Pourrat, Jenny, 54–56
Prussia, King of, 113

Quinet, 291

Randall, Miss Fanny, 231–32
Récamier, M., 264
Récamier, Madame, 195, 204,

INDEX

211, 223, 231, 248–52, 254, 256, 259, 261, 263–64, 267, 270, 272–74, 277, 309, 316–17

Religion Considered in its Sources, Forms and Development, 39

Restoration, the, 241–52, 310–11, 318

Revolution of July, 282, 293, 297, 311, 318

Rewbell, Jean François, 146, 159, 311

Richelieu, Duc de, 282

Rieu, Mlle., 103

Rilliet-Huber, Madame, 139, 141

Robertson, Dr., 314

Robespierre, 95, 107, 124, 141, 317

Robinson, Henry Crabb, 186–87, 190

Rocca, John, 233–34, 238

Rogers, Samuel, 202

Rollaz, M., 129, 309

Roman Polytheism in its Relation to Greek Philosophy and Christian Religion, 39

Rousillon, Camille de, 105, 143

Rousillon, Pierre de, 105

Rousseau, Jean Jacques, 10, 287–88

Rousselin de St. Albin, M., 147

Royer-Collard, 278, 281

Rudler, Gustave, 6, 22, 25, 30, 76, 87

Ruxton, Miss, 278

Sabran, Elzéar de, 195, 231

Sainte-Beuve, 12, 23, 99, 305, 309

Sainte-Croix, M. Louis Claude Bigot de, 55

St. Pierre, Bernadin de, 15, 17

Sanne, M. de, 199

Saurin, Madame, 47–48

Saussure, M. de, 15

Saussure, Albertine de (*see* Necker de Saussure, Madame)

Saussure, H. B. de, 128

Savary, Duke of Rovigo, 268

Schiller, 185–87, 211

Schlegel, Friedrich, 195, 313

Schlegel, Wilhelm, 190, 195–97, 209, 231–32, 238, 313

Scott, Geoffrey, 48, 50, 53, 77

Sebastiani, General, 261, 270, 317

Second Restoration, 254, 281–82, 289, 317

Sécheron, 218, 222, 225

Serre, Hercule de, 281

Sévery, M. de, 264

Sévery, Madame de, 17

Shelley, Percy Bysshe, 218

Siege of Soissons, The, 248, 316

Sieyès, the Abbe, 164, 166–67, 311

Signet, M., 160

Sismondi, Jean Charles, 137, 195–97, 204, 233, 265, 286, 313

Smith, Adam, 286

Soulavie, M., 128

Souza, Don Pedro de, 314

Speculative Society, The, 29–30, 39, 60, 144, 303

Staël, Madame de (Germain Necker), 13, 17–18, 46, 100, 112–13, 207–9, 314–16, 318; appearance of, 119–21, 195, 233; and Benjamin Constant, 115, 129, 136–41, 147–53, 155–57, 163–73, 181, 183–85, 188–90, 197,

INDEX

200–11, 213, 215–22, 224–34, 237–38, 242, 247, 252–54, 265, 295, 309; in Berlin, 189–90; birth of, 116; and Bonaparte, 162–63, 165, 168–69, 172–73, 179–82, 232, 310; character of, 152–53; and Charlotte von Hardenberg, 222–23, 226–27; at Chaumont, 231–32; as a conversationalist, 119, 129, 137; at Coppet, 194–97; and Count de Narbonne, 122–27; death of, 232, 277–78; denounced by Council of the Five Hundred, 148; derided by press, 170–71; dislike of Switzerland, 150; early life and education of, 119–20, 313; egoism of, 197, 215; expulsions of, 148, 161, 181, 184, 311; and French émigrés, 123–29, 136, 141–43; and Goethe, 186; in Italy, 197, 313; investments of, 253; at Juniper Hall, 125–26; and Mme. de Charrière, 112–15; marriage to Baron de Staël, 121; marriage to John Rocca, 233–34, 238; refusal to marry Benjamin, 181, 209–10; in Weimar, 185–86, 313; writings of, 113–14, 122, 148, 172, 181–82, 232

Staël-Holstein, Albert de, 124, 195
Staël-Holstein, Albertine de (Duchess de Broglie), 156, 195–96, 231, 253, 316–17
Staël-Holstein, Auguste, 122, 195, 208, 226, 231, 234
Staël-Holstein, Baron Eric Magnus de, 121, 141–43, 151, 172, 181
Stroelin (tutor of Benjamin), 19–20
Stuart, Lord, 271
Suard, Jean Baptiste, 32–34, 46, 52, 145, 248, 304
Suard, Madame, 32–34, 46–47, 52, 248, 304
Sweden, Crown Prince of (see Bernadotte)
Sweden, King of, 121

Talleyrand, 123, 125, 136, 157–58, 160–62, 164, 171, 182, 195, 245, 308, 311, 318
Tallien, 124, 145
Talma, François-Joseph, 174–75, 211, 226, 312, 314
Talma, Julie, 174–75, 178–79, 312
Tertre, Madame de (see Hardenberg, Charlotte von)
Tertre, Vicomte de, 199, 208, 216
Thélusson and Necker, 117
Thiers, M., 291
Thrale, Mrs., 125
Thureau-Dangin, Paul, 282
Tissot, Dr., 127
Trevor, Harriot Burton, 40–45, 59
Trevor, John Hampden, 41
Tribunate, the, 168
Tuffiakin, Prince, 231
Tuyll, Ditie van, 50
Tuyll, Isabella van Serooskerden van, 13, 48 (see Charrière, Madame de)

Uginet, Joseph, 149, 208
Uginot, Olive, 149

330

INDEX

Vaudois aristocracy, 3
Veaux, Bertin de, 150
Verménoux, Madame, 117, 308
Viennet, M., 297
Villèle, Comte de, 282
Vincy, M. de, 129
Voltaire, 6, 15, 72

Wallon-Gaulis, Madame, 151
Wallstein, 211
Wangenheim, Count and Countess von, 217, 219
Waterloo, Battle of, 254, 268, 315

Weimar, 185–86, 313
Wellington, Duke of, 271
Wemyss, Lord, 50
Wickham, Mr., 143
Wieland, 187
Wilde, John, 29–30, 60–61
William IV, Stadholder of the Netherlands, 83, 88–89

Zingarelli, Signor, 72
Zuylen, Belle de (*see* Charrière, Madame de)

f. Analysis: Dédoublement 7-8; 9, 23, 24, 27, 31, 33, 43, 44, 56, 60, 63, 68, 80, 102, 108-109; 185, 189, 196, 197, 199, 217, 219, 237, 245, 250.

"apt at deferred solutions" 178
spiritual loneliness:

Women: First mistress
    Mme Johannot
    Mrs. Trevor
    Mme Saurin (comedy)
    Mme de Charrière
    Mlle Pourrat }
    Mème   "

    Mlle van Cramm
        (marriage)

    "Caroline"
    Charlotte, Countess of Hardenberg
    Mme de Staël
    Julie Talma
    Anna Lindsay
    Mme Récamier

"a calculating egoist" -109
"of the most real people that ever lived"
"que la galère!" 156, 251, 256, 262,
old age: 20 duels, the last in arm-chair, 294; 176;
    "Bring yours along" 297

"amnesty to the past corrupts the future"

bons mots by Constant: On the Germans, 84; On the English, 63;
on royalty, 83; de Staël a swimmer, 123; the thing becomes an arena, 150; "a person who eludes one" 192; "When truth causes pain" 217; "Speech not his language" 233-34;
On the French, 237; On West Total-tarianism, 240;
"Neither the repose of virtue nor delight of transgression" 249
"An arbitrary act" - 288
Legend in Delphine, 182;